LIFE MADE REAL

LIFE MADE REAL

Characterization in the Novel since Proust and Joyce

Thomas F. Petruso

Ann Arbor

THE UNIVERSITY OF MICHIGAN PRESS

Published in the United States of America by
The University of Michigan Press
Manufactured in the United States of America

1994   1993   1992   1991   4   3   2   1

A CIP catalogue record for this book is available from the British Library.

Library of Congress Cataloging-in-Publication Data

Petruso, Thomas F., 1950–
    Life made real : characterization in the novel since Proust and
Joyce / Thomas F. Petruso.
        p.   cm.
    Includes bibliographical references and index.
    ISBN 0-472-10266-4
    1. Fiction—20th century—History and criticism. 2. Characters
and characteristics in literature. 3. Proust, Marcel, 1871–1922—
Characters. 4. Joyce, James, 1882–1941—Characters.   I. Title.
PN3341.P47   1991
809.3'927—dc20   91-34378
                                                                          CIP

Selections from *Call It Sleep* reprinted by permission of Roslyn
Targ Literary Agency, Inc., New York, Copyright © 1934, 1962
by Henry Roth.

Questo libro è dedicato alla memoria di Francesco Petruso, Antonetta Fera, e quel Tommaso che mi precedette.

How much more worth living did life seem to me now that it could be clarified. Life, which one lives in the shadows, brought back to the truth of what it was; life, which one unceasingly falsifies, in sum, made real in a book.

—Marcel

You can do it. I see it in your face . . . . Give them something with a bite in it. Put us all in it, damn its soul. Father Son and Holy Ghost and Jakes M'Carthy.

—Myles Crawford

Acknowledgments

I would like to thank Robert Alter and Ralph Rader for prompting me to think about character and simularity and for their encouragement from the earliest stages of this work, and I am indebted to Ross Chambers and Roy Nelson for their kind interest and invaluable feedback in the latter stages. Thanks also to Gian-Paolo Biasin, Steven Botterill, Leslie Simon, Denise Filios, and the participants in my Comparative Literature seminars at U.C. Berkeley for their good advice and healthy skepticism. Special thanks to Sam and Mary Petruso, to Joyce Harrison of the University of Michigan Press, to Mary Martin for her biographical expertise, and to Mary Weems for everything.

Contents

Introduction

Playwrights and novelists have long invited our imaginative participation in the destiny of their characters, drawing upon the need and desire to know others that we display in the world; but creating people is not just the prerogative of literary deities. All of us indulge in the practice, from the earliest age, attributing affective characteristics and personalities to teddy bears, animals, and imaginary friends. Furthermore, one might say that we constitute ourselves and others as characters, fashioning from our histories and inclinations the self-definition we present to the world, and likewise interpreting the character of others through a reading of their self-representations.

One of the most marked aspects of the twentieth-century novel is the legacy of two of its great institutions, Marcel Proust and James Joyce, who created masterworks of autoportraiture that equate to an unprecedented degree the concept of being an author (and, by extension, a character) with being, period. Aside from providing long meditations on the ontological status of author and character, the works also offer a wealth of innovation in characterization and novelistic poetics that bears close examination, particularly given the centrality of such concerns to the subsequent development of the genre.

Unfortunately, the aims of authors and those of critics and theorists are at times so divergent as to render certain areas of study in or out of fashion, regardless of their significance to the author in creating the work. Thus, from the New Critics' injunction against biographical and intentional considerations to the poststructuralists' preoccupation with textual antics, characterization—and particularly its relation to real-life models—has been either ignored or relegated to the category of literary gossip or anecdote. Those studies that have addressed the subject have mainly attempted to locate character in strictly textual or rhetorical phenomena, as if embarrassed by its representational aspect. Given the central position of portrait-of-the-artist type novels in this century—i.e., novels focusing directly or indirectly on the act of writing and artistic arrival—it would seem that a study of character as representation of life experiences is especially pertinent.

Against the grain of much contemporary theory, I will undertake a reading of several works as *novels*, that is, as character-centered narratives representing the experiences of artfully crafted subjects. I will be looking primarily at novels that belong, to varying degrees, to a developmental line in the tradition of fictionalized autobiography that can be traced from Proust and Joyce, along with some others included because of their importance to other modes of characterization. This book invites one, then, to a gathering of some of the century's more prominent and less well known imaginary people, beginning with Marcel, Stephen, and the Blooms.

Chapter 1

Babies in the Bathwater

While the wave of theorizing set in motion with the arrival of structuralism has done much to revitalize literary studies, "theory"[1] has betrayed certain inadequacies with regard to the novel. The genre has been described as beset by crises as various as the final collapse of bourgeois culture and/or the "dissolution of the subject," while theorists continue to round up and work over the usual suspects. Meanwhile, of course, novels of all stripes have persisted in appearing, from those unquestioningly entrenched in the principles of nineteenth-century realism to those enacting the latest theorem. Novels are received by critical communities that are characterized, according to A. D. Nuttall (1983), by the tendency to see all human culture as epiphenomenal to a set of factors available only to investigators of their particular persuasion. This tendency results often enough in the sort of prophetic absolutism that produces undercutting explanations, seeking to "account for the discourse of an opponent [or the work of an author] not in terms of that opponent's knowledge or ignorance of reality, but as determined 'from below' by factors of which he is unconscious" (Nuttall 1983, 7).

A curious paradox resulting from theoreticism is that while it is now considered rather naive and outmoded to discuss literary characters as representations of human beings, it is considered quite appropriate—chic, even—to endow "texts" with any number of human qualities, such as the ability to carry out "strategies" and betray "anxieties." How can there be any question of representational power, the argument goes, when the hapless author is being spoken, for example, by the language he pretends to master? The power, indeed, has been shifted from the author to the critic, who emerges as the revealer of a "deeper" truth.

Despite the insights that Marxism, Freudianism, and linguistics have brought to literary studies, each of these approaches has shown an inclination toward global claims extrapolated from successful local applications that have collectively contributed to a set of restrictive assumptions about the nature of both literature and critical methodology. While Marxism and Freudianism, insofar as they focus on the determining power of preexisting structures, are no less instances of structural analysis than the theories derived directly from linguistics, it is the latter that make the most pervasive claims on literature, on the obvious grounds that all works, regardless of their thematic or ideological orientation, are analyzable on the level of their linguistic surface. The overall effect of these currents, then, has been to deemphasize, if not to deny altogether, the place of both authorial intention and characterization in the novel, since each of these is centered on the individual agent and takes for granted literature's ability to represent and communicate something of human experience. Thus, much of contemporary theory has proven itself inept at offering any but the most reductive accounts of the sort of novels—beginning with Proust and Joyce and continuing through the century—in which authorial intention and autobiographical genesis of character are very much at issue.

Characterization, in general, is a sore point with theorists who are drawn more toward the medium of representation than toward its objects. Nowhere else, it would seem, is the viability of the novel, or of literature in general, as a representational medium more in question. Ever since Paul Valéry's attack on "literary superstitions"—defined as all "beliefs" that ignore the verbal condition of literature, including the existence of characters, "those beings without innards" (1960, 569)—French criticism and its American derivatives have led the way toward the reduction and exclusion of character, while shifting the focus of attention to strictly linguistic or rhetorical phenomena. In Anglo-American circles, the New Critics prepared the ground for the continental theorists by first isolating the literary work from its representational aspect. Their doctrines of the intentional, biographical, and affective fallacies, when applied to the novel, rendered it meaningless in the ordinary sense.[2] With the work cut off from the sort of commonsense assumptions about agency and intention that characterize our understanding of the world, it can become possible to validate all manner of interpretations. Or, as Frederick Crews puts it somewhat more cynically:

> If the author's inferable intentions are to be put out of mind, the only remaining guide is the theorist himself, now awash in literary data that will be compliant to even an eccentric and ill-considered idea. (1986, 123)

The novel, with its digressive and expansive nature and its formal fluidity, has proven to be especially troublesome for critics with an inclination toward formalism. Valéry, as quoted above, is simply complaining that novelists are not poets, as if fiction were somehow invalidated by dint of its verbal nature. Elsewhere, the linguistics-based theories have obfuscated generic specificity by reducing all types of literature to their linguistic components. One would not, of course, wish to deny the utility of descending from thematic abstractions and impressionistic musings to the page itself in order to ground oneself in the structural and rhetorical elements of a work. Indeed, the movement toward the textual surface, as exemplified and necessitated by *Ulysses,* must be considered the most characteristic gesture of twentieth-century literary thinking. But the tendency to regard literature as merely text has led by now to a somewhat sclerotic orthodoxy that often defies both critical tact and common sense.

The fervor with which linguistics-based theories were embraced in the sixties was a reflection not just of their utility, but also of a particular ideological context, namely, the desire to put the humanities on a more scientific footing. Linguistics provided the cornerstone of the endeavor, since it addressed itself to the common ground upon which disparate spheres of cultural activity might be reduced to quantifiable relational elements. The movement inherited from formalism certain epistemological difficulties, especially as applied to a literary-critical methodology, which it will be useful to examine in some detail. For the moment, however, I wish to call attention to a particular strategic advantage inherent in the emerging theoreticism. Robert Alter's description is to the point:

> The formidable intellectual apparatus of structuralism, moreover, lends a particularly powerful attraction as a method of

studying literature without the old embarrassing concern for value; for it offers the literary intelligentsia what any professional or priestly caste needs in order to maintain its own coherence and morale—an esoteric language, a set of elaborate procedures that can be performed only by the initiate, and the conviction that the specialized rituals of the caste have universal efficacy, or at least universal applicability. (1984, 6)

Here, then, is the latest version of the Rosetta stone, which, like Marxism and Freudianism before it (and so much the better when combined with them), can provide, as Fredric Jameson says of his own methodology, "the ultimate semantic precondition for the intelligibility of literary and cultural texts" (1981, 75) and even "the absolute horizon of all reading and interpretation" (17). If the tone of this assertion is somewhat dogmatic, it is, alas, not at all rare among theoretical initiates. The political implications of possessing the master key of intelligibility are obvious enough, particularly when the notion of "text" is expanded to include all cultural phenomena. One might be tempted, initially, to attribute this ideological fervor to the political climate of the years during which structuralism was emerging as a critical movement. The arrival of structuralism and its derivatives marks an intellectual revolution throughout the West coincident with the coming of age of the postwar generation, and provides the methodology of choice in what is seen as a radical reassessment of the dominant cultural paradigms. But an examination of the paradigms adopted by the structuralist and poststructuralist "projects" will reveal a play of forces much more nuanced than the simple advent of liberation and empowerment so often heralded by their partisans.

The application of linguistics-based formalizing theories to literature took place against a background of increasing attempts to adopt formalist models of the functioning of the human mind as cybernetics came to offer the example of the computer as an epistemological paradigm. It is my contention that to the degree that "theory" shares the premises of information theories and other neoformalisms, it renders itself ill-suited to the comprehension of that dimension of literature which makes it precisely unlike other forms of "discourse," and "theory" becomes, in effect, complicit with the dominant (i.e., technocratic) cultural apparatus. This is most clearly the case for the sort of early structuralist and later semiotic approaches that resulted in tidy formulae and flow charts, but even the poststructuralists who rejected the "scientific" footing of their predecessors have failed to distance themselves from the basic premises underlying the position. If poststructuralists have shown the impossibility of a literary "science," their systematic recourse to the irrational merely repeats the same impossibility in negative terms. Their gesture is one of self-empowerment, although the power is itself an illusion (except to the degree that it may serve one in the academy); in concentrating on the play of signifiers, the critic evades the real consequences of meaning, but the latter will not disappear for our refusal to recognize it.

The short-term political claims of "theory," then, are not really the issue. As Frederick Crews has said, "There is something distinctly odd about attacking a system of oppression by altering the rules of its literary criticism" (1986, 118). Furthermore, it is not at all clear that many "theorists" have even located the oppressor, although it would most often seem to be the author, who has presumed to tame language to representational ends. The point, though, is that in reducing writing to its textual surface (and the writing of the oppressed is leveled as easily as that of the elite), one simply concedes political relevance, thus supporting the status quo. A. D. Nuttall, who is generous in both praising and criticizing structuralism and its suite, has commented on a certain inherent conservatism of the movement:

> The impetus of the movement however is not lost. Its vigor is evident in certain joyous tabus, tabus which to our forefathers would have reeked of reactionary obscurantism, would have been the last thing to be expected from the young or forward-looking; empiricism is rejected, and so is truth-to-life and the free creative sovereignty of the author over his own work. Instead we have certain Gallic epigrams: literature writes itself, people are read by the books they suppose themselves to be reading, thought (not people) thinks, speech speaks, and writing writes.
>
> Thus the fundamental thrust of structuralism is conservative: what is done is done and our trivial individual interventions are mere expressions of a system which is greater than we. (1983, 6)

The task is to separate the practical benefits made available to the critic through the development of tools of narrative analysis from some exaggerated claims and assumptions resulting from a "fallacy of the successful first step."[3] That is, the fact that one has identified structural elements or patterns of a thing does not mean ipso facto that one has grasped the secret of its production, much less its meaning. The early structuralists, on the model of the formalists, were always on the verge of elaborating one or another "grammar of meaning" or "poetics of the story" based on their initial success at elaborating a partial taxonomy of textual elements. Poststructuralists, more subtly, noticed the futility of the search for the ultimate grounding of meaning in rational elements and took the opposite position, that meaning is ungroundable, and thus there can be no business as usual. Although the results of the two approaches are diametrically opposed, they simply illustrate the logical poles of formalism. As Jonathan Culler (1982, 223) cleverly shows, structuralism is a search for regularities that turns up anomalies (assumed to be regular on the next level), while deconstruction is a search for anomalies that results in (rather monotonous) regularities. In either case, one should distinguish between function and meaning, between description and understanding.

The development and popularity of "theory," and its claim to have radically altered our way of understanding, has a parallel in the field of artificial intelligence (A.I.) research, which shares structuralism's formalist premises. During the sixties a group of researchers staked out a rather healthy-sized bit of political and economic turf with the promise that, based on early success at formalizing and replicating elementary mental processes, fully "intelligent" machines were just on the horizon. Although generous Defense Department grants continue to flow in their direction, the A.I. researchers have long since discovered that the replication of human expertise on the basis of reproducing a sequence of discrete, decontextualized steps (like the structuralists' attempt to master the "production of meaning") is quite impossible, and attempts to formalize (render programmable) the "situation"—i.e., the spontaneous and intuitive grasp of context characteristic of the human mind—have proven no more successful. Nonetheless, the formalist model of mental functioning exerts its influence on the culture in various ways (including Italo Calvino's rather embarrassing attempt to describe a computer-age literature, to be discussed in chapter 4).

Again, it is not the practical utility of either computers or structural analysis that is at issue, but rather the consequences of theoretical postures based on erroneous assumptions resulting from the same. Hubert Dreyfus has done a thorough job of detailing the error of the philosophical assumptions behind A.I. Three points of his critique are especially relevant to recognizing the limitations of any formalism, including the literary one. Formalist models of human behavior rest on:

1. A psychological assumption that the mind can be viewed as a device operating on bits of information according to formal rules;
2. An epistemological assumption that all knowledge can be formalized, i.e., understood in terms of a logical calculus; and
3. An ontological assumption that everything essential to intelligent behavior must be analyzable as a set of decontextualized, situation-free elements. (1986, 156)

The digital computer has, in other words, come to supply a paradigm of mental processes—the information-processing model—in much the same way that laws of thermodynamics supplied the conceptual model for Freudianism. The structuralist ambition of deciphering the codes that produce meaning rests on the assumption that the mind operates on literature in the same way that a computer would: by comparing, classifying, searching lists, etc. It is important not to confuse information with meaning, or processing with understanding. Meaning and understanding can only be the results of the context—the preexisting organizational field of experience—in which human beings assign relevance to things. The fact that the context is conditioned by culture, as well as by the laws of chemistry and physics, does not mean that it is an ideological construct and that we are floating in a sea of indeterminacy. The "text" is precisely what remains of literature when it has been removed from its meaningful context, and structuralist and poststructuralist theories alike operate on the implicit assumption that such a decontextualized reading takes place at some level of our experience. Meaning thus becomes calculable, or incalculable (to the poststructuralist), in terms of situation-free elements (insofar as the theorist limits the situation to the text itself and excludes the world of which it is a product and in which it appears) as opposed to being determined by analogy to actual or imagined life experience.

Dreyfus situates his dispute with the A.I. theorists in the long tradition of conflict between rational and practical philosophers, or between philosophers and antiphilosophers. Poststructuralists, when championing playful Nietzschean nihilism, would appear at first glance to fall on the antiphilosophical side of the ledger, but as Culler so convincingly demonstrates, one cannot simply oppose the scientificity of structuralism to the purposeful irrationality of deconstruction. To turn something inside out is not to refute it; one rests on the same premises. The two theoretical positions are of the same coin: the one depends upon the elaboration of the rules behind phenomena, and the other reinterprets phenomena as a result of the rules' inelaborability.

Simply to substitute structural relativism for atomistic objectivism does not end the theorist's difficulty, although it opens new perspectives. It ought to be evident that the sort of formalist combinatorial schemata that Vladimir Propp derived from certain Russian folktales will not suffice to explain the modern novel to the degree that the latter moves beyond the framework of the action narrative or popular romances so widely read by semiologists.[4] Indeed, the evolution of the novel might well be described in terms of a shift from movement of plot to depth of characterization. When structuralism turned its attention away from the combinatorial possibilities of the plot, however, it still ignored characterization in favor of strictly linguistic and rhetorical phenomena and thus remained limited in accounting for the novel. In excluding the representational dimension of the genre, theory tends toward what Nuttall calls metaphysical structuralism. This is what Valéry, or more recently Hélène Cixous,[5] indulges in when he relegates character to nonbeing in favor of textual "realities." But as Nuttall points out, form can only be understood as form in relation to a well-founded conception of matter or content. If meaning is conferred through context, and not merely through signifiers that would be decodable by a machine, the ultimate context must be the world itself.

It would seem, then, that "theory" has relegated the represented experiential content of literature to its repressed unconscious. Questions of affect in representation or in response and questions of intended meaning are presumed to be as off-base in discussing the novel as they would be in discussing abstract painting. Academic criticism, where it has become preoccupied with revealing rhetorical features and gaps in the logic of representation, has in effect conceded the assessment of literary meaning and value to others. For it seems clear that novelists have continued to write for reasons other than the exercise of technique or the illustration of theorems, and readers continue to turn to the novel for purposes other than resisting representational chicanery and proving themselves secure against naive responses. Surely, a cultivated literary intelligence ought to include the ability to analyze technique—we are quite aware, after all, that we are studying a work of art and not reality—but to reduce the work to an impersonal, ahistorical, textual surface is truly naive, or else cynical. The novel as a genre is predicated on the simple commonsense notion that people enjoy vicariously participating in (i.e., witnessing, empathizing with, imagining) other people's possible experiences, comparing them to or imagining them as their own. That all of this is facilitated through certain technical means does not invalidate it.

As I have suggested earlier, there is a similarity between certain exclusionary postures of New Criticism and structuralism. Ralph Rader (1974) has noted that the mind is dependent on just the sort of interpretive assumptions about agency and intention proscribed by New Critical theory in its encounters with both literature and the world. The context that gives sense to our assumptions is that of storytelling; a voice is relating an account of experience that approximates our knowledge of the world. A. D. Nuttall offers a version of this argument in tracing the history of the dissolution of mimesis, pointing out that while it is true that one cannot verify one's intuition of an author's mood on the basis of a mood displayed in a work that is perfectly capable of being a complete fiction, it is nevertheless true that, for example,

> *certain expressions could not so much as "give the impression" of sadness if they did not in some degree reflect what people say or suffer when they actually feel sad. The New Critics, in their rejection of specific authorial intention, did not sufficiently notice the persisting force of hypothetical*

> *intention,* the cogency of which is rooted in ordinary behavior. (1983, 90; Nuttall's emphasis)

Nuttall likens the New Critical posture to certain attitudes of formalists that he describes as "logical Calvinism," in which there can be no middle ground: neither the attack on intention nor the attack on verisimilitude will allow for the hypothetical or the probable. The degree of relevance of our intuitions or deductions concerning authorial intent will vary greatly among works, although I will attempt to establish further on that there is a major subgenre of the novel that depends upon such consideration of the author to achieve its meaning. First, however, it will be necessary to examine the ideological and philosophical basis of the rejection of the standard of verisimilitude that underlies all of the mentioned critical movements. One would not dispute that there are individual works and modes of writing to which the notion of verisimilitude is irrelevant, but general literary theories that discount the validity of the principle and seek to undercut absolutely the representational aspect of literature should not be justified on that basis.

Structuralists, like A.I. researchers, have banked heavily on the model of the Chomskian theory of linguistic competence abstracted from human performance. The theory is that without having internalized the "grammar" of literary meaning one would be unable to wrest sense from the linguistic structures of the work, and that by abstracting from this process the structuralist will then expose the rules governing the "production" of meaning. The presumption is that the reader, once enlightened, will somehow be freer to supply new interpretations, as if the discovery that language is the medium of sense somehow changed that sense. Hubert Dreyfus, in citing Chomsky's theory as one of the underlying factors in the failure of A.I. to make good on its theoretical claims, identifies it as:

> a powerful conjunction of the Platonic assumption that the formalism which enables us to *understand* behavior is also involved in *producing* that behavior, and the Kantian assumption that all orderly behavior is governed by rules, both reinforced by the idea of the computer program. (1979, 332; Dreyfus's emphasis)[6]

Again, it is important to appreciate the distinction between identifying formal components of a work's artifice and explaining the work;

we are dealing with language, not pigment, and language necessarily has referents that cannot be excluded from an explanation. Theorists err in assuming that a formalism elicited to analyze a work can be projected back as the work's generating principle. If this were so, and if literature were reducible to a set of rules of meaning, our word processors would be writing novels and not just shuffling our words around. When we look, in subsequent chapters, at novels built upon even the most elaborate structuring principles—i.e., those that ought to come closest to the structuralist's ideal of form as meaning—we shall see that such attention to and at times emphasis on form does not in the least preclude mimetic intentions. In fact, one measure of the success of such works—starting with Proust and Joyce—is found in the extent to which they employ deliberate structural patterning to a representational end, combining a realist aesthetic with a novelistic poetics.

The competence theory stands behind "theory's" claims to radicalism. If meaning can be shown to be a "product" of the writing/reading "system," and if the means of production can be exposed as a cultural—hence ideological, not natural—phenomenon, "liberation" will become possible (as if writers, not governments and power elites, were the oppressors). The argument that power is a product of discourse or that it depends upon the logocentricity of thought categories will not do, since the expression of any opposition (or of theorists, for that matter) can come from none but the same structures. As Nuttall observes, the discourse of the left is as readily deconstructable as that of the right. The notion that opening new horizons of interpretation is in itself a progressive act—a notion that seems to enjoy much currency among theorists—is rather too simplistic, as it describes the *modus operandi* of fascism as well as anything else. The extent to which "theory" has been identified with political innovation is indeed surprising, given the feeble nature of the claim. There is a great difference between freeing an intellectual elite to justify new critical postures and freeing people from the very real oppression that persists in the world, with or without the complicity of novelists. In repudiating the author's intention, the reader's claim to interpretive validity, and the evidential grounds of debate, theorists, aside from defining a vacuum that they will then fill, exercise a nihilism that, by default, can only support the status quo.

When theorists, on the basis of the notion of literary competence, describe meaning as an ideological product, they are discounting the importance of literary history and tradition. That is, given that literature does not operate in the same manner as other language, one must account for the context in which the reader comprehends its "codes"; why, in other words, is it not incomprehensible? To the hard-line theorist, our understanding is facilitated by an ideological choice to follow the rules proposed by the text. It is but a step from this notion to the implicit belief in a hermeneutics of suspicion, suggesting that all human culture is supported by a widespread motivated cover-up of the truth, which it becomes the theorist's privilege to expose. This is the essence of what frequently passes for "empowerment." "The system" of language speaks the author and reads for the reader, upholding its built-in values, but the source of its ideology remains in the shadows. The interested parties in this scheme are apparently either everyone who has participated in Western culture since about the fifth century B.C., or everyone not espousing the privileged theory. It is undoubtedly a valuable exercise to demonstrate the borders of the culture that conditions one's interpretation of the world, but it is not clear why the knowledge that there are horizons should somehow radically disturb what lies within them, unless, of course, we're dealing with someone who has taken his or her culture to be a state of nature. What "theory" enacts, then, is the obverse of the conception of culture as the accretion of individual and collective creative acts.

Between the notions of the absolute sovereignty of systems and the absolute sovereignty of willful individual subjects there is room for understanding literature as a transhistorical phenomenon of which the practitioners form a continuous cultural community.[7] Even the novel, relative latecomer that it is, cannot be very well assimilated to any particular local cultural paradigm (e.g., the rise of the bourgeoisie) once one has recognized its place in a continuum of evolving narrative techniques. My point is that literature, as constituted diachronically, should be recognized not merely as a linguistic phenomenon, but as a tradition of storytelling. The novel in particular can be understood as coming from a tradition of recounting individual destinies and evolving through technical innovations in the representation of consciousness.[8] Critical sophistication cannot obscure the fact that people read novels out of curiosity about others and the world, among other reasons. To replace this tradition with the idea of a grammar of meaning production, for example, and to dismiss the interpretive context as ideology is a questionable gesture. The "ideology" in question is not local—like, say, that of the Third Republic, or even of industrial capitalism—it is rather the result of a history of storytelling and character illustration. It is such a tradition that authorizes our assumption that the goal of literature is the communication of some sense. What theory offers in its place will be a statement about language, or perhaps a repudiation of the "text's" ability to accomplish what any literate person will concede it accomplishes. The theorist may, as does Jonathan Culler (1975, 230), explain that the meaning one derives from reading novels from a character-centered framework is merely the result of an ideological prejudice, but the choice to decode it as a semiological artifact, or to "tease out the warring forces of signification within the text" (1982, 220), is no more objectively founded and is more than a little arrogant, as this "undercutting" is undertaken toward the end of endowing the critic with "feelings of mastery" (225) and "a powerful procedure for *producing* meaning" (248; my emphasis).

Culler's thorough elucidation of structuralism, for example, seems designed to make the teleological determination of "the project" quite clear. His jargon and a certain smugness would seem to indicate that the goal of reversing all of the usual assumptions about literature (whether gratuitously or not) has decided the findings of the theorist at every turn. Writing is to be opaque, any representational view of it must be based on ignorance, or complicity in a fraudulent and outmoded system. All terms are thus reversed: detail becomes "apparently insignificant," the narrator's viewpoint becomes "anomalous," understanding becomes "recuperation" or "naturalization." If the naive reader should find a work intelligible, that illusion is purchased at the exorbitant cost of missing the fundamental incoherence of the "text." Comprehension is, then, the result of no less than a "powerful strategy to prevent texts from becoming writing" (i.e., unattributable gibberish; 1975, 200).

Culler's best example of such a strategy (1975, 200–201) centers on the question of characterization, specifically on the technique of indirect focalization or limited point of view. He cites a passage from *Madame Bovary* (more precisely R. J. Sherrington's reading of same) to illustrate the sort of narrative confusion we must rationalize in order to attain sense. The problem seems to be that details focalized through a character's awareness are not strictly separated from the narrator's own diction or the author's aesthetic ends (as we shall see in an example taken from Roland Barthes) or from details that would seem to be of no relevance in illustrating character. For example, Culler catches Sherrington saying of the passage in question (Flaubert 1951, 310–11) that "only the details which force themselves upon Charles' awareness are mentioned." This might work as far as patterns of light or perspiration on Emma's shoulders go, but Culler draws the line at the mention of some flies crawling around on glasses and drowning in the dregs of cider therein. Surely there is nothing to deduce, he says, about Charles's character in this description, which comes between the two previously mentioned. Culler maintains that if we attribute the fly perception to Charles, we are engaging in circular reasoning—it is Charles's perception because it's there and vice-versa—and he goes on to impugn the sophistication of readers who would buy such a scam. What is passed over, however, is the necessity of attributing the perception to Charles at all (even though there's no good reason why one couldn't). It is not at all clear why attribution must be certain and completely motivated for anyone other than the structuralist, whose systematization, to be successful, must be complete. Indirect discourse and limited focalization do not function through some disappearance of the narrator, but rather via a usually subtle and intermittent conflation of voice and viewpoint. The light, the flies, and Emma—from whatever perceptual locus—are all presented to the imagination of the reader, and the presence of the flies, if it does nothing to enhance our knowledge of Charles, does nothing to undercut it either. What Culler calls the "considerable interest in the behavior and death of flies" (201) is in actuality conveyed in a passing sentence displaying nothing that would connote any special attention being given to the perception. It is perfectly acceptable to the reader as the sort of thing likely to be seen in a farmhouse on a sunny day in early spring. It is the impression that counts; its precise source is of little importance in this case.

Culler, though, worried by the narrator's instability, or perhaps by the unexplainable presence of the flies in the first place, given that there is nothing especially Charles-like about the image, determines that such a reading amounts to a "last ditch strategy for humanizing writing and making personality the focal point of the text" (201). The reader, then, is apparently following the lead of critics like Henry

James who have worked out the rationale behind the strategy. In any event, Culler explains the strategy as follows:

> If we cannot compose the text by attributing everything to a single narrator we can break it down into scenes or episodes and give meaning to details by treating them as what was noticed by a character who was present at the time. (201)

Led on by the presumption that the text makes sense, we will seemingly concoct any theoretical sleight of hand—such as claiming that the narrative voice has taken on a character's perspective—to achieve that end. The "we" to whom Culler refers are readers who want first of all to postulate a single narrator and who, when faced with inconsistency, resort to a "modern literary convention" made explicit by James and his followers. "Our" first choice, then, would be to "compose" the text by presuming a singular narrative point of view.

Whether the "composer" is general reader or critic, Culler is wrong. The "text" was composed by the author, who is notably absent from Culler's version. Obviously enough, readers, undisturbed by anxiety over univocacy and free-floating detail, understood *Madame Bovary* perfectly well before James explicated the technique of limited point of view. James described a technique employed by the author; he did not perform logical gymnastics in order to explain away incoherence. The reader may or may not be cognizant of questions of attribution but nonetheless understands the author's representation. The reader follows the indicators of the author's technique, based on previous experience of literature and of the general conventions of storytelling. The "text," in other words, is not decoded by a Martian or a hyper-rationalist, but read by someone who understands it as belonging to a certain tradition. If Culler's version is accepted—if we are resorting to strategems to produce sense where there would otherwise be only a schizoid narrative voice and incoherence—one must then suppose that either the author or "James and his followers" are acting in great ignorance or very bad faith. It should be no surprise that literature doesn't just go about "meaning" in the void, but that it requires a conditioned audience. Culler, while snidely deriding "extreme advocates of recuperation" and "representational justification which few sophisticated readers of novels would now allow themselves to employ" (201), has no more attractive alternative to propose than the notion of "writing" itself—that decontextualized, unattributable entity that will spring forth in all its radiant incoherence once we abandon our ideologically motivated obsession with meaning.

Culler has nothing to say, then, about Flaubert in his example. If we are wrong in accepting that particular moments in narration are meant to convey indirectly a character's perception or response, what are the implications? Is Flaubert a bad writer, or are we bad readers, or both? Is Flaubert merely sloppy—has he forgotten his feigned objectivity as narrator and identified with his character—or is he rather caught in a dilemma inherent in the impossible task of trying to get language to represent? One need neither worship the artist as lord of creation nor decry him for a fraud, one would hope. Readers who accept the logical demands of the author's technique are simply agreeing to the terms of the artifice for the satisfaction of the story, of participating in the world it evokes in the imagination, and they do so independently of any theoretical explication of their intuitive understanding. This understanding is based on the reasonable commonsense assumption that one is confronted with a meaningful representation.

These would thus seem to be the irreducible positions: the partisan of "theory" will accuse me of upholding the old teleology of meaning or of character, and I will claim its advantage over the teleology of non-sense on the grounds that the rewards of interpreting a work in the context of an evolving tradition of literary representation are richer than the rewards of "undercutting" that dimension in favor of restricting oneself to the play of various textual phenomena. Reading literature "transparently" (Nuttall's term for accepting the representational premise) does not preclude textual analysis, whereas theorists persistently declare previous modes of reading obsolete. In any event, the structuralists' approach to the novel is very weak in accounting for character, as Culler concedes (although he's quick to advance the reasons it doesn't want to), and equally weak in deciding what to do with the author, other than dismiss him and pirate the text. The author pretends to have something to say about life, and could be wrong; the theorist says that the only thing he can really talk about is language, and he is certainly right.

If indeed reading is dependent upon "models of intelligibility," those models are based on our experience of both the tradition of literature and the interactions, thoughts, and feelings of ourselves and others in the world. Culler does not offer any other possible source of intelligibility and is unable to describe clearly any advantage to be had from unintelligibility. Neither has the *nouveau roman* succeeded in embodying any alternative criteria. Culler disparages the sort of "recuperation" that seeks to make sense of Robbe-Grillet's works, for instance, by postulating the characteristics of the narrator responsible for the mode of a particular text (e.g., paranoia, obsession, etc.), but he offers no advantage to not doing so. If, "as Stephen Heath has admirably demonstrated," such novels become "thoroughly banal when naturalized" (200), Culler does not tell us exactly what they are without such "naturalization," nor does he offer any rationale for his implicit valorization of pure, formalizable linguistic product, namely, "*écriture.*" Once again, the "project," when it goes beyond its methodological utility and makes ideological claims, seems to be gratuitous: its ultimate justification would seem to be the power-grab itself.

There ought to be nothing surprising in the realization that literature makes use of specialized techniques that differ from those of everyday speech or from other written language, but somehow the fact that literature defies strict formal reduction causes great excitement for the structuralist. The notion of competence thus becomes crucial: if a particular approach or context is necessary to our way of understanding literature, then that understanding seems to be false, according to the logic. The source of this "illusion" is not seen as perception that has been conditioned by the mode of expression of the work—a notion common enough in the visual arts—that is, as a communicative process between author and reader, but as a misguided response based on naive assumptions (if not something more sinister, as if we were seeing figurative images in abstract painting, or hearing a narrative in a symphony). The language system is doing its thing, and reader and writer are equally victimized, evidently.

There is no question of the author in all of this. It is not deemed important whether or not Flaubert has succeeded to a greater or lesser degree with his technique—i.e., whether the overlapping of Charles's perceptions (if indeed they are such) with the narrator's voice or interests causes confusion or a breakdown in the reader's reception, renders a vivid and convincing impression, or what. Instead, Culler calls into question the existence of the technique, which emerges as an anomaly in relation to the structuralist's ideal. If one has not registered the anomaly, it is presumably because of bad (read: traditional) reading habits. Culler clouds the question of the agency of this bad reading, for while he seems on one hand to suggest that the "we" means all nonstructuralist readers, he at the same time blames James and his followers. Even if one allows that he uses "James" to indicate the articulator of what was already a widespread practice, the move is the same: Culler takes the novel as it is encountered in the practice of readers, declares the practice invalid and/or obsolete, and skips over the fact that the critics are simply describing, not prescribing, the way that the novels are read. It's not as if James had advanced an argument and the structuralists had disproved it; James described a current practice and the structuralists reject it on a value judgment. If a given critic does a bad job of explaining or if a given author does not produce a perfectly crafted airtight narrative, is the logical conclusion that the "sophisticated" reader can no longer accept any representational premise in literature? The standard of exactitude implicit in the structuralists' argument (any anomaly in an ideally regular theoretical schema is grounds for a cover theory and usually an ideological pronouncement) is their own theoretical creation; it does not operate in the practice of competent reading.

By choosing the most obvious point of attack in his example—that is, ridiculing the idea that the presence of the flies should reveal something about Charles's character—Culler overlooks what seems to be the true source of his irritation. The problem about the flies, although Culler doesn't name it directly and deflects it onto the issue of character and voice, is a problem of motivation; the flies remain for Culler an anomaly, a gratuitous, inassimilable detail. The underlying issue he's not addressing is that of verisimilitude: what is the structuralist to do with random elements of decor that cannot be assigned some symbolic or ideological value, that escape, in other words, the categories of a grammar of meaning?

This is, of course, the problem tackled by Roland Barthes in his well-known essay "L'effet de réel." Barthes, characteristically, poses an astute question from which he draws some curious conclusions. The basic issue in the background of the essay is methodological and serves to illustrate Dreyfus's point about the fallacy of the assumption that a formalism used to understand a thing must have been involved in the thing's production. Since seemingly random detail defies, according to Barthes, assimilation in the semiotic structure of the story, it threatens the integrity of the entire project. It is at such moments of confronting the limitations of its systematization that structuralism provides the jumping-off point of poststructuralism. Structuralism, in coming up against those elements that "exceed" the system, provides the "irregularities" that are the common currency of deconstruction. Both are predicated on the (im)possibility of rationally systematizing literature as a linguistic product.

Poststructuralism, no less than structuralism, springs from the search for grounding; it just takes off from the fact of its impossibility. John Searle (1983) notes that Derrida is correct in seeing that there aren't any foundations, but that he marks himself as a classical metaphysician by acting as if foundations were necessary, as if something were lost or threatened without them. The failure of transcendental grounding, as Wittgenstein shows (and Pascal knew), leaves everything just as it is. "Theory" does not successfully undermine novelistic representation, nor does it contribute to our understanding of the genre's central figure, the character.

Descriptive detail, then, when it cannot be easily assigned to a motivated informational syntax, is bound to provoke a great reaction as the theorist scrambles to circumvent the literary, as opposed to linguistic, conclusion—that description is serving a representational end, that the flies are there because that's just what you would expect. Quite often, description serves to add depth, that is, to convey or elicit a feeling, a sense of participation or empathy that is quite immeasurable and inadmissable to structuralism's textual analysis,[9] which is at home with the surface level of plot movement.

Early in his essay, Barthes admits the stakes. Whereas "superfluous" details could be "recuperated by the structure" and given an indirect functional value to the extent that they constitute "some indicator of character or atmosphere," something more precise is wanted:

> It seems rather that, if the analysis claims to be exhaustive (and indeed, of what value could a method be which didn't account for the entirety of its object, that is, in this case, for the entire surface of the narrative fabric?), it must, in attempting to reach the absolute detail, the indivisible unity, the fleeting transition,

in order to assign them to a place in the structure, inevitably encounter notations which no function (not even the most indirect conceivable) will allow one to justify: these notations are scandalous (from the point of view of the structure), or, what's even more disquieting, they seem to be accorded a sort of *luxury* of the narration, extravagant to the point of dispensing "useless" details and to thus raise, in places, the cost of the narrative information. (1984, 167–68; Barthes's emphasis)

There is a shrewd question behind Barthes's anxiety over proliferating detail: why one detail and not another? If details can in fact escape narratological motivation, and if the premises of structuralism exclude a mimetic purpose (going outside the text), and given that we cannot even consider the question of mood, then to what informational or rhetorical category can we possibly assign such elements? If we cannot so assign them, we will be left with no principle of selection—i.e., production—that will allow us to account for the presence of a particular detail as opposed to any other, or to an infinity of detail, for that matter:

> So soon as discourse would no longer be guided and limited by the structural imperatives of the story (functions and indicators), nothing else would be able to indicate why the details of a description should stop here rather than there; if it weren't submitted to an aesthetic or rhetorical choice, any "view" would be inexhaustible by discourse: there would always be a corner, a detail, an inflection of space or color to retrieve. (Barthes 1984, 171–72)

In other words, realistic description is always determined by aesthetic or rhetorical factors, rather than by verisimilitude, otherwise the border between representation and object could not hold. The realist description, in pretending fidelity to the referent, is simply preventing itself from slipping off in the other direction, toward infinite fabrication. Whether or not Barthes accomplishes anything other than establishing a category for the uncategorizable is open to question; the more important factor here is that he plainly mistakes analysis for production, applying the criteria of the one to the other. It is the structuralist who is preoccupied with the grounds for restriction of detail, not the author. A computer might go about composing a scene by referring itself to the totality of available information and then narrowing the field, but this is a preposterous model of human behavior. The writer doesn't start with the whole of reality, or even the whole of a part, and go about retrieving bits of it; description is rather determined by a representational end. How are we ever to determine "laws" governing artistic expression? Even in the case of painstakingly researched detail such as one finds in *Ulysses,* where it might seem at least tempting to say that details were chosen because they were in fact those present in Dublin on Bloomsday—in other words, the case that seems most like plain transcription—some inexplicable "choice" has occurred that is unaccountable to aesthetic or rhetorical justification. Why one storefront and not another? Why one street and not another? There may or may not be a straightforward answer to such questions—perhaps a particular detail was motivated by an unknowable personal detail of the author's life; no matter, the reader has no need to rationalize textual elements, as long as they pass as consistent to the conditions of the imaginary context, which is evaluated in a manner analogous to the way in which we evaluate the world. The point is that just because the critic is motivated to postulate a criterion of selection underlying a given descriptive element, that does not necessarily mean that a choice was made by the author or that intelligibility depends on assigning such a determination.

Barthes depends on such attribution because, as he says, his analysis is useless unless all details can be assimilated to the narrative surface. Without the "structural imperatives of the story" to account for the troublesome details, Barthes decides that they fulfill a purely aesthetic function and sets out to show that description has, since antiquity, been ornamental. Using his own example from *Madame Bovary,* he contends that literary realism is "submitted to the tyrannic constraints of aesthetic verisimilitude" (170), that is, it consists of a skeletal reference to its object, fleshed out with a lot of linguistic flourish. Barthes seems almost indignant at the discovery that literature is not photography, much less the presence of the original.

The scene, a description of Rouen as seen from a carriage entering the city, provides Flaubert the opportunity for a stylistic exercise, as if "all that were important about Rouen were the rhetorical figures" (170) it inspired. Barthes says that the scene, "impertinent" in regard to narrative structure, is motivated by literary rather than realistic "laws"; its sense depends not on conformity to a model, but rather on cultural rules of representation. He is too quick, however—and quite incorrect—to dismiss the scene as structurally irrelevant. He declares that the scene cannot be attached to "any functional sequence nor to any characterizing, atmospheric, or sapiential signified" (171), but the description—the narrator's metaphoric effusion notwithstanding—is clearly within Emma's focus. Even if one supposes that Emma, despite her preoccupation with romanticism, is incapable of translating her perceptions into what Barthes terms "jewels of rare metaphors"[10] for which "Rouen" is a mere background (as opposed to an authentically represented object, one presumes), Flaubert has taken unmistakable pains to put the narration within the frame of her consciousness.

The passage opens with two paragraphs giving an external description of Emma as she arises and goes to wait (impatiently) for the carriage that is to take her to Rouen and to Leon. After a brief omniscient description of the carriage en route, we enter Emma's mind indirectly:

> Emma knew it [the road] from one end to the other; she knew that after a pasture there was a post, then an elm, a barn, or a boater's shack; once in a while, in order to surprise herself, she would shut her eyes. But she never lost a clear sense of the distance remaining. (Flaubert 1951, 530)

"Finally" the city "was appearing" at a glance. Although Flaubert uses the impersonal pronoun *on* in attributing this view, the imperfect marks it as an ongoing process, and whose goings-on have we been witnessing, if not Emma's? Next comes the paragraph quoted by Barthes, the one containing the metaphoric account of the view, which does not mention Emma at all—the view is unmediated. The next paragraph gives Emma's reactions to the scene:

> Something vertiginous detached itself from these amassed existences, for her, and her heart swelled with abandon as if the 120,000 souls throbbing there had all together sent her the steam of the passions she supposed them to have. Her love was growing before that space, and was filling up with the tumult at

the vague droning that was rising up from it. She was spilling it over outside, over the squares, the promenades, the streets, and the old Norman city was spreading itself out before her eyes like an enormous capital, like a Babylon that she was entering. (531)

The paragraph goes on to describe her externally, and the following paragraph has her getting out of the carriage.

The paragraph quoted above is a classic case of focalized, character-centered narration: the words (and the population of the city) are rendered in the narrative voice, but the sentiments and the view inspiring them portray the inner state of the character. Whether or not Emma "actually" thinks of Babylon is unimportant; the simile serves as a correlative of her emotion, and provides a measure of ironic distancing on the narrator's part which itself contributes to the characterization. There is no reason to declare that the paragraph preceding this one, which contains the metaphors, is "impertinent" to characterization—despite the fact that no mention of Emma is made—when it comes sandwiched between paragraphs that are unquestionably focalized through her.

But even if one were to overrule my attribution conclusively, what would change? The plot is still advanced with Emma's arrival, the impatience evidenced in the external descriptions of her and the effusion suggested by the similes still convey her affective state, and the central paragraph provides a stylized description of the panorama of Rouen. The reader receives the elements of a visual impression of the scene and a sense of the character's emotional state that is relevant to the subsequent action. One does not turn to a novel to see what Rouen really looks like, nor does one turn to a photograph to sense the emotional state of a lonely, romantic, self-deluding provincial doctor's wife entering the city where her lover resides. Presumably, most readers have not had the pleasure of verifying the accuracy of Flaubert's version of coming upon Rouen in a carriage, but conformity to the model is not really the issue here. The description is acceptable, it is even probable, insofar as it does not defy any commonly held notion of natural law or geography: there are no palm trees, for instance; the islands in the river are not jumping about like salmon. In claiming that verisimilitude is supported by consensus rather than by his notion of fidelity to the real, Barthes passes over the fact that such consensus is governed by probability—

by what we expect of the world based on our experience in it—and implies that it is therefore an ideological construct.

Barthes's show of indignation at the "discovery" that Flaubert's Rouen is actually composed of metaphors is silly: didn't we know all along that we were dealing with linguistic artifice? One ought not mistake the elements of textual analysis for the "product" of the text. A description is realistic not because, as Barthes says, it interrupts the aesthetic discourse with a naked naming of the concrete real (making, as usual, the reader come off as the victim of some chicanery), but rather because it strikes us as a reasonable probability in its context, and our standard of reference is our knowledge of the world. Nuttall's response to Barthes's celebrated claim, in the same essay, that the "superfluous" barometer in Flaubert's "Un coeur simple" is there to announce "I am the real" is decisive: the barometer says, in fact, "Am I not just the sort of thing you would find in such a setting?" (Nuttall 1983, 56)

What both Culler's and Barthes's examples suggest is that structural analysis cannot, as the latter would have it, "account for the totality of its object" without being forced into theoretical positions whose logical consequences are so at odds with the actual practice of reading and writing novels that either the theory or the practice must appear ridiculous. "Scandalous" details such as the barometer or the flies can remain functionally unaccountable because they may appear without any reason at all, the way that a fly appears on my desk; the author may be imitating or suggesting the inexhaustibility of the world in creating a probable image. Barthes's solution, to declare this lack of reason a reason in itself, accomplishes little. These details are not added-on snapshots of the world used to justify a realist premise; they are elements in an imaginative whole for which a theoretical explication may or may not be possible. In any case, this is an area where the motivational hypothesis—and that is, in effect, what Barthes is seeking—almost certainly does not correspond to the process of the text's creation. There is no reason to expect, in other words, that the product of the human way of knowing—of immersion in a situation, the intuitive grasp, the imaginative leap—ought to be exhaustively explicable as a textual surface. Only a text generated by a computer (or a mind that patterns its functioning after a computer)—i.e., one whose every element is in fact justifiable in terms of a logical calculus—will meet the criteria of the sort of analysis Barthes proposes. Novels, on the other hand, are the product of and the representation of human awareness immersed in a referential totality, and we understand their details as elements of such a context.

Thus, the standard of verisimilitude must fall if structuralists are to account for nagging details of the text. Once the standard is overthrown, our understanding becomes an arbitrary construct.

Gérard Genette, in the essay "Vraisemblance et motivation" (1969), judges verisimilitude from a different, and somewhat more successful, point of view. Genette wisely associates the principle not with correspondence to the real, but with a standard of believable behavior on the part of characters, citing seventeenth-century quarrels over the propriety and likelihood of certain behaviors in *Le Cid* and *La Princesse de Clèves*. His argument concludes with the articulation of a formula—Value = Function - Motivation—in which motivation is the rationale offered in order to cover up the narrative function. For example, Cervantes makes Don Quixote an erudite in order to justify the intrusion of critical disquisitions in the novel. The reader or audience will begin to grumble when the cost, measured in willing suspension of disbelief, becomes too high for the functional return. According to this schema, the content of a work can only be a motivation, "a justification a posteriori of the form which, in fact, determines it" (96). This, then, is a full-blown formalism, and like most formalist grids has the advantage of great clarity and a functional model, and the disadvantage of a rather limited range of application. It is not coincidental that Genette's two major examples come from the seventeenth century—a play and an early novel, respectively. Although the formula offers an improvement over Culler and Barthes insofar as it attempts to account for characterization, its simplicity and its narrative focus limit its utility to the most elementary plots. The modern novel, as it becomes increasingly concerned with consciousness rather than events, will thoroughly frustrate the formula. Measuring the narrative value of Julien Sorel's attempt on his ex-lover's life, for instance, contributes little to our understanding of the character or Stendhal's novel. How are we to accept the notion that form determines content—including characterization—in novels that, taking off from Stendhal's fictionalization of a newspaper account of a crime, draw their content from actuality and, eventually, make a game of form?

As Hugh Bredin (1982) points out, all attempts to formalize

characterization are doomed to frustration if they leave out, as they must, psychological—in contrast to narrative—motivation. This does not mean that literary characters ought to be viewed as analyzable psyches conforming to the Freudian or other tenets of the critic/ analyst; it simply means that their behavior is quite often more likely to be understood as conditioned by a standard of possible human behavior in the world than as a retro-determined narrative step necessitated by the story's outcome. The novel, unlike the folktale, is not readily reducible to narrative functions identified with various "types" precisely because of the degree of individuation of its characters.[11] We accomplish very little by putting Proust's Marcel and Joyce's Dedalus together as, say, "young artists" or "seekers of epiphany" when what they do is of relative unimportance compared to their consciousness while doing it. It should be obvious that as plot becomes less determinate, assigning narrative functions becomes less instructive. Character is, in Bredin's strong formulation, substantial, not relational, and a cause of action, not caused. Structuralism's point, meanwhile, should be well taken: knowing now that characters are but the product of verbal artifice, one can better appreciate the magic of the medium's transparent opening onto imaginary worlds that tell us—through analogy—about our own.

Anglo-American criticism, which has traditionally demonstrated somewhat more faith (if occasional gullibility) with regard to character than its Gallic counterpart, has seen various attempts at reconciling the existence of character with the exigencies of textual analysis, including W. J. Harvey's influential *Character and the Novel* (1965). Harvey endeavors to establish a ground for a mimetic theory of the novel that would replace the discredited Victorian notion of the "Eternal Human Heart," and to do so borrows the Kantian notion of constitutive categories, to wit: time, identity, causality, and freedom. These categories provide the contexts that give meaning to the raw data of narration. They are elements of the structure of experience, comprising the basics of consciousness, the necessary focus of the evaluation of character, and they have the advantage of being stable enough within the history of the genre without resorting to claims of rational universality. These structures do not work through the individual in a deterministic way, but rather provide an interpretive frame for characters' manners, morals, passions, and thoughts. As

Rawdon Wilson (1979) suggests, there is an uncertainty to this approach stemming from the imprecision of the categories and doubts as to the range of their applicability. The category of "freedom" seems particularly troublesome, as it is apparently designed to suit Harvey's chief case studies, Sartre's characters, whose genesis as illustrations of philosophical theorems makes them perhaps too atypical. Harvey's approach does, however, respond to character as a dimension of "the whole book and nearly always a quality of long passages of the prose continuum" (1965, 200) whereas structuralism and New Criticism must concern themselves with short passages and more immediate textual phenomena.

The history of the novel to which Harvey refers coincides with the development of the liberal (Kantian, pluralistic) imagination. The liberal mind addresses itself to the conflicting, the partial, the relative, the human, in short, as opposed to the absolute. Implicit to it is the belief that the individual will always exceed the categories of any ideology. This is in contrast to the sort of theoretical monism that would reduce the individual to a single determining factor such as language. Harvey sees the novel's liberality as distinguishing it from poetry:

> Great poems have been written from a monistic position. If we shift our terms a little we can easily relate the monistic to Keats's "egotistical sublime" and the pluralistic to his "negative capability." The novelist, much more than the poet, *must* be endowed with "negative capability." . . . A poet *can*, if he wants to, make a final and total commitment to a single ideology; the novelist cannot. (26; Harvey's emphasis)

The point concerning the novel's pluralism is well taken (although one must allow for such experiments in monomaniacal narration as are practiced by Beckett, for instance), but this should not be allowed to obscure the fact that the novel does owe much to poetic techniques of representation insofar as the novelist may often employ variations on the dramatic lyric or monologue forms in fashioning a character or a narrating persona. The "egotistical sublime" of a Wordsworth might in fact make a more suitable paradigm for the modernist novel, given its accent on personal lyricism. M. A. Goldberg, in his analysis of Stephen's aesthetic in *A Portrait of the Artist*, notes that in that work "liberty and beauty are to be identified with self-perception and self-knowledge—not with the ardent interaction of self and object as with Keats" (Goldberg 1969, 155), and this analysis is as true for Proust and for an entire lineage of portrait-of-the-artist novels. These novels, while embracing the traditional pluralism of which Harvey speaks, also embody an "egotistical sublime" in their emphasis on the recounting subjectivity at work. Although Goldberg somewhat inaccurately describes *Portrait* as a "prototype of the stream of consciousness novel" (154), his account of its representational logic is valuable in understanding both that work and its descendants:

> *A Portrait of the Artist as a Young Man* seems to offer a representation of an ordering which is wholly internal. Even the aesthetic theory emerging in the final chapter is a part of the larger whole which is Stephen, a development from the songs and smells and stories which confront the "nicens little boy named baby tuckoo" at the opening of the text. From the single consciousness filter reality and worth. As long as the external world is subordinated to the internal consciousness and absorbed within it, values are relative to this inner being. (154)

With *Ulysses,* the single ordering consciousness—no longer embodied in Stephen, but evolved into a narrative presence in its own right (the "arranger")—is turned outward onto a world as rich and varied as any in the realist tradition and yet clearly "arranged" according to the artistic design of the presenting consciousness. The novel thus forgoes the tradition's pretense of naturalism without sacrificing its claim to verisimilitude. Joyce, then, initiates a trend in the novel—and one that confounds the structuralists' assumptions about the implications of literary conventions—by exploiting the representational potential of even the most conventionalized artifice.

Critical thinking about the novel has often been hampered by a too-narrow conception of the formal properties of the genre. Before one can succeed in rendering anything like Harvey's experiential account of characterization, there is a more basic formal level that must be considered: that of the work's implicit statement of its relationship to the real world. The novel has too often been judged from the perspective of the tradition defined by Ian Watt (starting with Samuel Richardson), which is taken as a standard from which exceptions are judged as deficient or primitive.[12] Not only has it been amply demonstrated that there has been a counter-tradition of self-conscious fiction in existence since Cervantes, playing on the reader's recognition of representational boundaries, but even within the tradition of novels that do not violate the fictional premise, a variety of formal stances on the part of the fiction vis-à-vis reality are in evidence, requiring corresponding conceptual adjustments by the reader.

Ralph Rader, in trying to formulate a single theoretical perspective that would clarify both the history of the genre and the relationships among its subcategories, has elaborated three novelistic models: the pseudofactual, the general action/fantasy, and the simular (1973). These categories represent differing modes of self-justifying intelligibility, in the novels' position, that is, with regard to the relationship between their fictionality and the world. The general action model describes the mainstream "traditional" novel, which builds upon a sense of the actual a story that answers to our inner desires, following a desert/fate curve of plotting that hinges on our moral judgment of the protagonist. We follow Pamela's story hoping that her goodness will be vindicated. Preceding this model historically, and frequently misjudged according to its standard, is the pseudofactual novel, represented by simulated autobiographies such as *Moll Flanders.* These novels, which formally embody a truth claim, are fiction in fact, but not in form; they present false natural facts as truth. In the general action model, the reader intuitively accepts the fictional device (the false "letters" in *Pamela,* for instance) as a condition of the illusion; in the pseudofactual model, nothing in the form of the work conveys the fictional nature of the narration. If the first case is analogous to theater—designed to be convincing within an acknowledged, then ignored, fictional context—the second is analogous to street theater—designed to be taken for reality. The third model, the simular, describes the sort of fictionalized autobiography found in the modernist novel. These novels are actually the diametric opposite of the pseudofactual. Whereas the pseudofactual novels present simulated truths, the simular novels present artificial simulations. Both types, in other words, project images of the actual as opposed to the fictional; the difference between them is that the pseudofactual is a formally nonfictional presentation of fictional fact and the simular is a formally fictional presentation of true facts. In the first case, false

natural facts (events in Moll's life) are presented as truth on autobiographical authority; in the second case, real natural facts (events in
Joyce's or Proust's life) are presented as fiction, as a narrated, third-
person, aesthetically determined artifice.

Where the pseudofactual novel seeks the transparency of historical documentation, the simular novel showcases its artistry. Thus,
the "detection" of the authorial presence in works of the respective
categories will have very different consequences. (In the action novel,
the authorial presence is a pervasive yet ignored condition of possibility: we do not ask the question of the story's agency, except in instances of breakdown, such as contradiction or over-intrusive com-
mentary.) Rader describes the results of authorial presence as follows:

> Our awareness of Defoe's presence in his works is contradictory
> and puzzling, and the more we become curious of his role in
> them, the more their intended effect diminishes. Our awareness
> of Joyce within and behind his novels is magically, lucidly perva-
> sive, and the more we become conscious of it, the more the
> effect proper to the work increases. (1973, 49)

Nonetheless, because of the critical prejudices ingrained by the doctrine of the "fallacies,"

> commentators have often omitted to follow out the full logic of
> the relationship [of life and art in Joyce] thinking of it as only a
> special instance of the kind of connection between life and art
> which obtains in any work rather than as the very principle of
> the form. (51)

Portrait and *Ulysses,* then, as well as *A la recherche du temps perdu,*
cannot be understood without at least tacit awareness that they are
accounts of real lives. (I will address the undoubted protestations of
Proustians in due course.) Here, the mainstream of twentieth-century
criticism, let alone the trendier theories, has proved reluctant to take
on the most salient and innovative feature of the simular novels, at
best ruling biographical reference interesting yet irrelevant. This
oversight has caused both the origins and the subsequent influence
of the simular novel to be obscured, and I would contend that an

understanding of these factors is crucial to following the development of characterization in the twentieth century.

New Critics would perhaps have gone farther in their readings of the novel if they had borrowed from lyric poetry models of representational logic rather than rhetorical forms, for the simular novel, as inaugurated by Proust and Joyce, is the logical extension of developments in nineteenth-century poetry. In defining the poetry of experience, Robert Langbaum (1957) describes the Romantic mind as growing out of a crisis of personality brought about by the consequences of the Enlightenment's separation of fact from value. The aim of Romanticism, then, is to reintegrate fact and value by "salvaging on science's own empiric grounds the validity of the individual perception against scientific abstractions" (27). Romanticism thus becomes a "doctrine of experience," meaning that its primary focus is on the imaginative apprehension gained through immediate experience. In Langbaum's opinion most of nineteenth- and twentieth-century poetry—not excluding that which is conceived as a reaction against Romanticism—participates in the project of redressing a split between thought and feeling that has constituted literature's response to science.

Constructed upon a disequilibrium between experience and idea, this poetry speaks not as the latter, but as the former. All of this is equally true of the simular novel, which sets the course of much of the genre's subsequent trajectory. Joyce and Proust, no less than the Romantics, address the question of defining and justifying values in the face of a collapsing tradition. They each recapitulate, in novels loaded with aesthetic musings, the history of literary theory as if from a state of panic, all the while proclaiming—and rather loudly—their own standard. The simular novel, then, in portraying the development and experience of the artist, always implicitly and frequently explicitly announces and displays its aesthetic standard. Artifice thus becomes a focal point of these works as technical, stylistic, and structural innovations are adapted to the purpose. The attention to artifice should not detract from the fact, however, that these works aim above all at a kind of self-defining and expression on the part of the author not unlike that of Wordsworth, for instance, and awareness of this expressive purpose is a necessary element of a thorough comprehension of such works.

The simular novel's genesis, then, is in the experience of the author, whose aim is the aesthetic representation of that experience. Simular novels are organized around moments of personal insight and artistic self-discovery on the order of Joyce's epiphanies, and it will be instructive to review Langbaum's analysis of the device. Langbaum defines epiphany as the manifestation (although one ought perhaps to say the representation of the manifestation) in the visible world of invisible life, and claims it as the essential innovation of Wordsworth's *Lyrical Ballads*. It is a means of apprehending value when value is no longer objective, as it grounds value in perception. Epiphany presents an idea along with its genesis, "establishing its validity not as conforming to a public order of values, but as the genuine experience of an identifiable person" (46). Thus, the poet's idea is conveyed, as a union of emotion and perceived object, without our having to pass judgment on its truth value; our task is rather to follow and comprehend the movements of the perceiving subjectivity. It is in fact precisely the portrayal of such movement, of the disequilibrium between the certainty of the moment of insight and the problematical abstraction of an idea from it, which is the distinctive feature of modern literature, according to Langbaum. The modern symbol, with its possible (as opposed to allegorical) meanings, becomes an object for imaginative penetration; its ultimate meaning is the observer's life inside it. In this sense, Mallarmé and Hopkins are not so different from Wordsworth, says Langbaum, and, I would add, neither are Proust's Marcel or Joyce's Stephen Dedalus, in the aesthetic purposes they announce.

What separates later Romanticism from both neoclassicism and the sentimentalism of early Romanticism—what separates later from earlier Wordsworth, for that matter—is the authority conferred to the poetic perception via the autobiographical connection. The dramatic situation of the poem is an exchange between two identities, the concrete landscape and the speaker, and the drama is convincing to the degree that we are able to accept its specificity and immediacy. Langbaum insists upon this localized nature of the moment of epiphany and it is just this aspect of the poetic model that lends itself so well to novelization. Epiphanies, as localized, specific events, become narratable as moments in the developmental history of an individual. The most obvious example would be Joyce's decision to use his compiled epiphanies to chronicle the steps in which, as Stephen puts it, "the soul is born" (1968, 203). In Langbaum's version:

The autobiographical illusion is important as precisely the plot—a plot about the self-development of an individual with whom the reader can identify himself . . . [and who is not always meant to be other than the veritable author, I would add]. The observer is thus a character, not in the Aristotelian sense of a moral force to be judged morally, but in the modern sense of a pole for sympathy—the means by which writer and reader project themselves into the poem, the one to communicate, the other to apprehend it as an experience. (52)

This observer, the speaker of the dramatic or expressive lyric, evolves into the protagonist/narrator of the simular novel, while simular novels in which the author maintains a more traditional distance among narrative roles, projecting self into a third-person character through an unidentifiable narrator, owe more to the dramatic monologue. In any event, it is Joyce who most directly adapts the various forms of first-person poetic voice to prose narrative. Rader shows that the terms of Stephen's triform aesthetic—the lyric, dramatic, and "epical"—are in fact carried out in the characterization of Stephen in *Portrait* (lyrical: the artist presents his image in immediate relation to himself), Stephen in *Ulysses* (epical: he presents his image in mediate relation to himself and others, or, Joyce's young self as another), and Bloom (dramatic: his image in immediate relation to others, or, Joyce's contemporary self in another person). In all of these examples, it is a very small step from the model of the dramatic monologue to the use of the interior monologue. In either case, we apprehend character in the psychological/moral sense—by inference from observed behavior (insofar as we might consider interior discourse a behavior, descended from the Shakespearean soliloquy via the nineteenth-century view of the soliloquy as a technique of character development, as opposed to an element of the plot in the stricter sense of Aristotelian poetics).

What Joyce achieves through his characterization, then, is in fact the logical end of the novel's tendency since Flaubert: the fashioning, through indirect discourse and interior monologue, of a third-person prose equivalent of the first-person poetic forms. The novel thus comes to combine the autobiographical premise of pseudofactual form with the artistic advantages of the general action narrative mode (i.e., omniscience) in carrying out the lyrical aims of Romantic poetry, with the authorial self as the effective poetic object.

The simular novel completes the nineteenth century's shift of emphasis from action to character; protagonistic perspective replaces the logical ordering of the action novel. What Langbaum says of the dramatic monologue is true of this sort of novel: meaning is no longer, on the Aristotelian model, to be found in the law that determines the character's fate, but now rather *is* character "in its unformulated being, in all its particularity" (181), or, we might say along with Dedalus, in its *quidditas*. Plot, in other words, has come to serve a self-expressive or lyrical purpose that is its justification. Herein can be found the underlying principle of simular novels: that the coming to be of the teller *qua* teller is the tale in itself.

It should be noted that while I have been focusing on the simular novel in particular, the general point I have tried to make about character will apply to other sorts of novels as well. The simular form per se is a mainstay of modernism, but the principle of fictionalization of the actual persists in many less flaunted forms. On the one hand, writers such as Truman Capote, Don Delillo, and dozens of lesser lights have created fictional versions of current events, usually crimes, thus extending Stendhal's legacy. On the other hand, there are many writers who have based novels on personal experience and on their coming to write, without necessarily building the relationship between life and art into the work as a formal principle to the degree that Rader shows Joyce doing so.

Langbaum further says of the dramatic monologue's speaker:

> [His] paradoxical particularity universalizes him, in other words, as sentience just because it is impossible to generalize him as concept. . . . His perspective must be, as a matter of fact, as far as possible from the general if the situation is to figure for both him and us as an experience rather than as the illustration of a principle. It is [thus] that the speaker's particular perspective leads us back to the most uncategorical possible generalization—the undifferentiated life common to us all. (204)

If one substitutes "consciousness" for "undifferentiated life," one will have elicited the pervasive object of representation in the novel as authors become increasingly concerned with techniques of rendering inner awareness, and the traditional third-person omniscient narrator's duties are given over to narration from characters' points of view. The novels I will be discussing go to some length in responding to the hypothetical question of what it would be like to be a given character. This has been the genre's legacy, to inform us of the particularities of other versions of the common denominator of consciousness. The protagonists of these works are individuated not only by the type of concrete localization particular to epiphany, but also by their social circumstance, which they themselves tend to perceive as exceptional or marginal. They are thus motivated by the sense of isolation, or exclusion, negative individuality, one might say, and their stories are in part chronicles of the characters' means of coming to terms with the troublesome aspects of their identities; the act of writing, of composing one's own story, plays an integral part in the process, whether at the first degree, as in the case of Proust, Joyce, or Christopher Nolan, or with a measure of indirection and analogy, in the case of Virginia Woolf, William Faulkner, or Henry Roth.

My point concerning the simular novel, then, is not that we all ought to go running for biographies, maps, and city directories in order to understand novels, but that the principles behind this model—fictionalization of the actual and personal lyricism—have been such significant factors in the novel in this century that one needs to consider the derivation and evolution of the form, and that mainstream criticism's reluctance to do so has left it without an adequate frame for understanding character. Harvey's attempt to schematize a "structure of experience" is severely limited in application precisely because it cannot accommodate the structure of the author's artful transformation of experience into a fictional correlative, or as Marcel would say, into life made real. How will Harvey account, for example, for Joyce's secondary characters in *Ulysses,* who remain opaque, autonomous, and eerily effective precisely because they are modeled on real people and represented in the way that we would encounter them in life?

While the simular novel calls attention to characterization by making a character of the author/narrator, there is another sort of novel, the self-conscious, or metafictive, which does the same by featuring characters who are characters. This metacharacterization follows the lead of early twentieth-century practitioners like Unamuno and Pirandello and takes as its focal point the logical distinction between the two senses of "character," to wit: narratological position and human qualities. Although this kind of novel would seem to be quite removed from the representational aims of those with a less playful approach to character, they are in fact mimetic of human beings in an unusual way, and, no less than the first group, can be understood as organized around the representation of consciousness. Between these poles, then, an approach to the novel that begins with characterization—rather than dismissing it as a narratological by-product or ideological aberration—will render a comprehensive reading of the novel through this century in the context of a developmental history of the genre.

Chapter 2

Hypercharacterization: Proyces and Jousts

*"A la Recherche des Ombrelles Perdues par Plusieurs Jeunes Filles en Fleurs du Côté de chez Swann et Gomorrhée et Co. par Marcelle Proyce et James Joust"*⁴

Thus Joyce, in a letter to Sylvia Beach (Ellmann 1983, 508), refers to the early volumes of Proust's monumental opus. Aside from displaying the same playful parody that Joyce will aim at his own works in *Finnegans Wake* ("shamebred music," "a poor trait of the artless," and "his uselessly unreadable Blue Book of Eccles"), this formulation interposes not only the titles of the various volumes, but the names of the authors as well, feminizing Marcel into the bargain. Whether Joyce intended any critical comment by this gesture and whether he was playfully acknowledging some affinity of their respective projects must remain unanswerable, if intriguing, questions. What is certain, however, is that these two authors beg comparison on several counts, starting with the fact that each stands as a literary colossus at the dawn of a century they have marked not only by the notorious breadth of ambition of their works, but by the legacy of the considerable "industries" they have spawned, right down to the singular phenomena of yearly pilgrims making the requisite stops around Dublin (not unlike the Stations of the Cross) and stopping to smell the hawthornes outside Illiers (now officially Illiers-Combray). Surely these two, who, to a greater degree than any other writers, studiously labored to turn their lives into art, would savor the delicious irony of that art thus perpetuating itself in life.

Certainly no one opening *Ulysses* or *A la recherche du temps perdu* at random could possibly mistake one for the other. Their authors are temperamentally worlds apart and each has a thoroughly characteristic style (styles, actually). Joyce's protean narration is not likely to be confused with Proust's relentless and familiar univocacy. If Joyce is, as Stephen Dedalus likes to say, the artist offstage "paring his fingernails," Proust is center stage, biting his. Joyce would be as lost in the Duchesse de Guermantes's salon as Proust would be at the bar in Barney Kiernan's pub. As their respective biographers Ellmann and Painter recount, the one time the two met, they had nothing to say to one another. And yet, therein lies a clue to their odd similarity: whatever would two such colossal, self-possessed artistic egos have to say to one another? If one looks beyond the differences of strategy, style, and milieu, one finds two works comparable only to each other as monuments to their authors' audacious self-confidence. Proust's work spans a generation but returns constantly to a single night; Joyce's work spans eighteen hours, but pulls the history of Western civilization (and then some) into itself. In essence, the one is telling the story of how he was afraid to go to bed at night, and the other is telling the story of how he fell for his girlfriend, and neither of them betrays the slightest doubt that his story—how these events lead to his being here telling the story—is anything other than utterly compelling. Proust and Joyce, like no others, have written novels that embody their personal identity in literature to an extent that makes the usual synecdoche of author for work (as in "Have you read Joyce?") seem uncannily appropriate. It is perhaps this sort of fellowship that Joyce was recognizing in playfully confusing the names of these practitioners of the fictionalized autoportrait of the artist.

Beyond important differences (which will be considered in due course), there is a profound similarity in the works of Joyce and Proust, centered on the relationship of art and life, specifically the question of novelistic creation as a record of, even a means of, establishing one's identity. *A Portrait of the Artist as a Young Man, A la recherche du temps perdu,* and *Ulysses* all focus, to a greater or lesser degree, on the attainment of the condition of possibility of their existence as works of art. That is to say, quite simply, that each of them revolves around the struggle of a protagonist to be able to write a book that is plausibly the one we're reading. Another way of describing the process is to say that the possibility of the novel being written serves as its generative principle. Events in the work are ostensibly motivated by their relevance to its eventual production; they need no more dramatic justification than having taken place in the protagonist's life.

For *Portrait* and the *Recherche*, T. S. Eliot's circular metaphor for spiritual autobiographies is apt: they are journeys in which we "arrive where we started and know the place for the first time" (1986, 2199). *Ulysses* presents a special case, for which Joyce's own geometric model of parallax is most appropriate; this work does not depend upon a protagonist's development through time to lead to its starting point, but rather upon a synthesis of two protagonists' attributes giving rise to the narrative voice.

The differences among the three works will require extensive elaboration. What can be said thus far is that beneath differences in structure and voicing all three are examples of fictionalized (as opposed to pseudo-) autobiography corresponding to Rader's definition of the simular novel outlined in the previous chapter. As such, they represent a distinct break with the tradition of the novel in the nineteenth century. It is precisely because of their autobiographical genesis that the protagonists of these works risk appearing stiff or overly serious if they are regarded as "heroes" in the conventional fictive sense. Because we understand them as instances of autoportraiture, we are sensitive to nuances of judgment on the authors' part. What would pass as an acceptable appeal to sympathy or antipathy in a more traditional work risks appearing self-righteous or ironic here. Largely on the basis of the distancing, or lack thereof, implicit in the respective authors' narrative modes, critics have frequently tended to read Joyce with too great a sense of irony and Proust with too little. Other critics have argued against these tendencies and shown the way to far richer readings.[1] What I wish to emphasize is that because the main tradition of the novel through the nineteenth century, as defined by Ian Watt or by Rader's general action model, is predicated on using characterization as a locus of moral testing (i.e., of the author's meting out of reward and punishment in anticipation of the expectations to be aroused in the reader), this model proves inadequate to understanding works whose purposes are, in essence, confessional and memorial.

Joyce and Proust do not require that the reader identify with the characters so much as they seek witnesses to their achievement. Unlike Balzac or Dickens or even a more subtle artist like Flaubert, they do not seek to elicit our affective response to the fate of the protagonists (although this is not precluded: who doesn't like Bloom or feel the anxious intensity of young Marcel?). They are rather describing an attempted solution to what is an existential dilemma. The choice and realization of the artistic vocation is no mere element in a larger design; it is the author's redemption, his self-justification, the foundation of his identity. Gérard Genette (1972, 260) points out that the *Recherche* differs from the *bildungsroman* by virtue of the fact that the development of the protagonist hinges on a sudden change, a recognition of truth in an instant rather than as the result of a long linear progression, and the same is true for *Ulysses*, although in the latter case the enlightening change is not directly represented as it is in the former. In either case, the artist arrives at a defining relationship to his vocation, to which the work itself offers testimony.

The difference in purpose from the earlier tradition that I am describing will perhaps help to explain the relative failure of Proust's and Joyce's earlier attempts at portraying themselves in a more naturalistic vein in *Jean Santeuil* and *Stephen Hero*. These earlier works suffer from the authors' attempts to stay too far out of the picture. Proust eventually solves his problem by recourse to first-person narration in *Contre Sainte-Beuve* and the *Recherche*, while Joyce turns to what Dorrit Cohn (1978, 26) has termed "consonant psychonarration" in *Portrait,* in which the narrator mimetically employs the character's idiom, and he goes on to use the more autonomous forms of interior monologue in *Ulysses*. It is no accident, then, that Proust and Joyce adopt narrative voicings from outside the tradition of the novel—Proust from the confessional essay on the model of Montaigne and Rousseau, Joyce from the poetic monologue forms—for their artistic purposes are in a crucial respect different from those of previous novelists and closer to those of many post-Enlightenment poets. Joyce and Proust could in fact be called novelists of Wordsworth's "two consciousnesses," i.e., of a past and present, recounted and recounting self.

Whereas the *Recherche* shares with *Portrait* the portrayal of the coming of age, aesthetically and otherwise, of its protagonist, it shares with *Ulysses* a triangulation of characterization that results in a parallactic view of the writer. The notable difference between the two cases is that Proust's projection of self into character and voice is diachronic while Joyce's is synchronic. That is, Proust has divided himself between Marcel the narrator and Marcel the narrated in a way that is analogous to Joyce's projection of aspects of himself into both Stephen and Bloom. The former pair, however, comprises past and present manifestations of the same character (who, in the present, is our narrator), whereas the latter pair consists of separate and contemporaneous characters who are, as we shall see, systematically conflated by the narrator/arranger.[2] This apparent discrepancy of technique is attenuated by the possibility of reading Stephen and Bloom, to a certain extent, as past and present manifestations of the author (i.e., Joyce at 22 and at 38), united by a pivotal event that makes realization of the book possible. In this sense, Stephen and Bloom function like the Marcels. Similarly, the Marcels are like Stephen and Bloom in that they can be read as irreconcilable aspects of self that can only be united by a third persona, the elusive "refiner of impressions" who, like Joyce's "arranger," is the sole producer of art. Thus we have a sort of Proustian trinity: younger Marcel who undergoes experience, older Marcel who narrates that experience, and between the two a self that inhabits an atemporal realm of artistic realization.

As Marcel narrates he focuses on those moments—not unlike Joyce's "epiphanies"—of aesthetic excitation associated with the involuntary emergence of a sublime sensitivity belonging to the artist. Marcel's story is ostensibly the story of his attempts to possess or stabilize that artist-being. Whether Marcel's announced endeavor represents the actual achievement of Proust's work can remain undecided for the moment; what is clear is Proust's insistence that such is the consciousness to which Marcel has always aspired. After the crucial "epiphanous" experience that leads directly to the possibility of realizing his artistic project (when he trips on a cobblestone in the Guermantes' courtyard), Marcel reflects on the nature of the entire series of such experiences:

> I slipped rapidly over all that, more imperiously solicited as I was to search out the cause of that happiness, of that character of certitude with which it imposed itself, a search I had postponed before. Well, that cause, I discovered it in comparing those various happy impressions that had this in common, that I experienced them at once in the present and in a distant moment, to the point of making the past encroach upon the pres-

ent, of making myself hesitate in knowing in which of the two I found myself; truly, the being who then savored that impression in me savored in it what it held in common in a bygone day and the present, what it had of extratemporality, a being who only appeared when, through one of those identities of past and present, he was able to find himself in the only milieu in which he could live, enjoy the essence of things, that is to say, outside of time [. . .]. He alone had the power to make me rediscover the old days, the lost time, before which the efforts of my memory and of my intelligence always failed. (4:449–50)[3]

Similar passages in Proust's final volume have received so much attention that a disclaimer of sorts is in order. Proust himself is largely responsible for the persistent search for key passages that would unlock the meaning of the entire work, having suggested both within and without the work that it could not be understood without taking into account the turning point of the final episode. The issue of his structural tidiness should not, however, obscure the fact that he is doing many other things along the way besides telling the story of his aesthetic enlightenment. Proust is nothing if not a master of narrative sleight of hand, continually identifying himself with a narrator who persistently denies his powers of observation and disclaims any ability to have produced the realistic passages that fill the book. In any event, within the context of Marcel's aesthetic development, the "being" of whom he speaks in the passage quoted above is The Artist, the same sort of artist, it would seem, that is the target of Stephen's ambition. How this artist persona emerges in the respective novels and to what degree it does in fact correspond to the visions of the young protagonists are principal questions to be addressed in comparing the two authors. The first point to establish is that in each case the emergence of the artist persona lies at the structural center of the novel.

In *Ulysses,* the joining of Stephen and Bloom, and of their concomitant attributes, results in the creation of the artist, in both senses of the genitive. This transformation or unification in turn serves as a figure for the real-life event that Joyce is memorializing, namely his first "walking out" with Nora on June 16, 1904. Many commentators—S. L. Goldberg, R. M. Adams, Ellmann, James Maddox, and Ralph Rader, among others—have contributed to our understanding of the repeated conjunction of Stephen and Bloom under the signs of the author (reflected as the face of Shakespeare in the bordello mirror, for instance) in the complex allusional network of the book. This sort of consubstantiality is typical of Joyce's adaptation of Catholic doctrine as a structural paradigm, and it is quite consistent with the aesthetic theories annunciated by Stephen in *Portrait* and "Scylla and Charybdis." The implication is that Joyce, in the figure of Stephen, is unable to achieve his artistic ends until his life is changed through Nora, who enables him to develop his necessary Bloom side. That is, Joyce, lost in the *"selva"*[4] of Stephenhood (unable to come to terms with the reality of his sociohistorical situation), finds Nora and is only consequently able to create a Bloom, a man involved in and accepting of the real world. When Joyce says that Nora "made [him] a man," this can be taken in the fullest sense. Through Nora, Joyce not only is "made man," but becomes capable of making a man in turn: he is able to represent himself as a father, to create the figure of Bloom as a "father" to Stephen, and also to become a father in the literal sense. The point is that the seemingly irreconcilable aspects of Joyce become unified and significant in relation to Nora, as symbolized by the image, in "Ithaca," of Bloom and Stephen, side by side, members in hand, looking up at Molly's silhouette on the window shade as they urinate in the garden, just before the narration disappears into her voice in "Penelope." Joyce points to Nora as the factor that made the artist, hence the book, possible.

In Proust's case the formula is somewhat more elliptic. The celebrated toe-stubbing incident in *Le temps retrouvé* that sets off Marcel's culminating reflections in the Guermantes' library is not the strictly necessary condition of his transformation into our narrator. It is but another in a series of such "epiphanies," any one of which could as easily have served as the pivotal event. Nonetheless, Proust, like Joyce, symbolizes his consciousness of himself as artist with a parallactic image of himself in relation to a pivotal female character, namely, Mlle. de Saint-Loup, the daughter of his childhood "sweetheart" Gilberte Swann, who serves as the paradigmatic object of Marcel's frustrated attempts at possession that dominate the novel. During his meditation in the library, Mlle. de Saint-Loup enters the room with her mother, and Marcel at first takes her for the sixteen-year-old version of Gilberte. This perception has the effect of removing him from time, which he sees materialized in the girl. Time has created a masterpiece in her, while it has merely "done its work" on him. She is, he says, "formed of the same years I had lost, she resembled my Youth" (4:609).

Mlle. de Saint-Loup thus affords Marcel a parallactic view of himself: she becomes the point of triangulation between himself as present observer and himself as observed, i.e., between Young Marcel and Marcel the narrator. Or, from another viewpoint, it is Gilberte who is figured in parallax and Marcel who occupies the atemporalized focal point between the images of mother and daughter that correspond to his present and past. Mlle. de Saint-Loup represents, in short, the closing and final sublimation of the cycle of desire that gives rise to Marcel's sense of artistic mission. Marcel realizes, seeing his youth before him, that time has escaped him and that he has no purchase on the present. Immediately on the heels of this realization, his narration shifts decisively to his artistic project:

> How much more [worthy to be lived] did life seem to me now that it seemed able to be clarified, life, which one lives in the shadows, brought back to the truth of what it was, life, which one falsifies unceasingly, in sum, made real in a book! (4:609)

With this formula, Proust would seem to be endorsing the valorization of art over life that has characterized Marcel's aesthetic quest from the beginning. Whether the book of which he speaks is meant to be the one we are reading is, as I have suggested, a matter of contention. I would say, in fact, that Proust is just being true to his structural pretext, and that what his book actually accomplishes is something quite different, of which he doesn't speak in regard to his own project (but of which I shall speak further on). Despite all the idiosyncracies and innovations of the authors, Proust and Joyce portray their protagonists as partisans of the most traditional of concepts in Western aesthetics: the idea of attaining immortality through art. The notion of time recaptured and "made real in a book" corresponds to Stephen's notion of "mansions in eternity." Marcel at the end of the *Recherche* is like Stephen at the end of *Portrait*, minus the wish to "forge a conscience for his race," perhaps. That is to say, he has arrived at the position of having committed himself to—and staked his identity on—his vision of himself as artist. While Joyce goes on to portray the consequences of certain untenable aspects of this position, Proust chooses to pass over them.

The critical difference in the two cases is that when Joyce writes *Portrait* he is writing of his youth, and his character can be accorded a certain measure of indulgence on the score of his youthful idealism. *Ulysses* gives Joyce the opportunity to show the problematic side of Stephen's position and to work out, or point the way to, his "redemption." Proust's narrator, on the other hand, like the author himself, is well past the age of youth. If Joyce, in Bloom, provides a more mature and worldly foil for Stephen, Proust provides nothing of the kind for Marcel. One would say, in fact, that far from tempering young Marcel's aims, the narrator is claiming at last to have made good on them. It would surely be folly to suppose that Proust, or anyone, would crank out a three-thousand-page work just to illustrate notions that he does not endorse. It is the author Proust, after all, who in actuality retires to the cork-lined room and expends his health and his last years in the service of art. On the other hand, one must certainly acknowledge a measure of distancing in a work the author has filled with hundreds of pages of aesthetic theorizing while the narrator flatly declares that a work containing theoretical exposition is like an *objet d'art* with the price tag left on. My own position on the matter is that while in his writing Proust acts on principles that have little to do with Marcel's doctrines of privileged moments and refined impressions and so on (these amount, in effect, to the sort of idolatry of art that Proust condemns), he does remain true to them as the generator of his narrative structure. He remains consistent in his characterization of Marcel, that is, for reasons of structural integrity in his "cathedral novel."

One need not accept a wholly ironic reading of *Portrait* or of Stephen in *Ulysses* to appreciate that Joyce, for his part, puts some measure of distance between himself and his artist-character. Stephen at the beginning of *Ulysses* is potentially capable of producing a great work, but he cannot do it yet. For the moment he is poisoned by the "spike bitterness." He has not worked through his guilt over his mother's death and seems unable to love, and he has been unable to wrest from the world (the nightmare of history) any recognition, or even minimal material reward, that would correspond to his ambition and sense of worth. Joyce shows Stephen's limitations without making him quite the figure of derision some critics would claim. If, as the presence of the author persona makes evident, Joyce has solved the dilemma that faces Stephen, he has no cause to be bitter toward the character in writing the book. The only person bitter toward Stephen is himself, troubled as he is by the "agenbite of inwit," and the condition will end only when he can (in "Circe") strike out at the figure of his guilt and then come to assimilate, in time, the compassion of Bloom.

It is notable, in contrast, that there is no similar bitterness in Proust. Marcel certainly derides society, but he shows little remorse of conscience. The distance between narrator and character here is temporal, but not psychological. The narrator betrays no ironic view of his former aims (although he does eventually criticize similar views in others). His psychological motivation and strategy are consistent throughout the work, and its coherence depends upon that fact. Nowhere does Proust suggest that Marcel the character cannot as he is become Marcel the narrator: he need only await the eventual "insight."

This difference in stance toward their artist-characters is, then, a crucial factor in understanding the working out of the authors' respective aims. Joyce implies that Stephen needs something that can only come from outside, from being taken out of himself, as in a love relationship. Proust implies that Marcel can in the end supply what he needs from within himself, in an act of aesthetic transformation. In *Ulysses*, Stephen's aesthetic musings frequently lead to the image of the seduction of Shakespeare by Ann Hathaway, Bloom's thoughts gravitate toward his seduction at the hands (literally) of Molly, and Molly's soliloquy, in turn, culminates in the parallel seduction of Mulvey/Bloom, all of which are figures for what took place between Joyce and Nora on June 16, 1904. Thus the entire work represents the redirection into reality of the desire originally sublimated in Stephen's aestheticizing ambition.

In the *Recherche* there is a continual metonymic shifting between objects of Marcel's desire. That is, the narration moves associatively from objects of enhanced perception (e.g., the hawthornes along Swann's Way) to objects of libidinal desire and vice-versa. What the two categories of objects have in common is their elusiveness, and Marcel's ambition is to possess them, to take them out of the world, whether by capturing an essence in art or by keeping Albertine prisoner in his house.

Stephen and Marcel each start out as proponents of an artistic posture that they have adopted as a kind of defense mechanism. *Ulysses* and the *Recherche* each begin with the protagonist reacting to the loss, in the one case literal, in the other figurative, of his mother. Stephen/Joyce's mother had died about ten months prior to Bloomsday, and Stephen is nearly homeless and haunted by May Dedalus's ghost. Marguerite Harkness, in *The Aesthetics of Dedalus and Bloom* (1984), follows the associative pattern of Stephen's thought between his mother and Swinburnian reflections on the sea, and she goes on, in her reading of "Proteus" as an exposition of Stephen's affiliation with Aestheticism, to situate his poetic vision in an overall defensive strategy first evidenced in *Portrait*. For example, the excitement he feels over his poetic breakthrough in composing the villanelle (similar to Marcel's enthusiasm over his insight in the Guermantes' library), is the result of sublimating the desire for E. C. that he had been incapable of expressing physically the day before. Thus Stephen, at a loss in dealing with his sexual feelings, becomes the singer of a transcendent femininity. E. C. may betray him for a priest, but he will become a "priest of the eternal imagination." At the beginning of *Ulysses,* then, we find Stephen, after his first abortive flight from Ireland, having lost his mother, faced with the betrayal of friends and the dissolution of his family, holding fast to his image of himself as artist.

Although the literal death of Marcel's mother is notably unrepresented in the *Recherche* (except to the degree that it might have served as a model for the famous passages concerning the grandmother's death and his reactions thereto), it was the real death of Proust's mother that was the watershed event in his life, after which he would at last dedicate himself wholly to his novel.[5] Within the novel, the loss of the mother is psychological. The novel begins with one of literature's great portrayals of diffusion of self. A protean consciousness, at first unembodied, appears in an atemporal, atopical "place" and takes on varied identities: a sleeper, a traveler, an observer of another's body, a seeming hermaphrodite. At the end of this associative chain the speaker's identity crystallizes in the memory of the primal scene of the *"drame du coucher,"* the bedtime drama that sets the pattern for all of Marcel's strategies of possession—both libidinal and artistic—which constitute the novel. This last night of lying with his mother, obtained through the father's passive concession to the boy's tantrum, is the one brief moment of complete happiness in the novel, and yet it is already under the sign of heroic futility:

> I knew that such a night would never be able to be repeated; that the greatest desire that I had in the world, to keep my mother in the room with me during these sad nocturnal hours, was too much in opposition with the necessities and the wishes of everyone, for the accomplishment that had been accorded my desire this evening to be anything other than factitious and exceptional. Tomorrow my anguish would return and my mother wouldn't be there. But once my anguish was calmed, I no longer understood it; and then tomorrow night was still far off; I was telling myself I would have time to take stock, even though that time could bring me no new power, since it was a question of things which didn't depend upon my will. (1:42–43)

Whereas Stephen adopts a posture of heroic independence, Marcel is heroic in his determination to avoid such a necessity. Not one to give in to the "wishes of everyone" and the demands of passing time, he will have developed before long a strategy for mastering just those "things which didn't depend upon [his] will." He will find a way, that is, to bypass the inconstancy of appearances and isolate "essences." In *A l'ombre des jeunes filles en fleurs,* for example, Marcel identifies Albertine and her friends, with whom he is obsessed, with a natural phenomenon to which he assigns an aesthetic value:

> They were for me the blue and mounting undulations of the sea, the profile of a parade in front of the sea. It was the sea that I hoped to recapture, if I went into some town where they would be. The most exclusive love for a person is always love for something else. (2:189)

It is as if when confronted with a person whom he desires, Marcel must respond by displacing that desire onto something else that, though still elusive, is more subject to his control, to the internal and voluntary "approfondissement des impressions." He internalizes the object in question in the guise of a perceptual essence—a shade of blue, a musical phrase—and eliminates or trivializes the original threatening object in the process. Marcel's strategem is a more innocent version of the thoroughly jaded and cynical posturing of Dandy protagonists such as J.-K. Huysmans's Des Esseintes, in *À rebours,* who cancels a proposed trip to London after having perfectly captured the city's essence in an English pub in Paris. Des Esseintes, who rarely leaves his home since the outside world is so ill-suited to his hyper-refined aesthetic sensitivity, represents a limit case of directing one's desire onto the senses themselves, as opposed to their objects. In Marcel's case, after a long series of disillusionments (i.e., proofs of his inability to control phenomena), he will focus on that thing which is most dependably accessible once triggered, namely, his memory, and he will have completely solipsized his desire. His ultimate aim, as he says, is not so much to describe the world in terms of its indwelling attributes, but rather to bring to consciousness the most intimate parts of himself. All of Marcel's many artistic models and mentors illustrate this same mechanism: the singular triumph of the novelist Bergotte, for example, is to have succeeded in expressing "the Bergotte in things," while Elstir's remarkable talent is to create perfect naturalist paintings in his studio with only his own mental images for models. Again, it bears mentioning that this position is not ultimately Proust's, or at very least that the author betrays a great deal more ambiguity on this score than does the character.

Throughout the *Recherche,* then, it is the solipsizing of desire in the guise of artistic inquiry that motivates Marcel, and on those occasions when he is unsuccessful at exercising his particular form of control, he is faced with the same crisis of identity that first set him in motion. For example, when forced to choose between leaving Venice with his mother or staying on alone to have a liaison with a servant girl (in *Albertine disparue*), he becomes reduced to "nothing more than a beating heart, an attention that anxiously followed the development of '*O Sole Mio*'" being sung by a nearby gondolier (4:231). This dissociative panic puts him squarely back in the state of the narrator at the start of the novel: the state of a frightened little boy faced with the solitude of bedtime.

Filial guilt is a prominent component in the psyches of Marcel and Stephen, and it is directly related to both their emotional isolation and their identification with writers of the Aesthetic/decadent movement. In his newspaper article "Sentiments filiaux d'un parracide" (1921),[6] Proust, in terms very similar to Joyce's dictum that *amor matris* is the only true thing in the world, praises mother's love and says that we are always guilty of killing the one we love most with the worry we cause that person. This notion is echoed in *Ulysses* through a series of allusions, traced by Harkness, linking Stephen to Oscar Wilde, who was also a very influential figure for Proust.[7] Harkness reveals a number of references to, and borrowings from, "The Harlot's House" and "The Ballad of Reading Gaol" in "Circe." The message of the latter of the poems is that "All men kill the thing they love . . . some do it with a bitter look / some with a flattering word, / the coward does it with a kiss, / the brave man with a sword!" (lines 649–54; Harkness 1984, 179). Harkness maintains that Stephen has killed his mother "not with a sword, but with a bitter look, or oedipally, with a kiss." But Stephen does, in fact, strike out at his mother's ghost with his "sword" in "Circe"'s culminating moment. The "sword" is, of course, his ashplant, with which he expresses his defiance of his mother and the "corpsechewer god" while doing in Bella Cohen's lamp in a Wagnerian fury. The ashplant itself is borrowed from Wilde. In his essay "Oscar Wilde: The Poet of *Salome*," written after the play's first performance in Trieste in 1909,[8] Joyce associates the "Apostle of Beauty" with his "famous white ivory walking stick." The essay contains a critique of the poet that describes the trap from which Joyce wishes to rescue his "priest of the eternal imagination," Stephen. This is where the character departs from any similarity with Wilde, as Stephen, anything but repentant, makes a weapon—not an adornment—of his stick and his art.

Joyce identifies in Wilde's first collection of poems the "youthful haughtiness and proud gestures by which he tried to achieve nobility" (1959, 201), and these are all signs of his "vain pretenses and [the] fate which already awaited him." No one would accuse Stephen, or Joyce, of aspiring to attain nobility, at least not of the pedestrian social variety. For Joyce, Wilde was a tragic figure whose misery was not comprehended by the English bourgeoisie for whom he was a clown. In his very grim account of Wilde's demise, Joyce emphasizes the betrayal of this public, which condemned "the love that dare not speak its name" (204) and abandoned Wilde to his fate; and betrayal is, we know, the one offense Stephen will not tolerate in art or in society. It is, in fact, the offense of Mulligan, who has himself become the clown of the bourgeois Englishman Haynes. Joyce attributes some of Wilde's predicament to the fact that his mother wished he were, and raised him as if he were, a girl. Thus Wilde was doomed to a life of masking himself, according to Joyce's thinking. This will perhaps help explain the veiled insinuations of homosexuality aimed at Mulligan: it is not a critique of sexual behavior on Joyce's part, but an indictment of the clownish Mulligan's insincere artistic posturing. We should not forget that Mulligan is himself a writer who is doomed to dilettantism because he, unlike Stephen, has the means to continue his medical education.

The real tragedy in Wilde's case, though, is that in the end he would betray himself:

> After having mocked the idol of the market place, he bent his knees, sad and repentant that he had once been the singer of divinity and joy, and closed the book of this spirit's rebellion with an act of spiritual dedication. (220)

One could get no farther than this from the spirit of Stephen's defiant *"non serviam."* It is notable that Wilde, who immortalized Huysmans's *À rebours* as a bible of Aestheticism in *The Portrait of Dorian Gray,* should come finally to live out the same reversal of position as the book's protagonist, Des Esseintes, and its author. Neither Huysmans nor his character comes to so unfortunate an end as Wilde, but all three share the ignominy of having to abandon their cherished principles and reembrace the bosom of the Mother Church. Their credo of living artistically turns out to be a kind of prolonged adolescent rebellion that only temporarily masks the submissive impulse. This is clearly not to be the fate of Stephen or of Marcel. Stephen is uncompromising, as was Joyce, in his differences with the Church; it is not a return to the fold, but rather an assimilation of Bloom's enlightened humanism that lies in his future. For Proust, the Church itself is much less of an issue; French Catholicism had long since ceased to be part of the sort of oppressive social apparatus that provokes Joyce's rebellion against Ireland and its clerics. Proust does, however, use an unmistakably religious vocabulary in his discussions of art, and reserves the term "idolatry" for the practices of die-hard aesthetes, although the circumstances of his own life would seem to indicate an abiding belief in the concept of the artist as a sacrificial figure, expending his life for the sake of his creation.

Joyce and Proust are each faced with the task of reconciling their positions and the artistic poses that afford a noble refuge to their protagonists at the time of their first awkward encounters with the world. In this respect *Ulysses* and the *Recherche* reflect a tension between the nineteenth century's poetic verities and the twentieth century's newspapers and machines. Both authors were, in fact, avid readers of newspapers, although this is apparent to a much greater degree in the work of Joyce, who had a predilection for the popular and sensationalist press, than in that of Proust, who wrote reviews and articles for the more staid *Figaro* (and we should not forget that Marcel's first published literary effort appears in that paper). Whereas Wilde, in the name of Aestheticism, decried modern journalism as vulgar, Joyce puts the newspaper right "in the heart of the Hibernian metropolis" and makes it, along with the hospital, library, bordello, and bar, one of the intersecting points of Stephen's and Bloom's paths. This is not incidental. Bloom's eminently practical connection to and use of newspapers (e.g., for arse-wiping) is emblematic of his Aristotelian attributes, which must come to temper Stephen's Platonic tendencies.

The "filial" association of Stephen to Bloom begins in "Oxen of the Sun." Joyce remarked to Frank Budgen, in one of his several elucidations of the book's structuring pretexts, that Bloom is the spermatozoan and Stephen the embryo in this chapter, which "mimics" the stages of gestation (and English literary history) and culminates in the birth of the Purefoy's son. Joyce plays fast and loose enough with his grids that one ought not to expect them to work out in exact allegorical equivalents, yet there is ample evidence to support the general lines of this schema. Bloom comes, in other words, from the artistic potency of Joyce to activate the thus far infertile Stephen. Bloom represents the kind of concern for Stephen's well-being in the world that is missing in Simon Dedalus, and Stephen provides an outlet for Bloom's frustrated paternal love. Stephen is "born" with the dramatic thunderclap and, "giving the cry" ("Burkes!"), heads directly for the teat (pub), as would any newborn. Joyce conjoins the symbolic and literal newborns in a manner typical of his consistently multireferential technique:

> The air without is impregnated with raindew moisture, life essence celestial, glistening on Dublin stone there under star-shiny coelum. God's air, the All-father's air, scintillant circumambient

cessile air. Breathe it into thee. By heaven, Theodore Purefoy, thou hast done a doughty deed and no botch. (1961, 423)

It is Stephen who steps "without" onto the Dublin stone into the air, but the reference is shifted to the newborn baby by the mention of Theodore Purefoy, making the sentence "Breathe it into thee" refer at once to Stephen and to the baby. While Ellmann (1983, 364) states that Purefoy's name was borrowed from a prominent Dublin obstetrician, thus fitting the chapter's thematic grid, it is an apt choice in another sense, as pure faith describes the abiding characteristic—rewarded in Joyce's artistic success—that will see Stephen through his ordeals. In this passage, then, one sees two threads of the narrative line (Stephen leaving the hospital and the baby entering the world) coexisting with the symbolic substructure that underlies every narrative event (Stephen "coming to life," faith being rewarded); and all of this is done in a stylistic parody of Carlyle that calls attention to the spirit of the "arranger." Theodore Purefoy is not the only one who has done a doughty deed.

Stephen goes on, then, to face the oedipal monster in "Circe." When his mother's ghost is conjured up by his onanistic ashplant dance, Stephen wants ultimate knowledge from her, the "word known to all [dead] men" (581). This is, in a sense, just a fancier version of the regressive impulse that haunts young Marcel. But Stephen reacts aggressively, striking out at the image of possessive motherhood (May Dedalus having meanwhile turned into the Virgin Mary), whereas Marcel seems rather to have identified with it.

In "Eumaeus" and "Ithaca," Stephen arrives at a tentative acceptance of Bloom on a simple yet profound level: Stephen needs a father, Bloom needs a son. Critics who harp on the banality or lack of communication in these chapters miss the fact that the exchanges between the two men, while inconclusive, are among the most genuine in the book, touching on their immediate circumstances and surroundings. The pair share a few simple moments of unbelligerent companionship in a world in which deception and pain are ubiquitous. The final image of the two urinating before Molly's window is as far as Joyce can carry his conjunction. He has brought the two projections of himself together before the figure of their unification (Stephen ends and Bloom begins with the discovery of Nora) and he shows that they are he. While they behold one another, we are given an image of infinite regression:

> Both were then silent?
> Silent, each contemplating the other in both mirrors of the reciprocal flesh of theirhisnothis fellowfaces. (702)

"This" face, then, which was earlier Shakespeare's in the bordello mirror, is now that of the common Allfather, Joyce, who has reached back—via Bloom—to father Stephen, to rescue his youthful self. Joyce emerges as the Creator, and like God, he has no origin outside of himself, yet he is at the same time a product of the world he has created. While having the aspect of eternity, he is entirely determined by history. The way to fulfill Stephen's ambition of escaping history turns out to be not the aspiring artist's way, i.e., transcendence, but Joyce's way, via the representation of the historical moment in all its minute details, and Bloom is the intermediary in the process. It is Bloom—the "noted phenomenologist"—who most connects us to the real world of Dublin. Joyce's trinity allows him to resolve the identity problem embodied in Stephen's filial guilt (i.e., the problem of one's origin in two parents) through art, which enables him to occupy the position of both father and son—in short, to become his own father.

Joyce's adaptation of Catholic doctrine as a model of self-characterization is not only typical of his ambition, but also indicative of an essential difference between him and Proust. Joyce, in resolving his character's oedipal conflict, identifies not with just any old father, but with God the father, and remains the son as well. This proliferation of his identity into three consubstantial personae, while structurally quite similar to what Proust has done, is symbolically quite different. Proust's denial of the father's role is as notable as Joyce's insistence upon it. To the extent that *Ulysses* is a novel of fatherhood, the *Recherche* is a novel of motherhood. Marcel's father appears only long enough to acquiesce to the boy's claim on the mother, and father-son relationships of any sort are notably absent from the work. Interestingly enough, Proust, like Joyce, omits any fictional equivalent of his real-life brother, suggesting that one of the psychological ends to be attained in fictional self-definition is the elimination of these most immediate rivals. Marcel is, meanwhile, closely associated with such female figures as the servant Françoise, his mother and grandmother, and Mme. de Villeparisis. True, his artist figures—Elstir, Bergotte, and Vinteuil—are men, but they remain abstract figures with whom he has little rapport. The artistic model with whom he most closely identifies is not a writer, but a character: Phèdre, the would-be incestuous stepmother in Racine's tragedy.

Proust's use of Racine in his novel is much like Joyce's use of Shakespeare. Each of them invokes the work of his culture's greatest dramatic poet as a paradigm of his own protagonist's psychosexual configuration. Joyce, characteristically, puts himself on at least an equal footing with the bard, using putative circumstances of Shakespeare's life to explain not merely *Hamlet,* but also Joyce's own work. Proust, in keeping with his injunction against biographical criticism, refuses to bring Racine himself into the matter. Each of these ploys reflects the general pattern I have been developing: at every turn, Joyce identifies with the father/creator figure, whereas Proust, continually refusing the father role (his analogy for writing is giving birth), is led for that very reason to deny insistently the relation of the author's life to his work, a denial that seems especially transparent in his case.

When Marcel, after much anticipation, at last sees La Berma's performance as Phèdre, he learns, he says, that in supreme art, the artist blends into the work. Like Joyce, he is going to use his theatrical model as a symbol of the conjunction of life and art. Every one of Marcel's relationships is set against the backdrop of *Phèdre:* his infatuation with Gilberte, he admits, is a transference of his love for the play; it is at a performance of it that his jealousy over Albertine is aroused; and it is with a line copied from the play ("Hippolyte/Albertine n'est plus") that he learns of her death. Eventually, in the final volume, Marcel explains Proust's use of the play, saying that it was "a sort of prophecy of the amorous episodes of my own existence" (4:43), emphasizing that his love was thus always under the sign of tragic impossibility, and more specifically, of jealousy. This is because his love is always an attempt to replicate the impossible triumph of the "drame du coucher." In explaining his fascination with the dynamics of jealousy depicted in the play, Marcel freely admits that his reading of it, like Stephen's reading of *Hamlet,* is designed to reveal more about the character of the interpreter than about the character in the play.

One might say that Stephen's Shakespeare theory also centers on the question of jealousy, focusing as it does on Ann Hathaway's alleged infidelity, but there is an important divergence from the Proustian model in this case. The salient point of Stephen's reading of *Hamlet* is that it announces an identification not with an oedipally paralyzed Hamlet (à la Ernest Jones's classic psychoanalytic interpretation), but rather with Shakespeare/Hamlet the father. That is, Joyce has Stephen claim that Shakespeare is doing exactly what Joyce is doing, namely, identifying himself with the father of his character, who must reach back and "rescue" the otherwise doomed son who will vindicate him in turn. Art for Joyce/Stephen/Shakespeare becomes, like Ulysses's bow, a means of punishing usurpers, of proclaiming one's identity. Stephen, Hamlet, and Telemachus all must heed the call of the father and, identifying with him, thus overcome the stasis that besets them.

The Shakespeare theory also reflects Joyce's odd wish to be cuckolded, as in the case where he apparently, though half-heartedly, tried to push his friend Roberto Prezioso toward Nora during the Trieste years (Ellmann 1983, 316, 356, 378, 437). It is as if Joyce wanted to be put in the position of being able to demonstrate, to enact, the triumph of the rightful husband and father. This is both similar and dissimilar to Proust's psychodynamic, which is more like that of a son asserting his right to what is the father's. One could say, then, that Joyce shows a fascination with feeling the torment of betrayal by the woman he loves, while Proust repeatedly has Marcel attempting to make himself loved by a woman who won't love him and preferably loves another woman, as he suspects of Albertine.

Without belaboring the point, it is fair to say that Joyce steers his hero toward a traditional "resolution" of the oedipal conflict—identification with the father and acceptance of a new "love object"—as the precondition of his artistic maturity, while Proust affirms his artistic identity through a resolute refusal of that route. Joyce points to his falling in love with Nora as the book's commemorative event, whereas Proust persistently shows all love as an impossible pursuit. The characterization in *Ulysses* is evidence of a way out of the self-involvement of Stephen in *Portrait* and in the "Telemachia." The circular form of the *Recherche* attests to the fact that Marcel finds his psychological state to be inescapable; he is now, at the end of the novel, as he was at the beginning and ever shall be. His insight concerning involuntary memory and the capturing of time provides a means—a structural pretext—of constructing the book of himself as he is.

Proust and Joyce, then, have each written into the form of their works a dynamic reflecting a particular psychosexual configuration. What I have described as Proust's solipsizing of desire might also be thought of as representing the complementarity of desires within an individual, in other words, an insistence upon the androgynous potential of all human beings. J. E. Rivers, in *Proust and the Art of Love* (1980), explains in great detail how androgyny and sexual transposition or inversion are central to the *Recherche* on the levels of structure, symbol, plot, and aesthetics. It is not simply that things are never as they first appear to be to Marcel, but that they are eventually seen as incorporating their opposite, thus forming a more complete whole than was at first expected. The synthesis of opposites permeates the work, from the culminating merger of the two "ways," to the transcendence of past and present in artistic representation. Among the many figures of inversion and merging noted by Rivers is the typical case of Marcel's description of the blending of sea and sky into an indistinguishable horizon in one of Elstir's paintings. Rivers demonstrates the limitations of reading Proust's characters in an overly gender-specific manner, whether as mere "transpositions" (e.g., reading Albert and Gilbert for Albertine and Gilberte), or as deficient cases of gender characterization. They are rather meant as whole psychosexual beings, embodying both male and female aspects.

Homosexuality in the *Recherche,* according to Rivers, becomes a metaphor for metaphor itself—for the process of establishing a common ground of identity among otherwise dissimilar elements. Homosexuality, and by extension androgyny, is the hidden principle that allows recognition and understanding of a previously unperceived sphere—the referential context of the "races" of Sodom and Gomorrah—in much the same way that the kinesthetic experience of the poet unites the scent of the lover and images of a port in Baudelaire, for example. Thus Proust's "hommes-femmes" are in effect poetic characterizations, opening onto a realm of perceptions much wider than that permitted by doggedly attempting to read the characters as representative of one or the other gender exclusively.

The "homme-femme" ought to call to mind Bloom's appearance in "Circe" as the "new womanly man," and in fact his "feminine" attributes (particularly contrasted with the "manly" specimens in "Cyclops") have been widely noted by critics. Joyce's version of Proust's androgynous aesthetic can be found in the principle of the complementarity of opposites—male/female, day/night, waking/dreaming—for which "Circe" serves as a proving ground. If, as noted earlier, Stephen must come to incorporate aspects of Bloom—if the two in synthesis comprise the authorial persona—it is equally true that that persona incorporates aspects of Molly, via Bloom. That is, Joyce, like Proust, shows in his way that the completed artist is one who has assimilated his "feminine" side. The artist must be capable of activating his/her androgynous potential, another way of describing "negative capability." On the most practical level, one would say that in order to create an opposite sex character of any conviction, one must be able to identify with the opposite gender component or polarity in oneself.

As Brenda Maddox indicates in her conclusion to *Nora* (1988), Joyce carries out Stephen's ambition of forging the conscience of his race by giving voice at the end of his works to female desire, specifically to the long-repressed Irish female libido, in the persons of Gretta Conroy, Bertha Rowan, Molly Bloom, and Anna Livia Plurabelle. The unredeemed Stephen of *Portrait* and the "Telemachia" cannot realize his aims because he, unlike Bloom, has not assimilated the characteristics of the "new womanly man," i.e., entered into a dialogue with the voice of female desire. If Bloom has his womanly side, Molly has a manly side, which has at times been read as a failure of negative capability on Joyce's part, but Maddox's point should be well taken: what Joyce accomplishes in Molly's monologue is of wider importance than the conformity of the character to overly narrow criteria of gender typology. Rivers's caution against restrictive sexual stereotyping in interpreting Proust (1980, 255) applies to the Blooms as well, and indeed to any fully drawn characters.

Joyce's characterization in Stephen and Bloom amounts to autorepresentation from an objective viewpoint: two versions of the self set in motion as fictional characters, on their own. Proust's first-person narration, on the other hand, is the essence of subjectivity. One sure measure of this is the degree to which Marcel's characterization is contained within the voice of the narrator. That is, the narrator reports Marcel's activities, but he is only minimally represented; his speech, for example, is rarely reported, whether directly or indirectly. This absence of more detailed external perspective is conditioned by the fact that we remain formally within the reminiscence of the first-person narrator, who never allows us to stray too far from his narrative present. This extraordinary difference in modes notwithstanding, the fact remains that the *Recherche* and *Ulysses* are quite comparable in the extent to which they make us aware of the mind of the author at work in the work. In sum, all of the differences in psychological orientation and modality of representation merely accentuate the extraordinary symmetry of the authors. Proyce and Joust (my apologies!) do seem to be opposite sides of the one coin of fictionalized autorepresentation, as Joyce's spoonerism at the head of the chapter playfully suggests.

The simular novel, as outlined in my first chapter, marks a decisive turn in the genre away from the moral testing of character toward the representation of character per se, in other words, away from a focus on the permutations and consequences of human interaction toward a focus on consciousness. This is not a sudden departure, however, for the way had been prepared by the development of increasingly fine techniques of representing the nuances of subjectivity on the part of exacting craftsmen such as Flaubert and formal experimenters such as Edouard Dujardin, whom Joyce credited with the "stream of consciousness." This shift of emphasis onto interiority obviously has an immense impact on temporality in the novel. As the plotting of a sequence of events (to illustrate the desert/fate curve of character development) becomes less important, temporal order is often reduced to a background condition of the fictional world, a natural law as it were, while the narration follows the free play of events in the consciousness of a character, which is not sequentially ordered, but organized into patterns of subjective relevance. What I am describing is the difference, often subtle, between portraying a mind in the world or the world in a mind. At the extremes, this is the difference between Balzac and Robbe-Grillet.

In the *Recherche*, temporal flux is evident from the start, in the freewheeling prolepsis and analepsis the narrator employs in identifying himself. This is, in fact, a kind of interiorized equivalent of the Balzacian "funnel" opening, which proceeds from the widest manageable panorama down to the specific locale where the action will begin, and which is mimicked in young Stephen's notebook in *Portrait,* only in reverse (Stephen Dedalus—Class of Elements—Clongowes Wood College—Sallins—County Kildare—Ireland—Europe—The World—The Universe). Marcel's consciousness occupies an atemporal position from which it can occupy any one of a number of like moments in its history before settling on the one in Combray. Marcel's memory is associative and involuntary, returning to central locations and events, and eliciting the affective responses thereto, which define the limits of his self-knowledge. Events take place, and characters make their appearance in the book, in accord with this principle. The previously mentioned shifts by which the narration moves from the hawthornes to Gilberte, or from the sea to Albertine, are nothing other than patterns of association between Marcel's affective centers of gravity, to wit, sensory pleasure and jealous anxiety.

Portrait's ordering is less patently associative. While the five chapters follow chronological stages of Stephen's life, recurring memories (the pandybat incident, being pushed in the ditch) as well as symbolic networks (water, birds, cows, etc.) and theme words organize the material into an atemporal gestalt that identifies Stephen. Both authors reach beyond what the character does to show how—or what—he is, which is obviously a much more slippery proposition.

The *Recherche* and *Portrait* are each limited to the perspective of a single interior focalization. Even though Proust takes liberties, occasionally providing details to which Marcel could not have been privy, he sees to it that everything in the book—including the detour of Swann's story—remains within the context of Marcel's self-reflexive inquiry. On this score, as on many others, Joyce's narrative technique is more rigorous (which is not to say more complex). There is nothing in *Portrait* that does not come to us through Stephen's mind; the conflation of the narration with the character's voice is complete. By the end, of course, Stephen's voice has in fact literally taken over in the form of the diary entries. Proust, on the other hand, grants himself license to report on characters other than Marcel as if Marcel had the omniscience of an unpersonified traditional narrator, thus reserving the advantages of either form. Joyce's rigor—and innovation—is to couch the narration thoroughly in the subjective mode of the character. The narrator's role is minimized; he need only set scenes—the reactions, commentaries, and vocabulary are Stephen's.

In *Ulysses* the narrator's role, in the traditional sense, is even further effaced, or rather evolves into that voice of the book itself known as the "arranger." In the most extreme case, "Circe," narration has been dispensed with in favor of stage directions. It might seem at first glance that "Aeolus" and "Ithaca," the other chapters

that borrow their format from alien genres—journalism and cate-
chism—have also dispensed with narration, but this is not the case.
Within their formats, there is still a conventional narrator who is
delivering the words and actions of the characters. Then there is
"Penelope," whose autonomous monologue has been anticipated in
bits and pieces by the semiautonomous monologues of Stephen and
Bloom throughout the book. This latter category is not fully autonomous because it is still propped up and interrupted by external narrative indicators.[9] These passages present the problem that confronts
all practitioners of "stream of consciousness": how to maintain the
mimetic pretense of inner awareness, which doesn't ordinarily register perception in discursive form, and still provide an adequate presentation of external "reality." As Dorrit Cohn points out (1978, 222),
Joyce partially resolves this problem by putting Molly in bed, where
her interaction with the external world is necessarily minimized, just
as Marcel begins his monologue from bed. The two cases are vastly
different, however, and their difference can be defined as one of
destination. Marcel self-consciously directs his "speech" to a reader,
true to the form of the work, while Molly's monologue has no outer
direction, true to the dynamics of inner awareness. Whereas Molly's
"speech" contains enough references for us to be able to follow outer
events (the use of the chamber pot, Bloom's movements in the bed,
etc.), we have no sense of a definitive real time and location of Marcel
as he speaks. In either case the minimal connection to external reality
affords the character, as does the analyst's couch, the freedom to
reflect associatively on the whole of her and his life, to organize the
nonsequential elements of selfhood.

There is another area where the reader, after Joyce, is confronted with the problem of deciphering external occurrences, and
that is in the passages—epitomized by "Oxen of the Sun"—where the
arranger's extremely stylized narration obscures plot to the point of
supplying a fair living for the writers of the guide books such as
Harry Blamires's *Bloomsday Book,* which gives a page-by-page account
of events. In *Ulysses,* culminating with "Circe," the plot is thoroughly
subordinated to the manifestations of consciousness. Indeed, the plot
must often be deduced through a systematic reduction of such narrative distortions as the epic exaggeration of "Cyclops" or the
dreamscape of "Circe." This movement toward subordination of plot
will be completed by the *Wake,* in which whatever "real" events there

are can only be arrived at from a procedure that amounts to a reverse psychoanalysis, working outward through the omnitemporality of the unconscious to reconstruct a temporal sequence. The *Wake* thus completes the movement from representation of the interiority of characters to representation of a hyper-awareness, that is, of a mind of the work itself—which is to say, of the author.

Stephen's definition of the lyrical form—"the form wherein the artist presents his image in immediate relation to himself" (1968, 214)—fits the *Recherche* as well as *Portrait* insofar as each is entirely focalized from within the protagonist who is a version of the writer himself. Stephen would, however, likely take offense at this comparison, finding the chatty confessional mode of the *Recherche* rather artless and heavy-handed compared to the refined indirection he has in mind. Indeed, the essence of Joyce's art lies in the objective distance the artist takes from his subject, most tellingly when that subject is himself, as born out by the two remaining categories of Stephen's aesthetic, the epical (the artist in relation to himself and others) and the dramatic (the artist in relation to others). These latter categories are illustrated in *Ulysses* in the characterization of Stephen and Bloom, respectively, who are in Rader's terms (1973, 61) the self viewed as another (i.e., the real Joyce in his own body) and another viewed as the self (i.e., a fictional character in an alien body).

The difference in Stephen from the end of *Portrait* to the beginning of *Ulysses,* other than the fact that he is now being viewed from outside (when we intermittently enter his focalization it is predominantly in direct quotation and no longer exclusively in a narrator's mimetic periphrasis), is a matter of heightened reflexivity. Stephen has bumped up against the world of others and is thrown back onto a somewhat obsessive cognizance of the distance separating him from realization of his artistic mission. While Marcel muddles along, despairing of ever becoming an artist due to his supposed shortcomings until he stumbles (literally!) upon a means to organize his work, Stephen has complete faith in himself, despite the unencouraging reception accorded him in the "nightmare of history," and he bides his time.

In the gap between the two works there is a two-year period in Joyce's life that is not directly represented in the fictional version. From Stephen's musings in "Proteus"—and from Ellmann—we learn of the abortive attempt at medical study in Paris, interrupted by the

death of May Dedalus/Mary Joyce, and of the subsequent disenchant-
ment with Dublin life. As James Maddox points out, the "Telemachia" is Stephen's attempt to distinguish an authentic selfhood from
the sort of inauthentic poses exemplified in "Merchurial Malachi"
Mulligan. Thus Stephen's monologue amounts to a continual review
of his actions, which, says Maddox, "follows so directly upon the
actions themselves that he is frequently unable to distinguish between
his impulse and the parody of the impulse which his mind [mediated
by the mature Joyce, I would add] offers him as immediate feedback"
(1978, 19). Stephen is, in other words, in a constant process of rehearsing transmutations of his experience, that is, possessing it in
representation to himself, measuring it against his self-defining image
of the artist. Most of what he sees is hitched to a literary allusion or
another element of his artistic credo. To cite a typical instance, when
Stephen spots a dog running toward him on the beach, his first
thought is pragmatic, concerning his safety, and it is followed immediately by an example of the sort of prophetic, self-defining procla-
mations that have caused many critics to suspect ironic mistreatment
of the character on the author's part: "A point, live dog, grew into
sight running across the sweep of sand. Lord, is he going to attack
me? Respect his liberty. You will not be master of others or their
slave" (45).

The brief paragraph in which this passage appears also contains
an allusion to Moses that, by the time we reach the series of Mosaic
references in "Aeolus," we will recognize as attributable not to the
character, but to the organizational mind of the work. At present,
however, I wish to emphasize the aspect of Stephen's thought that
has left him open to charges of priggishness. Our usual understanding of a person's inner monologue is more likely to correspond to
Bloom's, one would think. As the passage above indicates, Stephen's
inner discourse is at times a dialogue, as he formally addresses himself in the second person. Furthermore, one might well ask how many
of us go around delivering axioms and prophecies about ourselves
in our heads, but then we must also ask how many of us are carrying
around the raw material and determination that will produce a *Ulysses*.

Despite the many suggestions of Stephen's potential—Myles
Crawford's exhortation that he write something with "us all" in it
("You Can Do It!" in "Aeolus"), for example—the question of

whether Stephen hypothetically becomes the author of the book is moot. What is more significant is the way in which elements of his characterization point beyond him to the "arranger" of the material. I refer to both the conjunction of the character's thoughts with the allusional networks and his conflation with Bloom. The first of these devices is not confined to Stephen, but becomes rampant in the work as the arranger progresses from nods and winks in the reader's direction to outright commandeering of the narration. For example, in "Cyclops," the Citizen is quoted by the unidentified narrator who is an eyewitness character in the bar as referring to the "winedark waterway" (327), which is most unlikely coming from the Citizen, and is in fact one of Stephen's recurring phrases as well as an element in the work's overall Homeric substratum. In another instance, one of the chapter's parodies contains a partial quote from *Hamlet,* "to the manner born" (299), which is completed thirty pages later when John Wyse Nolan is reported saying "tis a custom more honoured in the breach than in the observance." Such devices fall into the category of metalepsis,[10] shifting between levels of the narration, and they constitute a transgression of the representational logic, thus calling attention, necessarily, to the organizing (or disorganizing, as the case may be) mind behind them. In each of the examples above, the characters' statements in themselves do not tax the formal premise or even our sense of verisimilitude too greatly, but our recognition of their derivation from or connection to another moment or level in the narration "exposes" the character as a creation. Pirandello calls such moments "holes in the backdrop" through which we see the mechanisms of artifice. In *Ulysses,* the "holes" form a coherent design. If Joyce's earlier work is a portrait of the artist as a young man, *Ulysses* is a portrait of the mature artist's mind at work. The novel's center of gravity is inevitably the organizing mind behind it, and Joyce doesn't let us lose sight of him, offstage "paring his nails."

The arranger is certainly not a character in any ordinary sense of the term, but "it" is nonetheless present as an identifiable intellect manipulating the various symbols, allusions, stylizations, and grids as a kind of shadow authorial persona. Quite apart from the myriad details of Dublin, it is Joyce's intellectual imagination itself that is a prime "object" of his representation. For Proust, it is more a question of the artist's receptivity than of his intellectual toil. For Marcel, the artistic sensibility matters more than any particular object of its representation. This sensibility will itself be the hallmark of the artist's works, and it will also serve to define the world for the artist. In a typical pronouncement from the final section of *Du côté de chez Swann,* for example, Marcel declares that it is the tenor of his recurrent mental images of things, rather than real outer circumstances, that distinguishes one era of his life from another (1:383). He goes on to say that such distinctions would not be at all apparent to one who only saw things from without, "that is to say, who saw nothing at all." Likewise, in his preface to *Contre Sainte-Beuve* Proust admits that he risks incomprehension on the part of those who, operating on intellect alone, don't realize "that the artist lives alone, that the absolute value of the things he sees is not important to him, that the scale of values can only be found within himself" (62). This scale of values, while thoroughly subjective, must nonetheless reflect universal truths that will render the reading of his book, as he says, a reading into the book of oneself. Proust will thus arrive at his artistic goal notwithstanding the specificity of a given object. His formula would seem to be just the opposite of Stephen's aim of expressing the *quidditas* of things, and this difference in orientation has consequences in most aspects of the respective works.

As opposed to Stephen's "ineluctable modality of the visible," the impinging of external reality on his awareness (although he loses little time in transmuting it), Marcel's catch phrase is the "deepening of impressions," which focuses not on the external object, but on the senses that register it. Marcel's problem is that his desire to reach or replicate exalted moments of perception or simply to confirm his preexisting notion of a thing frequently colors his perception. The history of his encounters with other people is one of continual conflict between his idealized images of them and their mutable and disillusioning reality. Marcel the character is in fact nearly always wrong about people. Characters are presented in terms of Marcel's notion and expectations of them, and their truer nature is only gradually revealed from the superior vantage point of his older narrating self. The narrator generally limits his information to the focalization of young Marcel until he's ready to lift the veil for us, but even so, we are often able, as in life, to arrive at conclusions that escape the character. For example, one has cause to suspect the homosexual aspect of Charlus's interest in Marcel long before the pivotal scene where the latter accidentally comes upon knowledge of the former's predilections. On the whole, though, the result of presenting characters through Marcel's focalization (as a character) is that character is ultimately unstable and characters unknowable, and this is one of the truths that Proust's refusal of traditional omniscient narration is meant to convey.

As Leo Spitzer has noted (1970, 454), the proliferation of hypothetical terms in Marcel's narration (*maybe, no doubt, as if, seemed to, appeared to,* etc.) is a technical necessity, given the formal boundaries of the first-person focalization. But the uncertainty and multiplicity of possibilities thus presented also have the effect of keeping the focus on the narrator's perception and on the limits of his knowledge. In one notable instance, cited by Genette, Marcel offers a complete inventory of possible interpretations of an elevator operator's silence: "He didn't answer, whether from astonishment at my words, attention to his work, worry about etiquette, hardness of hearing, respect of place, fear of danger, slowness of wit, or orders of the manager" (2:26). The effect of this indeterminacy is to confer upon the character a certain autonomy that, since it forgoes the omniscience and certitude unavailable to us in life, is in fact more truly mimetic of our encounters with people in the world. The attributes and behaviors accorded to secondary characters in the *Recherche* go beyond the traditional supportive role as described by E. M. Forster, for instance, and extended by W. J. Harvey and Baruch Hochman. While Forster's classifications of characters seem appropriate enough for the nineteenth-century novel through Henry James, Proust and Joyce alike created characters that made his analysis anachronistic five years before its publication.

Although many of Proust's characters seem to be reducible to types—even comically so, as in the case of characters who, like Dr. Cottard, consist mainly of exaggerated idiolects—he takes care to endow them with unexpected, seemingly inconsistent qualities. Forster cites Legrandin, for instance, as an example of a flat character who can be summed up in a single sentence, or motto. Marcel would be the first person to dispute this assertion. Just as we are becoming comfortable, along with Marcel, with the notion of having pegged Legrandin as the type of the provincial snob, Marcel's perception confounds the image. At a certain point Marcel sees Legrandin execute a rapid gesture (which he must have copied from his brother-in-law, thinks Marcel) causing a "muscular fluctuation of his rump" that suggests to Marcel the "possibility of a Legrandin altogether different from the one we know" (1:123). Marcel's study of Legrandin's musculature calls his attention to the fact that there is actually a flesh-and-blood animal under the social mask. While it may be true that this passing suggestion is not enough to change our typification of Legrandin, Proust is taking care to show that his characterization, like our knowledge of people in life, is necessarily incomplete, reductive, and provisional. He is deliberately avoiding the possibility that the reader should come to Forster's conclusion that a character is real when the novelist knows everything about it and conveys the notion that everything is explicable. In this case, Forster's idea that novels suggest "a more comprehensible, manageable race—giving us the illusion of perspicacity and power" (1927, 99) couldn't be less perspicacious.

The glimpse of Legrandin that confounds Marcel's previously fixed image of him is typical of his experience, and it belongs to a developmental line in characterization from Flaubert through Joyce predicated on presenting characters, increasingly, as they are perceived, without the benefit of privileged information. This makes it incumbent on the reader to deduce character from observation, to a certain degree. Flaubert and Proust eventually confirm or refute our impressions, while Joyce does not, as we shall see. What I am describing is the portrayal of characters as unknown sensory phenomena. Proust's particular version of this consists of portraying them as such only under the feigned protestations of Marcel, who keeps claiming to have no powers of observation. It is only in moments of "breakdown," when reality forces itself through his notions and idealizations, that Marcel focuses on the object of his perception, as opposed to his idea of it, but even then what he reports to us is the impact of the experience on his sensibility. When it's business as usual for Marcel, he is happily seeking out conformity to general psychological laws that are translated into his innumerable aphorisms and similes. The important point in this is that characters are presented in a primarily perceptual, not moral, aspect, no matter how skewed Marcel's vision may be in a given case.

In both *Contre Sainte-Beuve* and the *Recherche* Proust acknowledges a debt to Chateaubriand, Nerval, and Baudelaire for the central paradigm of affective memory being involuntarily unlocked by means of a random sensory impression. For Chateaubriand it is the song of a thrush, for Nerval a line in a newspaper, for Baudelaire the scent of his lover's hair that triggers the memories and impressions that comprise the content of *Memoires d'outre-tombe,* "Sylvie," and "La Chevelure," respectively. After these models based on hearing, sight, and smell, it is only natural that Proust should then cover taste (the madeleine) and touch (the stumble in the courtyard). Beyond the general comparison, though, Proust singles out Baudelaire for the voluntary effort of his method in a way that makes it sound very much like Marcel's "deepening of impressions":

> In Baudelaire, finally, these reminiscences, yet more numerous, are obviously less fortuitous, and consequently, in my opinion, decisive. It is the poet himself who, with greater choice and ease, voluntarily searches for, in the odor of a woman, of her hair and of her breast, the inspiring analogies which will evoke for him "the azure of the immense round sky" and "a port full of flames and masts." (4:498)

Marcel says he was going to try to remember in just which poems these lines appear (for his benefit, they're in "La Chevelure"), but unfortunately, he had by this time entered the Guermantes' ballroom and was otherwise preoccupied. Marcel is rarely ambitious enough to track down his references, in fact, but that is beside the point, which is that he is, as he says, quite proud to enter himself into such a noble association. The noble association with Baudelaire shows up quite clearly in Proust's use of metaphor. Marcel's descriptions of things and people, conditioned as they are by his propensity to extract general laws from his sensory experience, translate into prose equivalents of Baudelaire's "correspondences." I will cite one brilliant example of Proust's technique, which is also quite pertinent to his methods of characterization. It occurs early in the work as Marcel has begun to describe his early outings along the Guermantes' Way, following the Vivonne River:

> Soon after, the Vivonne's course is blocked by water plants. There are at first some isolated ones like a certain water lily that was left so little rest by the current against which it lay in an unfortunate manner that, like a mechanically activated ferry, it would only just reach one bank to be returned to the one from which it had come, eternally reenacting the double passage.

Pushed toward the bank, its peduncle would unfold, stretch out, spin, reach the extreme limit of its tension at the river's edge, where the current would retake it, the green rigging would fold back on itself and bring the poor plant back to what one can so much the better call its point of departure given that it wouldn't stop there one second before taking off again in a repetition of the same maneuver. I would find it again from walk to walk, always in the same predicament, calling to mind certain neurasthenics, in the number of which my grandfather counted my Aunt Leonie, who offer us unchangingly through the years the spectacle of bizarre habits they think themselves always on the verge of breaking but which they always keep up; caught up in the chain of their malaise and manias, the efforts in which they exert themselves vainly trying to escape do nothing but assure the functioning of, and trigger the mechanism of, their strange, ineluctable, and deadly regime. Such was this water lily, and also like one of those unfortunates whose singular torment, repeated indefinitely throughout eternity, so piqued Dante's curiosity, and of whose cause and particularities he would have had himself further instructed by the victim himself, if Virgil, striding away, hadn't forced him to catch up as quickly as possible, as my parents did me. (1:166–67)

Within the complex syntax of this passage's prose is a metaphoric chain much like that of "La Chevelure," for example, wherein the odor of the lover's hair triggers associations of exotic climes, hence of ships, water, colors, woods, and gems, with each new metaphor supplying a reference point back to another attribute of the hair. Proust moves from the lily to a mechanized boat, back to the lily, then applies the dynamic principle to human behavior as exemplified by the aunt and described as a mechanism, thus moving back to the lily, then to the damned souls, to Dante and Virgil, to himself and his parents. Proust starts with the object of Marcel's perception, extracts a general principle from it that is then applied to describe a type of human behavior for which he supplies a literary analog, which in turn serves as a metaphor for his process of observation itself, leading out of the metaphoric sequence back to the narrative present. Actually, one ought not say "back to" the narrative present, because along the way Marcel has, in typical fashion, rather cleverly slipped from a general description with no temporal reference to what must seem like a specific incident. Indeed, the strength of the associative chain, and the speed with which it moves, are such that the mixture of present, iterative, and preterite tenses passes rather naturally. Proust has also, casually and as if tangentially, used the passage to make points about Aunt Leonie and about Marcel, both directly and indirectly.

The oxymoronic fixed mobility of the lily supplies a general law that summarizes Aunt Leonie's eccentricities, which have been detailed in the preceding section of the book, and, as is true of most of Marcel's models of behavior, the "ineluctable malaise and mania" described here also apply perfectly to the obsessive dynamics of Marcel's own psychology. Not just the force of habit underlying the aunt's behavior, but the masochistically repetitive behavior of all the novel's lovers—Swann, Charlus, Saint-Loup—and its literary paradigms—*Phèdre,* as we have seen, and *François le Champi* (the George Sand story featuring the love of a mature woman for a young boy, which Marcel's mother read to him and which he finds on the Guermantes' bookshelves during his enlightenment)—mirrors the stubborn futility with which Marcel has been identified since the *drame du coucher.* Early in the novel one is inclined to conclude that wherever Marcel looks he can see only himself, but by the end it will be clear that he has found malaise and mania to be universal conditions of human life.

The allusion to Dante in the passage is particularly noteworthy. The "unfortunates" in the *Inferno* who fit the description of the lily's eternal repetition are truly the exception among the damned. The figures corresponding most closely to Marcel's description are those among the slothful—unwanted by Heaven or Hell—who are kept outside the Inferno on Acheron's far bank, eternally pursuing an aimlessly fluttering banner hither and yon in an enactment of their earthly lack of decision and commitment to one side (canto 3). Otherwise, almost all categories of Dante's damned suffer in utter immobility, with two exceptions. The first are the souls of the carnal sinners in canto 5, among whom are named several *femmes fatales*—Semiramis, Cleopatra, and Helen—and also Francesca da Rimini (alluded to in "Aeolus," 138), who was, as we know, seduced by a book. This group corresponds to Proust's image inasmuch as they are eternally buffeted by contrary winds on the banks of the Styx as they were by their passions in life, and are likened to starlings, cranes, and doves in their "up, down, here, there" motion. Proust, following Dante, is also using a principle of motion observed in nature to characterize a state of psychological torment. The second group of souls in motion are found in canto 15, in the third ring of the seventh circle, reserved for the punishment of sodomites. Here the condemned must remain in motion or face the prospect of remaining immobile for one hundred years under a rain of fire. They too, like Marcel, are walking along a riverbank, but in contrast to the bucolic Vivonne, the Phlegethon flows with boiling blood. The spokesman for the sodomites is none other than Dante's former mentor Brunetto Latini, who states that all of his companions in torment were clerks and "literati grandi e di gran fama," great and famous men of letters (15:107). In addition to the similarities in the nature of the sins and the punishments in these two circles, the cantos in question are united in portraying not only people who were Dante's contemporaries,[11] but also two of the occasions when Dante is moved to sympathy for the condemned. In each case, literature figures prominently, and the two categories of sinners correspond to the most frequent categories of Proustian lovers: treacherous women and homosexual men. Canto 15 also contains one of the *Commedia*'s several forecasts of Dante's eventual redemption and artistic success. Although Proust does nothing to elaborate all of the details dormant in the allusion, one cannot help, at the very least, being reminded that Proust, like Dante, is telling his story from the perspective of his journey's end when he so casually signals some familiarity with the *Commedia*.

The breathless skill Proust employs in bringing his metaphoric chain through Dante back to himself is matched, and nicely capped, by the comic image of the final simile "comme moi mes parents," as my parents did me. The likening of young Marcel leaving his poor water lily to catch up to his parents on the verdant banks of the Vivonne to Dante running to catch Virgil amid the sulphurous vapors of Hell is in a general sense similar to Joyce's profane equivalents of epic images, but the humor here is of a different cast. While Bloom is surely comically self-deprecating, Stephen is entirely serious when made to use literary allusions to his artistic ambitions. Proust, on the other hand, takes us immediately away from both the display of his erudition and the comparison of Marcel to Dante by reminding us of, and leaving us with, the image of a young boy dependent on his parents. The curious thing about Proust's simile, though, is that no such scene takes place in the *Commedia*. Although Virgil does take Dante to task on occasion, it is never specifically for tarrying, and Dante never describes himself running to catch up. Quite the contrary, the character thus described is in fact Brunetto Latini who, at the end of canto 15, must run to catch up with his companions after having tarried to satisfy his curiosity about Dante. It is quite possible that Proust's inexactitude of reference (not at all unusual in his work, as the Baudelaire passage has shown) is simply the result of an unmotivated confusion in memory of two scenes from the *Commedia* and of a wish to make use of the felicitous simile as a means of transition back to his narrative line. Nonetheless, he has willy-nilly supplied an analogy that, if read to the letter, would put Marcel in the ranks of the sodomites. While it is not typical of Proust to demand the degree of scholarship that Joyce routinely expects of his readers, and while his allusions are usually not carried out to Joyce's degree of detail, such an oblique reference to his own homosexuality would be consistent with his masking of the matter throughout the novel.

The allusion to Dante's image of raining flames recurs with direct reference to homosexuality in *La prisonnière*, in a passage detailing various characters' uneasiness about Charlus's pederastic predilections and meditating on the theme of homosexuality in philosophy and art. At a certain moment, Marcel offers his estimation that "the poet is to be pitied who—unguided by any Virgil—must traverse the circles of an inferno of sulphur and pitch, throw himself under the fire falling from the sky in order to bring back a few inhabitants of Sodom" (3:711). He goes on to imply that only latent homosexuality would cause one to choose the subject to begin with, and like so many of Proust's commentaries on literary practice, this one is self-reflexive, coming in a passage in which the author himself has chosen the subject of homosexuality.

The tendency to play detective and go hunting down the hidden significance of passing references and other arcana is perhaps a specifically post-*Ulysses* reading habit, but it is not without application to the *Recherche*. Proust was not above the occasional use of thematic signatures and encoded bits of autobiographic detail. There is a passage in *Sodome et Gomorre*, for example, that functions perfectly well within the work without requiring special explication, but that gains in significance—particularly in some of its seemingly "innocent" or unmotivated details—when read with the benefit of biographical data. The passage occurs in the middle of a chapter that seems to have been written with a thematic grid (as in *Ulysses*) whose field of reference is transportation, judging from the numerous mentions of flying, chauffeurs, horse riding, and an auto crash. While himself out riding, Marcel feels as if he is about to "cross paths with a mythological personage" when:

> All of a sudden my horse reared up; he had heard a singular noise, I had trouble controlling him and not being thrown to the ground, then I lifted my tear-filled eyes to the place where the noise seemed to be coming from, and I saw one hundred and fifty meters overhead, in the sun, between two great wings of shining steel that bore him, a being whose barely distinct figure seemed to me to resemble that of a man. I was as moved as a Greek might have been seeing a demigod for the first time. I was crying, too, because I was ready to cry from the moment I had recognized the noise coming from overhead—airplanes were still rare at that time—at the thought that what I was going to see for the first time was an airplane. So, as when you feel a moving phrase coming up in a newspaper, I was only waiting to have seen the plane to melt to tears. Meanwhile the aviator seemed to hesitate on his path; I felt open before him—before me if habit hadn't made me a prisoner—all the routes of space, of life; he went further on, glided a few moments above the sea, then briskly deciding, seeming to give in to some attraction opposite to that of weightiness, as if returning to his homeland, with a light movement of his golden wings he dove straight into the sky. (3:417)

The passage is, as I have said, completely comprehensible without the aid of external information, even if its lyricism does seem a touch overblown for the occasion. The transportation motif and Marcel's emotion assume a different meaning, however, if one considers that the gulf that Marcel overlooks is the one into which Proust's chauffeur, secretary, and lover, Alfredo Agostinelli, model for Albertine, crashed and died while taking flying lessons, paid for by Proust, under the ironic alias of Marcel Swann.[12] Proust is thus mourning, deifying, and memorializing his lover, sending him away from the sea and into the eternal skies. This is a fine example of a moment of fictional transmutation of life. Much later in the work, in "Albertine disparue," an echo of the real-life event occurs in a more conventional fictional equivalent when Albertine is thrown from the horse Marcel had bought for her, and he is plagued with guilt over her death. The difference in the two "versions" is that the second is a fictional analog for the real event, whereas the first is the real event transmuted: the aviator—the "mythological personage"—does not stand in the same relationship to the model Alfredo Agostinelli as does Albertine, and the same is true for the plane and the horse in relation to the real plane and horse, and so on. The first example is in fact oddly reminiscent of a passage in *Portrait* where Stephen, too, invokes Icarus without naming him. This happens just before Stephen comes upon the bird-girl, after his friends have hailed him in the name of "the fabulous artificer": "He seemed to hear the noise of dim waves and to see a winged form flying above the waves and slowly climbing the air . . . a hawklike man flying sunward above the sea . . . a new soaring impalpable imperishable being" (169). Each author is, it would seem, stepping into the Icarus myth to prevent the crash, to fashion an imperishable being. For the record, Agostinelli died in 1914, the year Joyce completed *Portrait; Sodome et Gomorre* appeared in the same year as *Ulysses*, 1922.

Dante provides a model for both Proust and Joyce in his portrayal of contemporary figures—including personal acquaintances—in his fiction. On a primary level, both authors, like Dante, make liberal references to artists and thinkers contemporary and historical (including a surprising reference by Proust to Molly's favorite writer, Paul de Kock [3:880]). The fact is, though, that the use of these figures is strictly ideological; they are not represented as actual characters as are Aristotle, Virgil, and the dozens of other historical figures Dante encounters on his journey. Although, to be sure, many of these are merely named and not represented, they are nonetheless understood to be present, and not merely references as they are in the modern works ("Circe" excepted). Both authors also make use of a controversial political figure to illustrate the protagonist's social alienation. Dreyfus and Parnell function in this sense in the role of Dante's various Guelphs and Ghibellines, again by reference and not figuration.

It is actually Joyce alone who follows the *Commedia*'s device of fictionalizing actual contemporary personages under their own identity, as I will show directly. For the most part it is *La Vita Nuova,* with its mix of artfully transmuted autobiography and aesthetic disquisition and its masking of or inexplicit reference to real people, that serves as a paradigm for many of Joyce's and Proust's procedures. Both of them, for instance, use a frustrated love—with E. C. and Albertine as catalysts—to precipitate a spiritual crisis that marks a decisive step in their artistic development. Joyce, like Dante, offers his poem as the direct artistic product of the crisis, whereas in Proust's case, the crisis is a rather long ordeal that produces no immediate text in which his desire is sublimated. The major characters surrounding the protagonists of both authors—Charlus, Swann, Gilberte, Albertine, and Saint-Loup, and Mulligan, Lynch, Cranly, and Cunningham—are sometimes direct representations of, sometimes composites of the real-life models.[13] It is not until *Ulysses* that one finds a true adaptation of Dantean fictionalized representation of real figures under their own name on a large scale,[14] although the technique had been on Joyce's mind for some time. In *Stephen Hero* Joyce has Stephen repeat his lecture from 1899 in which he defines the supreme artist as the one "who could disentangle the subtle soul of the image from its mesh of defining circumstances most exactly and reembody it in artistic circumstances chosen as the most exact for its new office" (78). This describes perfectly the genesis of *Portrait* and *Ulysses:* the "new office" is the representation of those moments in the life of the artist that become significant in light of his arrival as an artist, themselves reshaped in evidence of that artistry. Later in *Stephen Hero,* Stephen takes up Dante's model directly in meditating on a work that figuratively describes aspects of *Dubliners, Portrait,* and *Ulysses:*

> The ugly artificiality of the lives over which Father Healy was comfortably presiding struck this outrageous instant [i.e., the temptation to throw away his life and art in "lust-laden slumber"] out of him and he went on repeating to himself a line from Dante for no other reason except that it contained the angry disyllable "*frode.*" Surely, he thought, I have as much right to use the word as ever Dante had. The spirits of Moynihan and O'Neill and Glynn seemed to him worthy of some blowing about round the verges of a hell which would be a caricature of

Dante's. The spirits of the patriotic and religious enthusiasts seemed to him fit to inhabit the fraudulent circles where hidden in hives of immaculate ice they might work their bodies to the due pitch of frenzy. The spirits of the tame sodalists, unsullied and undeserving, he would petrify among a ring of Jesuits in the circle of foolish and grotesque virginities and ascend above them and their baffled icons to where his Emma, with no detail of her earthly form or vesture abated, invoked him from a Mohammedan paradise. (159)

It is clear that Joyce followed the spirit if not exactly the letter of this program in his subsequent writing. The great change from *Stephen Hero* to *Portrait* is one of indirection. In the latter work Stephen's attitudes and his project are shown, not announced; that is, they are carried—and not spelled—out. As Mary Reynolds has shown, *Dubliners* constitutes a Hibernian Inferno wherein Joyce casts the "patriotic and religious enthusiasts" and both condemns and commemorates the city from which he was exiled, as Dante did Florence. *Portrait* finds the tame sodalists and their circle of Jesuits eternally fixed in the stagnant city, and although Joyce stops somewhat short of rendering details of Emma's earthly form and vesture, she does serve as his Beatrice, the catalyst in his artistic ascension to the vantage point from which he mocks them. As for the "Mohammedan paradise," in "Circe" we find Bloom transported to a sort of levantine paradise through the intercession of the whore Zoe.[15]

In *Ulysses*, finally, one finds Joyce's fully developed use of Dantean characterization. Although the technique in question is not limited to any one section of the novel, I will draw my examples from "Wandering Rocks," where it is most prominent. In this chapter, the narrative "eye" looks down on the city, which is peopled with public figures and personal acquaintances of the author, as is Dante's work. Joyce's characterization surpasses Dante's in two important respects, however. Most obvious is his use of interior monologue coupled with the fact that Joyce, unlike Proust or Dante, is not limited to a single focalization through a first-person narrator. Thus his characters are presented not only from the perspective of the all-seeing eye over Dublin, but also secondarily, from the perspective of a character whose interior monologue we have entered. In another respect, Joyce has gone beyond Dante, or any other previous writer, in presenting

characters autonomously—i.e., without specific narrative motivation
or explication—in a manner mimetic of our encounters with people
in the world, on any city street. Thus, while Father Conmee and the
Earl of Dudley are public figures, presumably recognizable in name
if not appearance to their contemporary citizens, others, such as Dennis Maginni (the dance instructor seen in passing, p. 220), William
Gallagher (a merchant who salutes Conmee, p. 221), or the Reverend
Nicholas Dudley (who steps off a train, p. 222), may or may not have
been known to the author, were certainly unknown to the majority
of their contemporaries, and have for the reader nothing of the symbolic meaning of Conmee and the Earl, who represent the two great
oppressive institutions of Irish life. This group of characters, quite
likely retrieved by Joyce from *Thom's* or some other city directory, are
only identifiable to the reader through the labors of exegetes (in my
own case Gifford and Seidman [1974]); Joyce presents them, as I
have suggested, only in conformity with the phenomenology of perception. We see them as we would on the street, except that they
come with names. Their appearance is inexplicable and unmotivated.
When they are presented through another character's perception,
that character does not rehearse their moral qualities or his history
with them; they are merely presented along with any immediate reactions or associations they might trigger. We are nearing degree zero
of characterization in such cases; indeed, characterization here consists only of a name and perhaps an accompanying gesture. Some
characters, such as Dennis Carey (80, 626), have remained altogether
unidentified and seemingly extraneous. We are but one step removed
from the portrayal of anonymous passersby, for whom we would
have a description, but no name. The innovative aspect of this
autonomous characterization lies in the knowledge, admittedly and
necessarily external, that it is not "pure" invention, but a transposition from reality. One would have to say, in fact, that Joyce flaunts
this aspect of his work. I can hear, even as I write this, the howls of
protest from those who would insist that characters are textual elements and that their significance must be found within the text.
Clearly, Joyce does not share this opinion, and he has, quite self-
consciously, put himself in rather exclusive company: what would
anyone know, for example, of Pier da Medicina (an acquaintance of
Dante's, named only, in *Inferno 28*), or of Guido del Cassero or Agno-
lello di Carignano (minor small town politicos, same canto), not just

now but in their own time, based on internal evidence? They pass or
are simply numbered among the damned, and their significance lies
not so much in the specificity of their presentation as in our knowledge of the work's "background condition," namely, that its figures
are drawn from life. The fact that we could "track them down,"
whether we do so or not, changes everything about them. These
characters fulfill none of Forster's or Genette's functions, and with
them Joyce attains a higher degree of mimesis not just of Dublin on
a given day in 1904, but also of the perception of the first-degree
characters whose vision we borrow.

There are two other types of characters in *Ulysses*. The first are
the ones who have been transposed to Dublin from another place and
time in the author's life. Thus, in contrast to characters who were
unknown to Joyce but found in Dublin, there are characters known
to Joyce elsewhere who are transposed to Dublin. One such example
is Almidano Artifoni (228), Joyce's Triestine Berlitz School director,
who appears as a voice teacher to offer Stephen friendly counsel. In
"Circe" Joyce again follows Dante's lead in exacting a measure of
personal revenge by consigning figures (and names) of his real-life
tormentors to a hell. Two prominent examples are Private Carr,
made to bear the worst aspects of belligerent British imperialism in
payment for the offense to Joyce perpetrated by his namesake in
Zurich (Ellmann 1983, 426–29), and Father Dolan, of pandybat fame,
who pops out of a jack-in-the-box in a passage whose Dantean resonance is nicely explicated by Reynolds (1981, 136).

There is, finally, a category of characters that are fictional in the
traditional sense, although these are extremely rare, and Joyce covers
them with real names from the Dublin directory. Such are the Pure-
foys, for example, whom I have discussed above. It is as if Joyce, from
the beginning of his career, would not or could not conceive of a
character except on a natural model. As is so often said regarding
science fiction, all literary representations are ultimately derived from
natural models; Joyce's hallmark is the studied and systematic correspondence of figure and model.

Throughout his career, then, Joyce evolved the Dantean project
announced in *Stephen Hero*. His commitment to the fictional transposition of characters and events from life took him far beyond the concept in its original form, however. Once Joyce began crafting his
fiction from the people and places around him, he followed the logic

of his mimetic principle to its inevitable culmination in the autonomous monologue of "Penelope." The exacting precision of reference that has gone into the dozens of persons and places—in both Dublin and Gibraltar—mentioned in the chapter is extraordinary, when one considers that it isn't in the least necessitated by the demands of fiction as we know it before *Ulysses*. As fiction, the chapter would work as well if all of its references had been cooked up from a lively imagination and a sketchy notion of Gibraltar's geography. The point is that from the beginning Joyce's work is not fiction, but a form that flaunts its derivation from the actual. In the process of disentangling "the subtle soul of the image" and reembodying "it in artistic circumstances chosen as the most exact for its new office," Joyce concluded that the most exact circumstances for his art were those of everyday reality (1963, 78).

The fact that Joyce described his projected hell as a caricature of Dante's does not in the least mean that he did not take the project quite seriously. Indeed, what Joyce, the deliberate exile and voluntary Italian, learned from the Florentine was the audacity of representing the people immediately around him in high art, among a roster of cultural icons, and of making himself the hero of an epic quest. From the beginning, Joyce viewed literature as a spiritual portrait, whose art consisted of inscribing the sign of the artist in every detail of his creation, like the God of the medieval cosmos. In *Stephen Hero* he attributes to Ibsen just those qualities he would come to embody in his own work:

It was the very spirit of Ibsen himself that was discerned moving behind the impersonal manner of the artist: a mind of sincere and boyish bravery, of disillusioned pride, of minute and willful energy.... Here and not in Shakespeare or Goethe was the successor to the first poet of the Europeans, here, as only to such purpose in Dante, a human personality had been found united with an artistic manner which was itself almost a natural phenomenon: and the spirit of the time united one more readily with the Norwegian than with the Florentine. (41)

Seventy years after the publication of *Ulysses,* one would amend the statement to the effect that it is the Dubliner rather than the Norwegian who has more readily reflected the spirit of the time. It is apparent that Joyce took himself seriously as a successor to Dante, or to Homer, for that matter. The epic caricatures of *Ulysses* (the outstanding example of which is the Citizen's mighty, world-sundering heave of the biscuit tin in "Cyclops") do not mock modernity by implied comparison to a mythic past, or belittle contemporary forms in favor of the classical, so much as they show that the author sees himself, in immortalizing the drunks, blowhards, and Jesuits of Dublin, as participating in quite the same process—and with just as much right—as Homer, when he portrayed spear-chucking Greek mercenaries and adventurers as sons of gods. His point is not that we live now in a world without heros, but that heros only ever were so by virtue of the teller's art.

The question of whether grandeur is a property of art or its object is one that greatly troubles Marcel. It is at the center of his eventual self-realization as an artist, when he, like Joyce, finds that the matter of art lies in those things closest to hand. Proust was, of course, no less celebrated than Joyce for his mastery of literary pastiche. In a well-known passage that is a fine set piece, he mimics the Goncourts' social chronicles and uses the occasion to have Marcel meditate on the distance between his perception of the members of the Verdurin circle (whom he has known no short time) and the version of them that appears in print, and he wonders if indeed he would have found all of the great personages described by Balzac, or Sainte-Beuve, or Baudelaire just as mediocre had he met them. Furthermore, he wonders if the perceived mediocrity of the real model would be the result of some defect in his nature, or if rather the magnificence of the figures was only ever the product of the artist (4:300–301). True to his teasing form, he is, along the way, prompting us to pose the same questions of his characters drawn from life, and of his skill at characterization.

Marcel is confronted with a double bind: either his judgment or art has been falsifying nature; in either case, reality is not as he thought it to be. This realization precipitates a crisis that puts Marcel in a sanitarium. He has, he realizes, been taking *figures,* principals, for *figurants,* supporting characters. This conflict of perception and representation recalls Marcel's aunts, way back at the beginning of the work, who refuse to believe the stories about Swann that portray him as a frequenter of the aristocracy, since they have seen him for years in their own home and know him to be bourgeois like themselves. Even undeniable evidence of his noble associations does nothing to alter their perception of Swann; it merely debases the nobility in their opinion. Marcel, however, has never had such faith in his perception and is here exposed as an "idolater." Roger Shattuck (1974) remarks that this passage is the meeting ground of social and artistic snobbery, thus serving to deflate two of the three areas of "idolatry," or false belief, that have preoccupied Marcel and most of the other characters throughout the work. The other form of idolatry—possessive love—is typified when Swann realizes that he has wasted years of his life in mad—and successful—pursuit of a woman who isn't even his type. Likewise, Bergotte realizes, while contemplating a small detail of exquisite realism in Vermeer's *View of Delft* (which has been much discussed elsewhere in the book, and a copy of which, coincidentally, hung in Joyce's Paris apartment [Ellmann 1983, 592]), that he has spent his career pursuing the wrong goal—i.e., aestheticism, "expressing the Bergotte in things"—and then drops dead on the spot. Marcel, in turn, must learn the lesson of this disillusionment, as must Stephen: art does not refer to anything purer than life. Marcel, too, must simply jump in and "do, but do." The stuff of art is a boyhood memory; the way to the stars is through the mind of an undistinguished Dublin salesman.

To recapitulate, then, the major lines of characterization found in Joyce and Proust: their novels are simular; they highlight the connection of their fictional representation to the life of the author. As such, their primary mode of characterization is fictionalized autobiography in both the protagonists and the major secondary characters. Younger and older Marcel, and Stephen and Bloom, function as components in the characterization of a unified authorial persona in a relationship of hyperstasis to them, and the respective works turn on a pivotal realization or event that is the precondition of such a unification. The secondary figures, also predominantly drawn from life, depart in many ways from the traditional notion of supporting characters. In Proust's case, the characters tend to repeat or prefigure the dynamics of Marcel's psychosexual configuration and they are, true to the logical limits of Proust's first-person focalization, largely unknowable. That is, our vision of them is determined to a great extent by the limitations of Marcel's understanding, although at times we do see more than he (as character) does. Thus the restriction of the narrator's limited point of view paradoxically adds to the characterization, conferring a certain autonomy to the characters insofar as we concede to having a merely partial knowledge of them. They are like complete creatures whom we know partially, as opposed to the more traditional "types," who are like partial creatures whom we know completely.

In Joyce, too, we perceive characters through other characters' interior monologues, although they are at times presented by a narrative voice not localized in a character. The great departure of *Ulysses*, however, is the appearance of characters, albeit of minor stature, who are completely autonomous in the sense that they are represented without any particular narrative motivation and with minimal or no explanation within the work. Such information as is available must frequently be gleaned from very attentive, investigative reading of the work's seemingly incidental details. These characters appear as they would in the world, external and inaccessible. Within Joyce's interior monologues, especially Molly's autonomous monologue, thought is presented in conformity to the norms of spoken language (although at times minimally, e.g., Bloom's telegraphic, often inverted syntax), but without intrusive and artificial references to outer reality for the reader's sole benefit. Joyce attempts, in short, to present us with the equivalent of the results of psychic bugging, within the necessary convention that inner awareness be rendered as coherent language.

The effect of the authors' respective modes of characterization, via different routes, is a higher degree of mimesis in characterization of both the first-person or first-degree observing mind and the observed personage than had been attained previously. In *Ulysses* in particular, the autonomy accorded characters confounds the critical commonplace about the order-imposing purpose of novels by mimicking the random and incomplete nature of the world as we find it, giving the impression that the fictional world, like the real one, will carry on just the same without us. In the *Recherche*, by way of contrast, all is wrapped up and resolved in Marcel's voice, the work's beginning and end. In each case, the author has made himself the object of a hypercharacterization, that is to say, he himself is the ultimate referent of his work.

Chapter 3

Heirs Apparent: Quentin, Davey, Janie, Everyman and His Brother

Joyce and Proust each took great pride in their work as rigorous artifice—a well-deliberated construction. The source of such pride is perhaps more readily noticeable in *Ulysses,* which has, in a sense, an exoskeletal form: the structuring frames and grids upon which the narrative hangs are left visible, or at least readily traceable with the aid of the various extratextual keys Joyce was careful to leave around. The forms and grids are meant to be admired, to such an extent that many critics have taken them to be, in fact, the book's story. In Proust's opus, the subjectivity of the narrative voice, its constant and lengthy digressions and self-reflecting meditations, obscure the formal design except for the grand circular scheme of the entire work. It should be noted, though, that Proust's original plan was quite tidy, structurally. For better or worse, his rush to finish the huge project before he himself should expire left him with a great deal more time to accumulate and embellish material than to edit it. A more accurate appraisal of his structural vision might be based solely on the work's core: *Du côté de chez Swann* and the last section of *Le temps retrouvé.* But ultimately, Proust's great strength lies not in formal design, but in his persistence in mining every nuance of his alter-ego's subjectivity.

These are novels in which form comes to justify or give proof of content (as opposed to determining it, as Genette claims; see chap. 1). That is, Joyce and Proust represent their protagonists (and biography seconds the notion in each case) as staking their identity on becoming writers, then setting out in search of the means and material to realize the goal, and the stories become, structurally, the record of their attainment. But it is the "simularity" of the works that separates them from the traditional *künstlerroman* wherein the artistic arrival is simply thematic; in our case, it is performative, inasmuch as the form announces itself as proof of the content: "The protagonist did indeed succeed in his ambition, and here is the evidence of it." The artifice is proof of the artist.

A great many critics have remarked on the lack of dramatic resolution in Bloom's encounter with Stephen, and despite Proust's valiant effort at endowing his moments of illumination with great drama, they are in the end rather banal. The stories of the authors' attainment have little drama because there are no real obstacles; artistic realization is the a priori condition of the works' being. Thus without drama, the stories have no inherent shape, i.e., no climactic moment or opposing potential outcome, as in Greek tragedy or a general action–model novel. Shape must thus be supplied more deliberately; the burden of artistry shifts from fabulation per se to ordering. Filling in a form, that is to say, meeting the terms of an arbitrary constraint, begins to take precedence over crafting a plot. The notion of literary creation as an exercise in formal constraint could be categorized as a neoclassicist reaction against perceived excesses of Romanticism and naturalism. In Joyce and Proust, as in Flaubert before them, the line between parodying and practicing a previous aesthetic is often hazy.

In any event, the traditionally open form of the novel becomes at the beginning of the century the target of critiques as diverse as those of a rationalist such as Paul Valéry and an irrationalist such as André Breton. In effect, gimmicks such as automatic writing or pulling verses out of a hat and the constraints of classicism are alike in constituting arbitrarily imposed form as a work. This line of development finds its ultimate expression in the work of the Oulipo group, which was founded by Raymond Queneau and mathematician François Le Lionnais and included in its membership Georges Perec, Italo Calvino, and a number of writers of lesser stature dedicated to research into "potential literature" generated via combinatorial and constraining mechanisms, from medieval poetic forms to Tarot cards to computers. It is in such exercises that Genette's idea of form determining content is truly illustrated. If, on one hand, works that entirely subordinate plot and characterization to formal premises risk a certain tedium and lack of affective engagement, it would be difficult, on the other, to accord high artistic merit to works—even those of high dramatic interest—that continue along in the nineteenth-century general action tradition as if attention to formal artistry had never become an issue.

The standard set for the novel by Proust and Joyce includes both formal artistry and rich characterization. It is my intention in this chapter to examine how some writers of the succeeding generation of novelists—who began publishing in the late twenties and thirties—responded to this standard. The question of artistic influence is without doubt frequently imprecise and hypothetical. Some authors, such as Malcolm Lowry, who was quite nearly paranoid on the score of his originality, are insistent about just what they hadn't read and at what point they hadn't read it, while others, such as Raymond Queneau, are continually tipping their hats in acknowledgment of their chosen forerunners. My purpose is neither to advance a *post-ergo-propter* argument nor to try to document any writer's prepublication reading habits, but rather to follow the development of forms and techniques in the novel after Proust and Joyce and to note their impact on characterization in particular.

Ulysses has left a dual heritage, reflected in the broad divisions into which the work's criticism has fallen, the realistic and the mythic. I prefer to substitute *simular* for *realistic,* since I would argue that the book's realism is first and foremost a consequence of Joyce's wish to be faithful to his own experience rather than to external reality, independent of him. This is an important distinction because the writers I will discuss in this chapter belong to a tradition of representing in a realist format the experience of a protagonist who bears the marks of authorial identification, whether strictly autobiographical or not. These writers also draw upon the mythic aspect of Joyce's work—the use of allusions, subtexts, and so on—to varying degrees, but their emphasis on subjective mimesis in characterization distinguishes them from a second tradition exemplified by authors, beginning with Raymond Queneau, whose concern for formal innovation is not directed toward subjective realism or identification in characterization (the subject of chapter 4). This second group is not in the simular line of development, although they may use techniques derived from Joyce's simularity.

Another way to describe the dual legacy in the novel is to say that it comes to employ a formal objectivity while portraying a highly self-reflexive subjectivity around which the material is organized. If this consciousness or mind at the heart of the work is not always a formally fictional representation of the author's self (the simular), it is nonetheless usually a mind that serves as a stand-in or mouthpiece for the author. A fine example of this sort of protagonist would be Zeno Cosini, the creation of Joyce's friend Italo Svevo (*La coscienza di Zeno*, 1925), whose narrative takes the form of a memoir written during the course of a psychoanalysis and later published by a vindictive psychiatrist (a variation on the found-manuscript ploy of the pseudofactual form). Through such protagonists the author is able to carry out or represent an inquiry into the nature of his art and its status in the world—both literary and historical—that it enters. It is no accident that these characters tend to be well-versed in literature (if they are not writers themselves), since this is the necessary condition for the author to comment on literature, to articulate aesthetic principles, and to connect underlying literary allusions to the thoughts and discourse of characters.

The authors I will discuss in this chapter are traditionalists in the limited sense that they stay within the formal bounds of third-person narration for the most part and do not resort to explicit metatextuality; in other words, they do not violate the conventional fictional premise. They do, however, all make use of symbolic patterns and allusions as components of a character's identity, quoted and semiautonomous monologues, and other innovations in the representation of inner experience. The pervasive use of interior monologue—in its more and less direct forms—that is the basis of such techniques tends to make characters out of narrators, and vice versa. The impersonal narrator gives way to the characterized narrator or the narrating character. As the character becomes the vehicle of our perception of the fictional world, the novel's story becomes, beyond the events portrayed, the perception of them or their impact on a given psyche. Plot, in other words, is subordinated to characterization (not effaced, not subordinated to form), completing in the novel the movement from Aristotelian to post-Romantic poetics described by Langbaum.

William Faulkner, Malcolm Lowry, Henry Roth, and Zora Neale Hurston are examples of the second generation of novelists in the tradition I have outlined. Having absorbed the lessons of the "simular" novels, they each retreat a step from the line between fiction and the actual. That is, none of the protagonists of *Absalom, Absalom!, Under the Volcano, Call It Sleep,* or *Their Eyes Were Watching God* is a novelist, much less the implied author of the novel he or she is in. Only Lowry, in *Dark as the Grave Wherein My Friend Is Laid,* attempts to follow Proust down the path of directly cannibalizing his writing experience to generate a novel (although he does give his character a name different from his own). Roth's and Hurston's works are spiritual biographies of formally fictional (but not simular) characters of some autobiographical resonance, who, like Faulkner's Quentin, serve as analogs—not portraits—of the artist. That is, they occupy a position relative to their story that is like that of the author to the novel. Their stories are grounded in their own composition, in their own ability to give order and meaning to the events of the plot. They are, in effect, intermediate figures between author and reader, who partially stand in for both. This gives them a self-reflexive—but not metafictional—aspect that adds a dimension unavailable in characters in the more conventionally realist or overtly metafictive modes.

Technically, each of these authors represents the state of the art of the time. It is the aesthetic described above—combining formal innovation with characterization—that separates this group from others of the period who emphasized only one aspect of the dual standard while operating in a realistic format. Dos Passos, for instance, is a writer of great formal innovation (perhaps more so than any of the group I have mentioned), but his *USA* trilogy lacks a subjective center, thus remaining strictly sociological in scope. His characterization is only historical in dimension; we get no more of an inner sense of his fictional characters (who amount to a sociological cross-section) than we do of the real-life subjects of his "newsreels" and thumbnail biographies. While this technique does have the virtue of leveling the conceptual field—according his fictional characters the same status as the public figures lends them an external verisimilitude—the result comes closer to making a documentary out of a possible novel than the converse. Steinbeck, on the other hand, offers deeper characterization in *The Grapes of Wrath,* and a subjective center of sorts in Tom Joad, but his lack of concern for formal artifice and attention to style make him something of a belated naturalist.

Faulkner

William Faulkner's works exhibit all the signal traits of the modernist novel—mythical substructure, literary allusion, highly refined interior monologue, incremental exposition of effects and causes through multiple viewpoints—in the service of rich characterization and historical drama. Faulkner is a storyteller first and a formal and technical experimenter second. Raymond Queneau, who is rather the opposite, was fascinated by the genesis of novels and poses a useful but often overlooked question in a preface to a French edition of *Mosquitoes:* "From where do novelists come up with what they tell us?"[1] While it is true that knowing that Stendhal derived the basic plot of *Le rouge et le noir* from the newspaper account of a murder case does little to enhance our appreciation of his artistry in creating Julien Sorel, the question becomes more pertinent with regard to post-Joycean novels in which the relationship between the narrative text and a pre- or subtext becomes a crucial factor in our understanding of the work. What most intrigues Queneau is the role of imagination—as opposed to autobiography—in the process.

Queneau's purpose in applying the question to Faulkner is to try to understand the gap between the relative mediocrity of the author's early work and the mastery suddenly evidenced in *The Sound and the Fury.* Queneau pauses at intervals throughout the essay to wonder "if Faulkner ever sailed on some 'Nausikaa,' invited by some Mrs. Maurier." His suggestion is that *Soldier's Pay* and *Mosquitoes* correspond to the all-too-predictable first two steps in a budding (and often unpublished) novelist's career, namely, the youthful autobiography[2] followed by the self-as-artist sketch (Joyces and Prousts who can construct an entire magnum opus of these subgenres being exceedingly rare). Between *Mosquitoes,* then, and *The Sound and the Fury,* what happened to Faulkner that elevated him to greatness? What creative realization did he undergo? Queneau quotes Faulkner as saying that he simply thought it would be interesting to imagine the thoughts of some children on the day of their grandmother's funeral, and Faulkner has remarked elsewhere that this thought was triggered by the image of a little girl with dirty drawers. Next, says Faulkner, he had the idea of a being who would be more than a child, "a being who, to solve the problem, wouldn't even have at his service a normally constituted brain, in other words, an idiot," hence Benjy (quoted in Queneau 1965a, 128). From there it was his love for his character Caddy (one thinks of Flaubert's infatuation with Emma) that inspired the scale of the work. What Queneau wishes to signal in this process is its genesis in an unmotivated act of imagination, and I would add that it is in fact an act of characterization, a response to the question of what it would be like to be inside a given person in a particular circumstance. Both Queneau and Faulkner remain silent on the score of form and technique, but it is abundantly clear that *The Sound and the Fury* owes its reputation at least as much to these as to what Faulkner termed his "sombre story of madness and hatred" itself. The artistry of the story's telling lies in the use of interior monologue that moves the narrative associatively toward affective centers of gravity in the major characters, wherein the dramatic events are exposed piecemeal, through increasingly revelatory perceptions. These are all techniques found in *Ulysses*—for instance, in the way the story of the Blooms' courtship can be pieced together through the parallax view of the events offered by Leopold and Molly's numerous memories of them—but the difference between Faulkner's characters and Joyce's lies in their tragic aspect. That is, whereas Joyce shifts much of the burden traditionally born by plot onto the connection of his representation to actuality (details and events justified on the grounds that they are thus, rather than by their relevance to an unfolding story), Faulkner depends on the underlying drama as the motor of his narrative. In consequence, his characters are modern in their portrayal, but not in essence. They are not the everyday characters that we find in *Ulysses;* they have more in common, perhaps, with figures from drama and general action fiction insofar as their actions and consequences are of great import. Later, with *Absalom, Absalom!,* Faulkner takes a step back from his dramatic core, framing it in the view of at least two characters, Quentin and Shreve, who are much more typical of modernist characters in many respects.

Faulkner, unlike Joyce, or even Proust, who also treated the decline of a class and the passing of an era, portrays history as high tragedy. This is most true in *Absalom, Absalom!,* in which he also makes use of extensive literary allusion and mythical subtext as elements of characterization. For example, Thomas Sutpen is described variously as a Greek tragedian, a "stiff-jointed Pyramus" (and not a "widowed Agamemnon"), an "ancient, varicose, and despairing Faustus," and of course, the would-be King David alluded to in the book's title. Thematically, the conflicts within his family and society recall several Greek and biblical prototypes, including David-Absalom-Amnon, Cain and Abel, Polyneices and Etiocles, and Antigone. The "Negroes" are a race sold into bondage, and the South is a land that has displeased the gods. The Greek analogies are explicit, the biblical implicit, and they are clearly never far from the minds of those characters who are, in fact, interpreting and composing the Sutpen story—Rosa, Mr. Compson, Quentin, and Shreve—steeped as they are in biblical lore and classical studies. Thus, it should be noted that the characterization of the "players" in the Sutpen story is formally all done at the second degree, and it does not go beyond the flat, mythical dimension described above. The Sutpens and company are dramatic figures in the Aristotelian sense, pawns of fate caught in intersecting lines of force. Indeed, Faulkner's drama within the novel is not unlike the transposition of Greek dramatic *topoi* by contemporary playwrights like O'Neill and Cocteau.

It is not, then, the Sutpen crew—all of whom are dead (or effectively so, in Henry's case) as the story unfolds—who are fully characterized in the novel, but rather the tellers or assemblers of the story. It is they who give us the impression of gaining a partial view of complete beings. It is Rosa, the Compsons, and Shreve who exist as characters—who reveal their inner state and movements—by means of their attempts to characterize the Sutpens, et al. The "tellers" are in fact doing an author's job, fleshing out a basic plot structure, ascribing motivations, and testing out behavioral hypotheses. The Sutpen calamities serve as mythos—the figurative expression of a people's understanding of itself in the world—and it is Quentin's reception of the story and its meaning to him that is the first-degree subject of the novel.

Quentin and Shreve inhabit another world altogether—temporally, geographically, and spiritually—from the lost South, and they freely indulge in the creative effort of storytelling, embellishing the basic narrative, rehearsing dialogues, and criticizing one anothers' interpretations. The formal lines of Faulkner's narrative are quickly obscured, however, once any given character begins to get involved in his telling of the story. The effect is like the common cinematic technique of shifting the visual image to a story being told by a character while that character's voice continues momentarily to narrate, until the second-degree story takes over, effacing the framing narrative for its duration. Faulkner formally commits himself to narration of the Sutpen story via the characters, but proceeds to deliver the material, for the most part, in the same voice, that of the distinct, latinate, baroque, syntactically complex, poetic Faulknerian narrator. This narrator could have been limited, strictly speaking, to a "stage-managing" role, leading us from scene to scene, handing us over to the various storytellers; but Faulkner does not choose this path.

Rosa, the most eccentric of the first-degree characters, the oldest, and the only woman, has the most distinctive voice, the one that begins the tale, but it is not sustained for long. Faulkner partially solves the problem of avoiding extended passages of characterized voicing by keeping the storytelling scenes focalized through Quentin, so that the univocacy might be justified technically as indirect discourse: a Quentinization, as it were, of what he has heard. Faulkner sets this up carefully in the first chapter, stating that as Quentin listened, it was as if two voices were having a dialogue inside him, and immediately thereafter the italicized print designates Quentin's "translation," his inner retelling, of Rosa's speech and the parenthetical remarks within the passage (his second voice) reveal his variations on her original:

> the two separate Quentins now talking to one another in the long silence of notpeople, in notlanguage, like this:
> *It seems that this demon—his name was Sutpen— (Colonel Sutpen)— Colonel Sutpen. Who came out of nowhere and without warning upon the land with a band of strange niggers and built a plantation—(Tore violently a plantation, Miss Rosa Coldfield says)—tore violently. And he married her sister Ellen and begot a son and daughter which— (without gentleness begot, Miss Rosa Coldfield says)—without gentleness. Which should have been the jewels of his pride and the shield and comfort of his old age, only—(Only they destroyed him or something or he destroyed them or something. And died)—and died. Without regret, Miss Rosa Coldfield says—(Save by her) Yes, save by her. (And by Quentin Compson) Yes. And by Quentin Compson.* (9)

Obviously, this is not a technique one could comfortably sustain for long, and Faulkner doesn't. The passage does accomplish two things, however: aside from foregrounding the aural reception of the story, it illustrates (and graphically) a cultural and historical disjunction embodied in Quentin. The first of Quentin's "voices" is that of the present—of the Harvard student who recognizes the dismal reality of the historical situation and who neutralizes Miss Rosa's more colorful expressions—and the second is that of the past—of a young boy enthralled by a story, by the glory of its world and the stature of its heroes, and who insists on fidelity to Miss Rosa's account. For present Quentin, the story is a story; for past Quentin, it is myth and ideology. It is notable that near the passage's end the roles seem to reverse: beginning with the incoherent resumé of Sutpen's (or somebody's) end, the first Quentin is relegated to parenthesis and the second voice seems now to be dominant.

The passage thus demonstrates the great conflict in Quentin we understand, having read *The Sound and the Fury,* will lead to his suicide. Quentin recognizes the death of the South and the bankruptcy of certain of its values, as well as the cast of mind that must make heroes or demons—legends in either case—out of men like Sutpen, and yet he recognizes himself in all of that. He is both appalled by the story and dying to know its outcome.

After this passage, Faulkner, ever striving to strike a balance between the frame and the story, is content just to interrupt the quoted passages every now and again in order to remind us that Quentin is listening. The fact that the discontinuous passages recounting the Sutpen saga are versions—constructions—becomes most evident in the Harvard chapters, from the sixth on, as Quentin and Shreve try out different narrative possibilities and styles, including an aestheticist version, à la Wilde and Beardsley, offered by Shreve (193), and a mocking schoolboy version that he delivers in his Canadian parody of Southern speech. On the whole, though, the Sutpen story drifts into a common voice, as if the narrative impulse had gotten the better of Faulkner, despite his formal pretext, in the heat of composition. Faulkner himself was aware of the problem; the characters are made to notice a creeping univocality in the narration, although why the author should want to call attention to the phenomenon is a bit puzzling. After an italicized passage consisting of a letter from Quentin's father that supplies some new details, Quentin and Shreve, on the strength of that sample, go on to accuse each other in subsequent chapters of sounding just like Mr. Compson. This leads to a very obscure bit of metaphysical speculation on Quentin's part that is not without metatextual implications: "Maybe we are both Father.... Yes, we are both Father. Or maybe Father and I are both Shreve, maybe it took Father and me both to make Shreve or Shreve and me both to make Father or maybe Thomas Sutpen to make all of us" (261–62).

Indeed. Or perhaps it took a pipe-smoking gentleman at a typewriter, who, like Quentin, is torn between his critical view of the story he is telling and his identification with it—between the twentieth-century United States and a nostalgia for a mythical South whose horror he knows all too well.

The fact that Faulkner blurs or steps across the lines of his formal design, however, ought not obscure three important points. First, the logic of the design makes the piecing together of the Sutpen story a communal endeavor. The people of Jefferson, for whom Sutpen has been an enigma awaiting a legend since his arrival, are both creating and interpreting their local mythology in telling the story. They define themselves and the community as they delve into the meaning of events, and reveal their personal psychology by the way they color their narrative and characterize the figures in it. For Quentin, the story is emblematic both sociologically, as I have said, and psychologically (it is, after all, a tale of near brother-sister incest, his particular weakness, as we know). Quentin is, tragically, one of the "ghosts" he speaks of in the first chapter: one of those surviving inhabitants of a dead world, part of a people with a place, perhaps, but with no more time. As Quentin "composes" the myth, its meaning is clear: he is the spawn of a damned race, with no recourse but to end it all in the waters of the Charles, insisting to himself to the end, as he does repeatedly at the close of *Absalom, Absalom!,* that he doesn't hate the South.

My second point, then, is that the whole of the novel is centered on Quentin, who becomes a character with all of the hallmarks of a modernist protagonist: acute self-consciousness, literary awareness, and social alienation. The first two of these are closely related; as we have seen in Quentin's case, characters who are highly self-conscious can easily give rise to metalepsis in the narrative, i.e., to remarks of ambiguous meaning that can refer to the narrative itself. When characters start talking literature, they will eventually get around to the bit of it they're standing in.

The third point concerning *Absalom, Absalom!* is that Faulkner's use of what I have called post-Joycean techniques results in a modernist version of the historical novel. Just as the modernist *künstlerroman*—so far as the works of Joyce and Proust might be so categorized—adds a performative dimension to its traditional predecessor, so *Absalom, Absalom!* presents not just a historical drama, but the process of its composition and reception in the mind of the protagonist, and in doing so relies upon selected literary subtexts to illustrate its themes.

Lowry

Malcolm Lowry was, as I have suggested, rather sensitive about his position vis-à-vis Joyce, particularly after early reviewers of *Under the Volcano* were inclined to consider the work derivative. In a letter to Jacques Barzun (1965a, 143), who had found the novel "imitating the tricks of Joyce, Dos Passos, and Sterne," Lowry retorted that he had never finished *Ulysses* nor been able to read more than a page of *Tristram Shandy*. He considered *Ulysses* needlessly cluttered, and it was not until 1952—five years after the end of his ten-year struggle with *Volcano*—that he would acknowledge having finished reading it. In a letter to Albert Erskine (319), he sarcastically hurls the charge of derivation back at Joyce with the assessment "¿*Le gusta esta Dujardin?* Why is it Joyce?" parodying his character Geoffrey Firmin's mistranslation of the Mexican public notice that is one of *Volcano*'s leitmotifs and its final statement.[3] So much, then, for any notion that Lowry studiously mined the work of his predecessor, although as several critics have noted, he was most likely schooled in Joycean techniques by his mentor, Conrad Aiken. Be that as it may, there is no doubt that Lowry was quite aware of Joyce's shadow as he set about adapting modernist principles, which Joyce had no small part in establishing, to the long process of crafting his 1936 short story into the successful novel of 1947.

The fact that *Volcano* and *Ulysses* are similar types of novels that elicit similar modes of reading is underscored by a curious parallelism in the criticism of the works. Lowry, like Joyce, suffered from a near persecution mania concerning the difficulties of having his work accepted and understood and tended to see himself as a lone laborer in the service of his art, although with little of Joyce's unshakable faith in his ultimate vindication. Lowry's masterpiece has given rise to an "industry" with all of the characteristic subdivisions of the Joycean enterprise, though the industry, like the novel, is somewhat more streamlined than Joyce's, and we are unlikely to find costumed Lowrylaters descending on Cuernavaca on All Soul's Day to reenact the Consul's dipsomaniacal odyssey, much less to be thrown into the fatal ravine at day's end. (There are, of necessity, limits to life's imitation of art's imitation of life.) Lowry has his Gilbert—David Markson, a personal friend who wrote the first Lowry thesis and an exhaustive exegesis of the novel's allusions and symbolism (1978); his Harry Blamires—Dale Edmonds, whose "*Under the Volcano:* A Reading of the Immediate Level" (1980) gives a linear plot summary (including a rather staggering inventory of drinks consumed); his Gifford and Seidman—Ackerley and Clipper, who have compiled a greatly detailed set of notes entitled *A Companion to "Under the Volcano"* (1984); and his Ellman—a distinguished biographer, Douglas Day (1973), whose study reciprocally illuminates the author's life and fiction. Oddly enough, Lowry also had an Ibsen—a Norwegian literary idol to whom he made a pilgrimage—in the person of novelist Nordhal Grieg. Finally, in a parallel that will warrant further attention, Lowry has a Nora: although the Consul's ex-wife Yvonne, the catalyst of his travail, is drawn from Lowry's first wife and borrows only a few biographical details from his second wife, Margerie, the latter is subtly saluted in the novel as the catalyst of its realization.

As is true of *Ulysses,* the first extratextual explication of *Volcano* is found among the author's letters, specifically in one written to his eventual publisher, Jonathan Cape, in 1946 (Lowry 1965a, 56–88). In the letter, Lowry rebuts a somewhat unsympathetic reader's report with an elucidation and justification of the novel's form and techniques in a chapter-by-chapter summary. It is significant that Lowry faults the reader for having read the book as if it were traditional—for having overlooked or undervalued its modernism, in effect—and cites T. S. Eliot as a precedent, asking "who would have felt encouraged to venture into the drought of *The Waste Land* without some anterior knowledge and anticipation of its poetic cases?" He aligns his work with a tradition that requires the reader to be prepared to "grapple with the form of the book and the author's true intention." Since these are not evident at the onset, he suggests that the published novel might include some "solid but subtle elucidation in a preface or blurb." Such apparatus is justified by the poetic structure of the work, that is, by precisely that aspect of it which constitutes its evolution from the linear and formless narrative of the original short story. In fact, Lowry pleads, the book's main "defect" is that "the author's equipment, such as it is, is subjective rather than objective, a better equipment, in short, for a certain kind of poet than a novelist." This "certain kind of poet" is none other than the poet of experience, as described in my first chapter, who creates a novel of subjectivity plotted through a sequence of epiphanous moments—glimpses of the divine, or in the present case diabolical, in the life of the protagonist. For Joyce and Proust, the "divine" is the transcendent power of artistic sensitivity; for Lowry, the diabolic is the entropic, destructive power—in individuals and societies—that emerges in the absence of *agape*. Unlike his predecessors, Lowry displays no belief in the redemptive power of artistic representation per se; in his protagonist he represents an artistic vision, but not a portrait of the artist *qua* artist.

The Cabala provided Lowry with a formal skeleton for his novel that would also underscore the theme of hidden forces and patterns at play in the world. He explains to Cape that his structure is based on the number twelve, the universal unit. Thus, the book has twelve chapters and opens twelve months after the framed story of the Consul's last twelve hours. The form of the whole, he says, is a twelve-spoked wheel, and Sherrill Grace, to name one critic, has detailed the transfer of the formal concept into narrative leitmotif, with wheel and circle images turning up in every chapter (1982). Perle Epstein's definitive work on Lowry and the Cabala (1969) shows a much more esoteric application of occult studies to the novel, tracing an elaborate symbolism of initiatory stages, black and white magic, and the like. In her analysis, the Consul becomes a fallen magician, and his drunkenness is equated with the abuse of secret knowledge, his hallucinations with occult perceptions. Lowry, for his part, insists to Cape that knowledge of the Cabala is not at all important to understanding the work. Ideally it should function as the book's "hidden anchor," endowing it with a symmetry and unity that would be intuited rather than consciously recognized:

> Is it too much to say that all these chords, struck and resolved, while no reader can possibly apprehend them on first or even fourth reading, consciously, nevertheless vastly contribute *un-*

consciously to the final weight of the book? (1965a, 84; Lowry's emphasis)

His purpose, then, is the "opposite of Joyce's," namely, "a simplifying, as far as possible, of what originally suggested itself in far more baffling, complex, esoteric terms" (66).

What Lowry objects to in Joyce is, in effect, the detectable hand of the "arranger," which he would deem intrusive. His own intention is that the reader admire the beauty of his "Churrigueresque Mexican cathedral" without being distracted by its underlying framework. He does not trade on the reader's familiarity with his structural subtext in the way Joyce does with Homer, for example. Like Joyce, however, he does depend on the reader's knowledge of the literary canon to justify his novel's elaborate use of allusion.

Dante is one of the more obvious literary presences in *Volcano*. Lowry outlines for Cape his original plan for a Dantean trilogy, in which *Volcano* would correspond to the *Inferno*, a never-realized amplification of the novella *Lunar Caustic* would be the *Purgatorio*, and *In Ballast to the White Sea*, the manuscript of which was lost in a house fire, would be the *Paradiso*. By 1951, in a lengthy "Work in Progress" statement, he had conceived a much grander scheme (all the more unrealizable) for an arch-work called *The Voyage That Never Ends*, in which *Volcano* would be the centerpiece of an eight-volume series, mostly consisting of assembled and rewritten poems, short stories, and notebook material he had on hand, in varying degrees of incompletion.

While Lowry's ambitions, spurred by *Volcano*'s long-awaited success, no doubt, clearly outstripped his ability to bring works to satisfactory completion, he did succeed admirably in making *Volcano* resound with the echo of the *Inferno*. The novel begins at the Casino de la Selva and ends with the characters lost in an obscure wood, and Quauhnahuac, the fictional Cuernavaca, is rent from one end to the other by a chasm (*barranca*), as is Dante's underworld. The Consul's would-be guide out of darkness is named Dr. Vigil, and the book is studded with devilish images on beer bottles, and so forth. Chapter 6, which Lowry signals as "the middle and heart of the book," begins with Hugh quoting the *Inferno*'s opening line at the start of an interior monologue in which he takes stock of the spiritual desolation besetting him in his thirtieth year. The microcosmic first chapter, which provides the story's half-frame and prefigures most of the plot and themes, ends with the sound of a bell tolling "*dolente . . . dolore*," words that end the first two lines of Dante's third canto, the famous inscription over the gates of Hell. David Markson (1978) observes that the "Hell Bunker" that "yawns" on the eighth fairway of a golf course, where Jacques Laruelle stumbled upon Geoffrey Firmin and a girl, is an echo of Dante's eighth circle, where a well "yawns" in the middle of a field and holds naked sinners in its bottom. In this instance the allusion serves as an emblem of the Consul's sexual anxiety and generalized guilt. His feelings toward his boyhood friend Laruelle are ambivalent at best, for the latter has cuckolded him with Yvonne. The Consul is unable to "perform" sexually, except with a prostitute shortly before his death, and his mezcal-induced phantasms, like Bloom's, contain many sexually ambiguous, if not plainly homoerotic, images. Laruelle describes the scene in the bunker as "bizarre" and eliciting much laughter, although no details of the activity are supplied, and notes that it marked Geoffrey's first public drinking and a rupture in their friendship. As Mary Reynolds (1981) has shown Joyce does in "Circe," Lowry here makes use of a specific allusion to the *Inferno* in order to characterize an analogous "sin."

After Dante, Lowry draws upon Marlowe's *Dr. Faustus,* the Eden myth (with allusions to the Bible, Milton, and Doré), the New Testament (the Samaritan and the Agony in the Garden), Don Quixote, and Oedipus (via Cocteau's *Machine Infernale*), to provide mood and meaning in the novel. Lowry uses allusion both to create a metaphysics—a set of principles governing the destiny of his fictional world—and to assemble a mosaic of attributes that constitute character. According to Markson:

> The guilt of the protagonist of *Under the Volcano* is that of Adam after the expulsion, his agony is that of Christ at Golgotha, his fealty Don Quixote's. Through degrees of highly specific analogy Lowry's hero so to speak "becomes" Faust, Dante, Prometheus, Heracles, Buddha, Oedipus. He is Aeneas, Hamlet, Noah, Judas, Prospero, Narcissus, Trotsky, Macbeth, Shelley, Scrooge, Quetzalcoatl, Bix Beiderbecke, Candide, Moses, Gogol's Tchitchikov—if not to add Peter Rabbit and the Fisher King, among many more. (1978, 6)

Detailed research notwithstanding, Markson may be overstating his case. There is an infinite difference between resembling and becoming. My objection is not just semantic but goes to the heart of the question of the identity of characters in highly allusive works. Elsewhere, Markson is careful to insist that *Volcano* enacts a fusion of surface and symbol, that aside from (or above) the indeed remarkable density of allusion, the work functions perfectly well on the immediate narrative level; but the passage quoted above betrays a tendency to obfuscate the specificity of the character in favor of symbolism. Markson, too, is concerned with the inevitable comparison of Lowry to Joyce, a matter he addresses in his preface. He tries to assert Lowry's independence from "the master" with the claim that *Volcano* succeeds where the *Wake* does not, that is, as a work of multimythic richness held in coherent focus and integrated into the traditional form of the novel. This would make the Consul a sort of Here Comes Everybody to Cuernavaca if it were the case, but the works are of different kinds. The Consul does not "become" any of the figures listed in Markson's roster in the same sense that Earwicker is Finn MacCool, for example. In concentrating too intently on the concept of myth—and allusion is not ipso facto mythography—Markson lets escape what should be his most useful point, namely, that the novelistic tradition and form that are successfully maintained in *Volcano* are found in the story's grounding in characters, not archetypes.

In *After Joyce*, R. M. Adams notes the potential for conflict between the structuring devices of post-Joycean novels and depth of characterization. What he says of grids would also hold true for allusion, if it worked as Markson describes:

> It is a device of depth in that it leads our eye into the infinite cyclical recessions of the past, but it is a device of fictional shallowness, because it may diminish characters, reducing them to momentary manifestations of an eternal principle or fragments of a three-dimensional mosaic that is bigger than all of them. . . . Paradigmatic structure does not deepen our sense of character or plot but usurps on, and diminishes it. (1977, 46)

This last remark may be true of Nabokov's *The Defense*, Adams's immediate example, and it is certainly true of *La vie mode d'emploi* and many gimmick-works, but it need not always be the case. I have only to cite as counter-examples Stephen and Bloom, who inhabit a paradigmatically determined world and yet are among the most highly individuated characters one could think of. The fictional depth of a novel will be determined by an author's technical skill at "filling in" character, and not by the underlying grid. In Joyce's case, his mastery of internal monologue and his ear for voicing define the characters far more than any of his paradigms. Bloom may "be" Ulysses, or Elijah, or half of Shakespeare, but what we remember about him are his attitude toward himself and others and some of the things he says.

Markson would apparently agree with Adams's idea that characters can be reduced to momentary manifestations of an eternal principle, but he would find it a virtue, it seems. There is no inherent reason why showing characters to be such manifestations need necessarily result in fictional shallowness. Indeed, handled deftly, it could result in a keen analog of the human condition. The novel as a genre cannot help but impose order (however vague it might be in some cases) and pattern on its fictional life; this has been its merit. The problem Adams is aiming at is the one that arises when the underlying pattern becomes too deterministic, thus ceasing to be mimetic. Life that follows the rules of chess is a very weak analog of human life.

Adams also objects that grids are not in the minds of the characters, who assume they operate freely, but he does not allow for the possibility that this can lend itself to a convincing mimesis of the limits of human understanding. It might be pointless to set a character who operates within our conventional notion of human being into a world of rigidly or narrowly determined order that bears little resemblance to our own, or it might be quite amusing and instructive, as is the case with Italo Calvino's *Cosmicomics*. Again, it is the technique of characterization, not the paradigm itself, that will decide the issue. Calvino's lesson is that a few basic details of inner life ably presented will often be enough for us to claim the fictional creature as one of our own.

As Adams says, grids are not in the consciousness of characters; they are a structural component, and as such are the affair of the author, except in cases of infinite regression or first-person narratives such as Proust's, where the character is putting together his own story and is free to comment on his shaping of it. With literary allusions, however, the situation is somewhat more complicated. Allusions may fall into systematic patterns, thus making them a part of the work's structure, but they are often presented from within a character's consciousness. This does not create any problems as long as the two levels are kept separate, that is, as long as the allusion is operated through, and not by, the character. For example, Stephen may parody Homer (e.g., looking at the "snot green sea"), thus presenting an allusion, but he is unaware of the overall pattern of such allusions, that is, he does not recognize the controlling analogy between his world and the *Odyssey*. Joyce is careful to keep within the limits of his hard-earned psychic realism; it is precisely because he keeps the focus of character and arranger clearly separated that his occasional merging of them is so effective.

In earlier forms of the novel, wherein chatty narrators assumed much of the burden of representing the otherwise inaccessible reaches of character to us, similes would often do the work later done by allusion. For example, an earlier narrator might tell us that a character "rode off to do battle against the phantom evil, like Don Quixote," whereas a post-Joycean writer would simply stick a windmill quietly in the background, or have the hero stop to have his car repaired at the Rocinante Brothers' Garage, or, as in my previous example, have the character himself provide the allusion. The task of interpretation is left to the reader as the narrator becomes more of a facilitator, shuttling the narration in and out of characters' minds. Difficulties begin to occur when the narrative voice and the character's voice can interfere with one another. The challenge for the author is to make the point about the character—to provide the intended interpretive keys—while conveying a sense of the character's independence. I am referring, then, to the necessity of striking a balance between the representing voice and the represented consciousness in indirect discourse, or narrated monologue, to use Dorrit Cohn's term. In *Portrait*, Joyce avoids the problem with his use of consonant narration (again Cohn's term), the mimetic narrative voicing that encourages the identification of narrator and character. In *Ulysses*, Joyce's move from narrated monologue to directly "quoted" interior monologue eliminates any possibility of overlapping. The new techniques he employs are necessitated by the dual protagonists, whose utter distinction must be established, thus making the use of a common narrative voice that would indirectly present their thoughts most undesirable. At the same time, the author becomes all the more free to indulge his own literary voice in the many parodies and inter-polated passages. All of this amounts to two simple observations: first, narrated monologue, or the free indirect style, works best when focal-ization is limited to a single or consonant viewpoint; and second, works with multiple viewpoints depend upon optimum distinction among the "voices" of the characters and that of the narrator, other-wise all will simply blend into a singular voice.

I have taken this excursus into details of structure and voicing in order to discuss certain problematic aspects of *Volcano*. Two kinds of overlapping occur in the novel, lending it a unity that may not be entirely desirable. First of all, there is overlapping of structure and allusion, i.e., of authorial and figural roles. Recognizing the analogy between the fictional world and the *Inferno*, for example, is a process taking place between the author and reader, even in cases where the character supplies the analogy. So when Hugh thinks of himself as Dante, he is not reinforcing the analogy; by making it explicit he is begging the question, seconding the authorial function in a redun-dant manner. Bloom does not think of himself as Ulysses. In *Volcano*, even neutral descriptions or details of the countryside are already heavily shaded with the Consul's vision; so any further reinforcing of the work's controlling analogies only clouds the issue. This sort of problem could have been avoided in great measure had Lowry simply limited his focalization to the Consul instead of alternating his view-point with that of the other principals. Second, aside from the Consul, the characters' voices are neither strong enough nor individuated enough. Their dialogue, particularly Yvonne's, is often stiff, and in indirect quotation their voices are not distinguished enough from the narrator's, so they tend to blend into a flat reportage.

Lowry justifies his overlapping characterization by positing an aesthetic to cover it, although a search of his works does not provide convincing evidence of technical skill that would allow any other choice. Lowry tells Cape that he has "not exactly attempted to draw characters in the normal sense—though s'welp me bob it's only Aris-totle who thought character counted least" (1965a, 60). Later, though, he joins with the philosopher, saying that character is for him, as for Aristotle, the last consideration. Echoing another of Cape's writers, Sean O'Faolin, Lowry notes the "comparative unim-portance of character anyway," and calls for the novel to reform itself by "drawing upon its ancient Aeschylean and tragic heritage." The sense in which he finds the novel having roots in Greek tragedy remains unexplained, but such a return would amount, he says, to another Renaissance. So then, if his characters are weakly individuated, it is because they represent "aspects of the same man, or of the human spirit" (60). Hugh and Geoffrey are doubles, Hugh is Everyman, and Yvonne is "the eternal woman." Defenders of Lowry's theory of character often come close to a kind of Jungian meltdown that melds novelistic detail into archetypal generalities so vast—or elemental—that they seem barely articulable in meaningful terms. Sherrill Grace says that "the development and etiology of characters is [*sic*] not important, compared to the symbolic, allegorical level," since the characters are, in fact, "ideological positions as well as concepts such as freedom and necessity" (1982, 37). Grace puts the cart before the horse: a work in which allegorical value takes priority over character is not a novel. Abstract qualities are derived from character, not the reverse; Grace's concepts may or may not be interesting, but they will only be as successfully developed as the persona in which they are embodied. Readers do not pick up novels seeking a tête-à-tête between Mr. Freedom and Ms. Necessity. Critics who become too enthralled with symbolism per se risk sounding as if the novelist's greatest achievement were the reduction of the genre to a sort of miracle play.

Lowry himself pleads to Cape that "there are a thousand writers who can draw adequate characters till all is blue for one who can tell you something new about hell fire." This may well be true, but again, hell fire in the abstract would be of paltry interest—if even representable; it can only be known in its embodiment in the thoughts, words, and actions of characters. Furthermore, Lowry is confusing traditions: his audience is not conditioned to interpret character as a flat persona serving as a locus to immutable forces of destiny, but rather to seek out the vicissitudes of existence as Geoffrey Firman, person, and whatever principles might be abstracted from it are secondary. When, in the Renaissance, poetry and drama "returned" to the model of their antique prototypes, it was a renewal of generic forms; the novel has no such antique heritage, Aeschylean or otherwise.

Lowry need never have issued his disclaimer about characterization as far as his portrayal of Geoffrey Firmin is concerned. The weak point of his characterization is found rather in the two other members of the central triangle, Hugh and Yvonne. The Consul is in all respects a well-drawn and enduring figure that can stand without apology alongside any fictional characters this century has to offer. His vitality as a character stems from his "simularity"—his provenance as an artful rendering of the author's own consciousness—and from the masterful focalization that brings the fictional world to life through his perception. Lowry's problem derives rather from the fact that the Consul so dominates the work that the other major characters suffocate in his proximity. Lowry is no doubt correct when he tells Cape that the reason for the reader's disapproval of the chapters focalized through Hugh and Yvonne is that the Consul was so compelling that the reader was probably impatient to get back to him. There would not be any debate over characterization had Lowry simply given the whole book to the Consul, but having decided to share focalization with the other two principals, he did not develop the latter sufficiently to support the burden.

The problem with Hugh and Yvonne is that the exposition of their character does not take place on the level of their immediate interaction with the fictional world. Their pasts and selves are instead presented in lengthy blocks of passive reflection—his while lying in bed, hers while daydreaming at the bullfight—that amount to gratuitous flashbacks. Much of the Consul's past is presented through Laruelle's reminiscences in the first chapter, but in that case the perception of him is external and serves to create an air of enigma around him; even within this flashback, the Consul is also revealed through the several pages of his letter to Yvonne that Laruelle is reading. The point is that we do not depend on the sole block of Laruelle's reflections to define the character to the degree that is true of Hugh's and Yvonne's autocharacterizations. Lowry is again dead-on in his evaluation when he concedes to Cape that some readers might view the flashbacks as a "belated attempt to draw character and at that a meretricious one" (80). What he did not learn from Joyce is the art of creating distinct fictional "otherness" of the sort achieved by imagining—on real models—particular bodies and assigning them their own unique voices, as is the case with the Blooms. Another crucial factor in Joyce's characterization is that Bloom's and Stephen's self-images are not developed in arbitrary blocks, but piecemeal, as immediate experiences elicit thoughts and feelings associatively. Joyce's characters are developed organically, through exacting psychological and perceptual mimesis; Lowry's are developed through an elementary expository device that is not nearly up to the standard set elsewhere in his novel. One is tempted by the corollary of Lowry's analysis of the reader's reaction, namely, that he was himself so anxious to return to writing about the Consul that he just disposed of Hugh and Yvonne in the most expedient way and got on with it. Still, it should be said that Yvonne is by far the most successfully realized of any of Lowry's female characters, who are mostly vapid, smiling accomplices who speak little and generally live up to their silly names: Primrose Wilderness, Lovey L'Hirondelle Cosnahan, and Tansy Fairhaven, to name the most embarrassing.

Jacques Laruelle is a more successful character than Hugh and Yvonne because he has less narrative weight to carry; his chapter is set apart from the story itself, in which he plays a minor role, and there is no need for him to enact a long memorial review of his past. As Lowry indicates to Cape, Hugh and Yvonne are weak precisely because the rest of the work is so well executed. His other explanation—that he meant the characters to be as they are the better to represent Everyman and his eternal love-interest, or what have you— does not hold up, and his spur-of-the-moment Aristotelian aesthetic is even less likely. As I have said, though, secondary characters such as Dr. Vigil are everything they need to be, and incidental characters such as the Oxbridge chap who finds the Consul lying in the street or the denizens of the Farolito are excellent, the latter by virtue of the odd ideolects Lowry invents for them, justified by their broken English. Ultimately, though, *Volcano* is Geoffrey Firmin's story, and the character more than carries it.

Douglas Day, in the preface to *Dark as the Grave Wherein My Friend Is Laid,* observes that on occasion Lowry did try to invent characters, but "he did not know enough about any other human being to do this." Geoffrey and Hugh Firmin, like the "Marcels" and Stephen and Bloom, are in part projections of stages of the author's life. Hugh represents much of Lowry's young manhood, before his first marriage, while the Consul depicts the author's drunken despair in Cuernavaca and Oaxaca after his first wife left him. The character Yvonne comprises aspects of both of Lowry's wives, but her situation in the plot is that of Jan, the first wife, who, although she never returned to her husband as Yvonne does, did leave her husband after a turbulent marriage marked by repeated infidelity on her part. The story itself begins—after Laruelle's retrospective/preview in the first chapter—with Yvonne's reappearance in Quauhnahuac, where she hopes to effect a reconciliation. The Consul is thus given an opportunity to save himself from desolation in conformity with the expression that is one of the novel's leitmotifs, *"no se puede vivir sin amar,"* one cannot live without loving.

There is another, albeit shadowy, presence of Lowry in the work, that of the author looking back on the entire episode in his life from the vantage point of British Columbia, where he is living in a squatter's cabin with his second wife during the relatively sober period in which he is reworking the story. This perspective shows up in a recurrent vision—shared by Yvonne, the Consul, and even Hugh—of potential happiness that might be found if the couple went away from Mexico together. The vision, a literal description of Lowry's life with Margerie in Canada, is first described in chapter 1, in an unmailed letter to Yvonne that Laruelle has found in a volume of Elizabethan plays (in the pages of *Dr. Faustus,* to be precise) borrowed from the Consul a year earlier:

> I seem to see us living in some northern country, of mountains and hills and blue water; our house is built on an inlet and one evening we are standing, happy in one another, on the balcony of this house, looking over the water. There are sawmills half hidden by trees beyond and under the hills on the other side of the inlet, what looks like an oil refinery, only softened and rendered beautiful by distance. (36–37)

This description continues for another page, in terms identical to those of the story "The Forest Path to the Spring," the closest Lowry would get to realizing the *Paradiso* section of his mediated *Commedia.*

Later, while Yvonne is horseback-riding with Hugh (thus affording Geoffrey the occasion and excuse to take advantage of a bottle of tequila he has stashed in his garden), she tests out the idea of a new life in Canada on Hugh, who throws cold water on the notion. Lowry uses Hugh's sarcasm as a vehicle for his own contempt for the city of Vancouver, but eventually Hugh takes Yvonne's dream seriously and adds to it, again in images belonging to "Forest Path":

> I can see your shack now. It's between the forest and the sea and you've got a pier going down to the water over rough stones,

you know, covered with barnacles and sea anemones and starfish. You'll have to go through the woods to the store. (122)

The vision continues in an italicized passage of interior monologue as Hugh rides on:

The woods will be wet. And occasionally a tree will come crashing down. And sometimes there will be fog and that fog will freeze. Then your whole forest will become a crystal forest. The ice crystals on the trees will grow like leaves. Then pretty soon you'll be seeing the jack-in-the-pulpits and then it will be spring. (122)

Later, while sitting with Geoffrey at a bullfight in chapter 9, their last moment alone together, Yvonne takes up the vision again, filling in more details of the Lowrys' life together. Still later, in the final chapter, at "half past sick by the cock" according to one of the Consul's fellow drinkers in the Farolito, after the Consul has made love with a prostitute who has, he assumes, surely given him a dose of something that definitively forecloses any possibility of ever making love with Yvonne again, he sees a calendar on the wall with a picture of a man and woman in a birch bark canoe under the moonlight in what he is sure must be Canada. This provokes one last brief review of the vision, but this time it is precluded as a possibility, couched in the past conditional:

British Columbia, the genteel Siberia, that was neither genteel nor a Siberia, but an undiscovered, perhaps undiscoverable Paradise, that might have been a solution, to return there, to build, if not on his island, somewhere there, a new life with Yvonne. (353)

The passage of the vision from the figurative—in the imaginations of the characters—to the literal—in the calendar picture—is a typical Lowryan procedure. David Markson (1978) notes that the figurative *selva* of Hugh's meditation becomes the literal woods of the last chapter, and that the image of the backward-turning wheel of time that ends the first chapter becomes literalized in the backward-turning Ferris wheel and the *maquina infernal* that the Consul rides at a carnival. In the case of both Canada and the *selva*, however, the terms first appear in a concrete form, then pass through the figurative back to a concrete manifestation. The *selva* first appears as the Casino de la Selva, and the initial appearance of Canada in the story proper is as a sticker from the Canada Hotel, where the Firmins were staying when Yvonne left, on Yvonne's suitcase when she arrives in Quauhnahuac.

Between hotel and calendar, then, Canada represents a vision of love actualized, but it is an impossible vision in *Volcano*. The separate passages, which form a continuous description, employ images of greenery, water, and cold, crystalline beauty that are completely antithetical to the hot and sinister images of Mexico and to the Consul's intoxicated visions. The harmony of the pair in Canada is in contrast to the unbridgeable gaps between the characters in the story. Lowry looks back from his paradise to his hellish despair not to rescue his fictional self, but to exorcise the ghosts of Jan and his self-destructive tendencies. The great irony, though, is that despite having found his paradise in Canada, the author did, in the end, fall prey to those tendencies, true to his fictional self-portrait.

Lowry's actual life at the time of his writing is thus figured in the novel as an unrealizable potential; the will to love and accept love is not sufficiently strong. The Canadian wood is an *anti-selva,* or if Mexico is a *selva oscura,* Canada is a *selva chiara.* The Consul is like Dante at the beginning of the *Inferno,* but he is a Dante without a Beatrice. Yvonne, the potential Beatrice, is herself lost in a dark wood (figuratively and literally). She and the Consul might save one another, but the world of *Volcano* is diabolical, characterized on every level—moral, historical, political, spiritual—by a lack of sufficient compassion to overcome the will to destruction. There is no Samaritan who can help the dying Indian by the roadside; neither Moctezuma nor Chamberlain can forestall imminent holocaust; Cardenas's effort to aid the peasants will be crushed by Mexican fascists and their foreign cronies; the Spanish Civil War, as Hugh frequently reminds himself, is being lost by the forces of dignity; and a man cannot quite forgive himself and the woman he still loves. If there is a Beatrice in the book, it is the one who remains unnamed, Margerie, as she is represented in the novel's countervailing vision of paradise.

Such, then, is the basic structure of Lowry's transformation of life into art. The Consul, like Quentin Compson, is a character with-

out any redemptive artistic power. The notable difference between
the two is that Lowry's projection is simular—it is not an invention,
but a representation of the actual, artistically rendered—whereas
Faulkner's is a traditional fictional character who is made to embody
the problem of historical identity that troubled the author. Quentin
must commit suicide because, unlike Faulkner, he has no ability to
release himself from the stranglehold of the South's ghosts by turning
them into art. The difference between the Consul and Lowry is the
latter's will to endure the hellfire for the sake of representing it. The
Consul and Quentin—the latter in a more limited sense—can join
Bloom as versions of the artist as a nonartist.

Actually, Bloom and the Consul have much in common, starting
with the fact that each spends his day in a peregrination, obsessively
meditating on the state and history of his marriage, while astutely
observing and commenting on the life around him. Each is haunted
by cuckoldry and a deeper guilt: for Bloom, the deaths of his father
and son, for the Consul, the strange, Conrad-like incident of the
Germans burned aboard the *Samaritan,* as well as almost anything
having to do with sex. Just as Joyce concretizes Bloom's anxiety over
infidelity with the recurrent Plumtree's Potted Meat ads, Lowry confronts the Consul throughout the day with posters for the film *Las
manos de Orlac,* the story of an artist (musician) with murderous
hands. Ron Binns (1984, 35) notes that the Consul, like Bloom, employs Greek *e*'s, talks to a cat, is followed by a dog, quotes Hamlet,
and is pursued by phantom authorities (although the Consul's phan-
toms become quite fatally real). The Consul's library and budget for
the day are detailed, as are Bloom's, and at one point Hugh even
remembers having aided a seagull, as did Bloom. Not least of all, the
Consul and Bloom are each featured in privy scenes.

Lowrey's toilet scene, paradoxically, makes much more extensive use of Joycean narrative techniques than Joyce's. The Consul sits
on a stone throne, in what he calls "the Cave of the Winds" and the
"eternal library" and entertains an eminently Bloomworthy thought:
"Where else could man absorb and divest himself of so much at the
same time?" (293–94). During the scene, which extends for about
eight pages, the Consul is reading a travel brochure, overhearing the
voices of Hugh and Yvonne floating in from the adjacent restaurant,
and also having auditory hallucinations consisting of remembered
bits of conversation and the voices of his "familiars," the spirits of

delirium. Thus the narrative form of the passage consists of psychonarration, quoted monologue, internal voices presented as if external (technically still quoted monologue), external dialogue, and quoted (graphically distinct) excerpts from the travel brochure, all presented as they would occur in the Consul's perception, with no narrative explication. All of this material is united thematically: Hugh and Yvonne's conversation concerns the treachery committed against the Indian and speculation about the local fascists' activities, and the brochure refers to Tlaxcala, the land of the people who betrayed Moctezuma to the Spanish. The brochure also refers to the area's Churrigueresque colonial architecture, providing the basis of a metaleptic reference to the novel itself. Hugh says to Yvonne that the Aztec civilization, as good or better than the Spanish, had a "deep-rooted structure." So, too, the novel, under its "Churrigueresque" (baroque, overloaded) style, is upheld by the deep structure of its formal esoterica. In an earlier bathroom scene in chapter 5, Lowry comes yet closer to infinite regression by suggesting a conflation of the Consul and the author:

> Yet who would ever have believed that some obscure man, sitting at the center of the world in a bathroom, say, thinking solitary miserable thoughts, was authoring their doom.... Or perhaps it was not a man at all, but a child, a little child, innocent as that other Geoffrey had been, who sat as up in an organ loft somewhere playing, pulling out all the stops at random, and kingdoms divided and fell.... (146)

Much of Lowry's narrative flexibility is facilitated by the Consul's alcoholism. The fact that he is passing in and out of various stages of delirium allows Lowry to employ a number of "Circe"-like effects. The Farolito bar in the last chapter even exceeds Bella Cohen's brothel as an infernal nightmare of menacing figures, incoherent dialects, and shifting levels of reality. At times the Consul thinks he is in one place only to find himself suddenly in another; scenes are presented, then exposed as hallucination as he comes back to himself. The overall effect is to create a fluid reality that magnifies the already sinister atmosphere of a foreign land full of political intrigue and naturalizes Firmin's rather matter-of-fact paranoia. A person accustomed to the presence of "familiars" would not find it unusual to be followed by characters in sunglasses all day.

Thus, the alcoholism is technically expedient, providing the means of portraying a world of diabolical signs and forces, and also simularly necessary, since it was, in fact, a determining factor in the author's experience. Lowry even insisted that verified premonitions, which the Consul experiences on occasion, are not uncommon phenomena to one suffering the d.t.'s. Among other things, then, *Volcano* is the story of an alcoholic viewed from the inside. In a preface to the French edition, Lowry states that "the idea I cherished in my heart was to create a pioneer work in its own class, and to write at last an authentic drunkard's story" (quoted in Hill 1980, 141). This explains his anxiety over the appearance of *Lost Weekend* before his own work was published.

Art Hill's informative study "The Alcoholic on Alcoholism" (1980) shows how much of the Consul's eccentric or otherwise inexplicable behavior is in fact quite characteristic of an alcoholic. His behavior is essentially oriented toward achieving maximum consumption with minimal interference. For every drink he's seen taking by those around him, he manages to take several more on the sly. His myth concerning mezcal—that he will be all right as long as he avoids this one serious potion—is a typical alcoholic self-delusion. Even without counting the prodigious quantity of mezcal he imbibes, there is still enough other alcohol in his regimen to fuel a moon rocket, when he finally gives in and orders a mezcal, it is simply the signal that he has abandoned all pretense of restraint. Hill points out a crucial scene at Jacques Laruelle's house, in which the Frenchman gets up to escort his guests to the door, while the Consul tarries a moment on the grounds that he needs to have a word with Jacques before joining the others. Once the other three people have left, the Consul, who had not touched his drink while they were present, gulps down not only his own but the remainders of the others' drinks in a clearly premeditated maneuver. This scene is typical of Lowry's technique in that the motive that triggers this particular surrender to his craving as well as his engineering of the favorable circumstances for it are not made explicit, but are left to the reader to reconstruct, just as we might pick up on or miss entirely the meaning of a person's behavior in life. The Consul finds himself in the company of his ex-wife and two of her erstwhile lovers—his friend and his brother, at that—at the very location of one of the adulteries, and it is more than he can handle. He is filled with contempt for the three of them, and as usual, the brunt of his aggression is self-directed.

Volcano, like *Ulysses,* gives one the overwhelming impression of its own dynamism. Unlike a traditionally fixed fictional locale, Quauhnahuac, like Dublin, seems to carry on without us; it is a world we enter, observing what we may, while much else goes on unnoticed yet implicit all around us, just as it does in the real world. Lowry follows Joyce in presenting apparently unmotivated and unexplicated details, leaving it to the reader to see and understand. One can go through *Volcano* after a first reading and reconstruct separate threads and subplots, discovering the relationship of isolated details to the whole. This aspect of the novel makes it of a kind with *Ulysses* to a degree that few other works could match. We are at once taken into the depths of the Consul's toxified subjectivity and given the pieces with which to reconstruct, as if from an aerial perspective, the mean-derings of the three principals, the Indian and his horse, the shadowy informers, the old woman with the dominoes, and Weber, the red-neck American arms dealer, through the day to their final rendezvous at Parian.

As in *Ulysses,* many details of *Volcano* are unlikely to be perceived in their integral patterns on a first reading. To cite one example, having finished chapter 12 and returned to the story's beginning in chapter 2, one would recognize the unidentified voice that Yvonne hears coming out of the Bella Vista bar saying "—just a bunch of Alladamnbama farmers!" as that of Weber, who was consorting with the fascists in the Farolito at the end of the book, and one would then recognize him as the American, mentioned by Hugh later on, whom he met on his way from Texas. Finally, as in *Ulysses,* the depth and complexity of the novel's structural design and symbolism make it a seemingly inexhaustible mine of artifice. Ron Binns (1984), for one, has turned up a systematic use of the color blue—which shows up everywhere from a light bulb, to the "Saint Louis Blues," to Jacques Laruelle's penis—in association with sexual jealousy and aggression. In sum, Lowry need not have fretted over Joyce's shadow; there is no shame in assimilating the lessons of a master and putting them to one's own good use.

Despite some critics' efforts to prove the contrary, Lowry was basically a one-novel author. (I am excluding from my discussion his youthful *Ultramarine,* which Aiken suggested he name *Purple Passage,* after his own *Blue Voyage.*) Everything that appeared after *Volcano,* other than the collection of stories *Hear Us O Lord from Heaven Thy Dwelling Place,* which was nearly finished, was published posthumously from manuscripts in varying degrees of incompletion. *Dark as the Grave Wherein My Friend Is Laid,* for example, was pared down to a modest 255 pages from 700-odd pages of manuscript by Douglas Day and Margerie Lowry, and while it would be unfair to judge it as a finished work by Lowry, a brief discussion of it will better illuminate the artistic success of *Volcano* and shed light on Lowry's overall aims.

In *Dark as the Grave* the distance between lived experience and fictional representation is greatly reduced as Lowry approaches a technique of speaking in his own voice through a thin fictional pretense. The work is based on Lowry's return to Mexico with Margerie in 1946, when he composed his letter to Cape and eventually received word of *Volcano*'s acceptance. In this case, Lowry employs his favorite alter-ego, Sigbjorn Wilderness, with Margerie figured (badly, one hopes) as his wife Primrose. Wilderness is the author of *Volcano*'s alter-text, *The Valley of the Shadow of Death,* and he has gone to Mexico to face his old demons—drink and a vaguely articulated guilt—while searching for his friend Juan Fernando Martinez. Martinez is modeled after Juan Fernando Marquez, Lowry's Zapotecan friend whose awkward anglicisms ("Throw away your mind") and philosophy of "la vida impersonal" are given to Dr. Vigil in *Volcano,* and he shares with that book's murdered Indian Marquez's dedication to the land reform movement of the thirties. The story culminates with the discovery that Martinez had died sometime previously, causing Wilderness to repair to a church—rather than a bar, notably—and grieve. The final scene has Wilderness looking out a bus window at blossoming orchards that are the fruit of Martinez's courageous efforts on behalf of the *Banco Ejidal,* the land agency that was the target of the fascists' ire in *Volcano.*

The novel is noteworthy first of all for this brief portrayal of successful, compassionate social action that points the way out of *Volcano*'s world of treachery, although this portrait pales in comparison with the protagonist's anguished self-examinations. Second, the work is notable as an example of novelistic self-consciousness handled awkwardly. Probably because Lowry did not live to see the work to completion, the layers of composition are sometimes painfully in evidence. As it stands, though, it is apparent that the novel consists of raw compilations from notebooks and the author's travel log, like an extinct *Volcano,* i.e., without the sort of artifice that characterizes its predecessor.

The novel is focalized entirely through Wilderness, but without the Consul's macabre, playful mind and vivid visions he is rather uninteresting. Wilderness turns up again as the author persona in the story "Through the Panama," in which he is now the author of *Dark as the Grave* itself, thus making him an author reflecting on the writing of his last work, which comprised reflections on the work before that; it's not hard to predict the next step in this potentially infinite regression. This sort of autocannibalism reveals the dreary side of metatextuality: it is the easy refuge of an uninspired writer.

Lowry makes Wilderness the spokesman for pseudomystical notions about the relationship between life and art. Successful simular novels lend a special aura to this relationship that is a symbol and product of their own creative ability, but Lowry depicts conjunctions of life and art as signs of a greater external power governing his life. Lowry was greatly taken by coincidences that amounted to the discovery of aptly literary symbols in his life, such as the Shell sign with a burned out "S" that stood over the refinery across the inlet from his cabin, or the fact that Margerie unknowingly rented them a room in the house that had been the model for Jacques's house in *Volcano.* Wilderness, too, sees such occurrences as deeply significant, but with precious little sense of irony. He cannot get over the fact that he is walking around in the setting of his novel, running into people who had served as his models, and is given to voicing his perplexity in heavily metaleptic terms:

> Was he the director of the film of his life? Was God? Was the devil? He was an actor in it, but if God were the director that was no reason why he should not constantly appeal to him to change the ending. (249)

> It was impossible to escape the conviction that there was tremendous meaning in all this, indeed meaning in all our lives. (234)

The ponderousness of such statements effectively robs them of any philosophical relevance. Metalepsis is a trope that is most effective when presented with a wink, in the manner of Diderot's Jacques, for example, who is always excusing his behavior on the grounds that it is so written that he should act that way. There is more meaning, even if less "tremendous," in Wilderness's recognition of the compassion that Martinez had had for him and of the tangible results that his friend's life had produced in the countryside and in the lives of the peasants, but there is no strong indication that Wilderness recognizes that his search for the "tremendous" has caused him to overlook the more mundane but more relevant value of community.

In "The Forest Path to the Spring," which was to have become the coda of his arch-work, Lowry again obliquely broaches the subject of community. The story's unnamed first-person narrator, a musician and recovering alcoholic, is at work on what he considers a breakthrough opera entitled—not surprisingly—"The Forest Path to the Spring" and lives with his wife in the setting of the northern vision from *Volcano*. The squatters' settlement is called Eridanus, after a ship from Liverpool grounded in the vicinity—one of Lowry's few references to his native city. In the story all of the symbols that characterized Quauhnahuac are reversed: Eridanus is all peace and light, nature outside of history and outside the "hell of ugliness" of civilization. Popocatepetl is replaced by its "northern cousins," like Mt. Baker. The Farolito is replaced by a literal lighthouse, "the highest symbol of civilization," toward which a deer swims in the final scene, and the devil imagery now has its angelic counterpart. There are no sinister figures in Eridanus, only strong, silent Northern European types. The inhabitants of the settlement are united in their affection for the place and by their marginal status vis-à-vis the nearby threatening metropolitan area. Within the community mutual aid, respect, and tolerance reign; it is ostensibly just the sort of place where an artist willing to endure some discomfort can have complete leisure in a setting conducive to cultivating impressions of beauty and harmony, and dry out, in this particular case. If anything, Eridanus is too serene; it is no accident that Lowry's great work, *Volcano*, depicts personal and political chaos and danger, among violent and demonstrative people.

Lowry's paradise found proves to be insubstantial to a degree that renders the story rather inconclusive as the culminating piece in what he considered a unified progression of stories in *Hear Us O Lord*, much less as the final statement of the projected life's work.

Life in Eridanus represents at best a temporary evasion of the world; it is an unsustainable vision, particularly in comparison with the suggestion of social change—as opposed to evasion—offered at the end of *Dark as the Grave*. If the world's "garden" in *Volcano* was being destroyed by its inhabitants, the gardeners in Eridanus face the constant threat of eviction by the municipal authorities. The community will endure only so long as the larger community of which it is willy-nilly a part is distracted by the demands of World War II and its aftermath. The story's concept of community is specious in a work without any of *Volcano*'s sociohistorical dynamics.

In *Volcano* Lowry addressed, as did Joyce and Proust before him, the problem of artistic sensitivity in the farce or nightmare of history, but his later works that feature artist protagonists do not succeed at portraying a resolution of the conflict via the creation of an enduring work. Proust and Joyce were voluntary exiles—the former from the Parisian society he had long cultivated, the latter from Ireland and family—whose works are sublimations in the classic sense of reproducing the lost "object" in representation. Faulkner, too, though not an exile, artistically reproduces the community of the lost South in his Yoknapatawpha County. Each of these authors, then, defines his place in the historical world. The Consul and Hugh, as well as filmmaker Jacques Laruelle, another artist in exile, are people without a community. Hugh's political actions, providing information to the British and sailing (belatedly) for Spain, are attempts to take part in history. Laruelle, as he leaves Mexico, hopes to see Paris again, but has little interest in the outcome of the impending war: "one side or the other would win . . . . And in either case one's battle would go on" (9). The Consul's battle, like Lowry's, is first and foremost the battle of the bottle. The protagonist of "The Forest Path" suggests that with the battle won, love and creativity might carry the day, but the suggestion is a weak one. The Consul's battle is given cosmic proportions, and his fate is made to represent the fate of humanity. Lowry's subsequent protagonists, in their attempts at happiness, place no premium on reintegration into history, into a functional community beyond barroom or love-nest. Lowry left "Eridanus" in 1954 for an extended European visit, eventually returning to England, where he lost the decisive battle with alcohol in 1957. There is little indication, in his art or his life, that once having repudiated his destiny as son of a wealthy industrialist (which paradoxically financed much of his writing) he ever succeeded in attaining an integrated social identity, and the high priesthood of art was no longer a credible option in the postwar world.

Lowry's later career helps to demonstrate the fragility of the simular form. When well crafted, the "presence" of the author as a sort of guarantor of the representation, and our sense of the purposeful aura surrounding the slightest details, combine to create a rare vitality and characters who are memorable not by their actions, but by their nature. A great deal of artifice is required, though, to sustain the weight of the author's presence, and a measure of restraint is necessary to avoid *longueurs* of the type found in some of Joyce's more extended parodies, or Proust's less edited out-loud thinking. Again, one must allow that Lowry would have endowed his later works with more artifice had he lived to see them through to publication—*October Ferry to Gabriola,* while still incomplete and unsatisfying in many respects, is the most structurally and symbolically crafted of the post-*Volcano* works, and suggests a fruitful direction—but as they are, the post-*Volcano* stories suffer from a lack of imaginative transformation.

Roth

The question of community and social identity is at the heart of Henry Roth's *Call It Sleep* (1934), and it was also the decisive factor in his career, which he abandoned after this one novel, later explaining that he had done so out of a sense of loss of communal identity. The impact of *Ulysses* on Roth's work, as elsewhere, is not hard to spot and has been frequently noted; a more pervasive influence, however, can be traced to *Portrait. Ulysses*'s influence on *Call It Sleep* is not structural, but found rather in techniques of voicing and representing the unconscious and wide-angle urban activity. Roth does not employ grids or subtexts, nor does he make much use of literary allusion (except for the climactic use of Isaiah 6), at least in part because his tight focalization on the six-year-old protagonist would not facilitate the insertion of such references. The novel is organized in the manner of *Portrait,* around symbolic motifs and recurrent imagery, and has a great deal in common thematically with Stephen's story.

Although *Call It Sleep* represents a much shorter time than *Por-*

trait—something over one year in the main action—it is a spiritual biography of no less depth, and greater dramatic intensity. Each of the works portrays a conjunction of familial, social, religious, and sexual tensions as a spiritual crisis whose resolution is marked by the boy's synthesis and mastery of the symbols that have shaped the story. It makes little difference that David Schearl's characterization will not formally support a hypothetical identification with the authorial voice, as does Stephen's, for the novel's culmination clearly locates the genesis of the work's governing images in the protagonist's consciousness. Thus *Call It Sleep*, like *Portrait*, is a story of psychological coming-of-age in which the protagonist attains an integral and stable self-definition when he becomes the fashioner of his own images.

Roth's story depicts the development of David Schearl's self-awareness as he confronts the mystery of sexuality and three impinging sources of aggression: his tense family triangle, the boisterous children of the immigrant neighborhood, and the alien culture that surrounds all of them. After a prologue showing the arrival of David and his mother at Ellis Island and their unpleasant reception by Albert Schearl, father and spouse, the novel is divided into four books (within which each distinct scene constitutes a chapter). The books— "The Cellar," "The Picture," "The Coal," and "The Rail"—are named for the thematic nexuses representing stages of David's understanding and attempts to secure himself against internal and external threats. The titles also identify groups of symbols and images that form motifs throughout the work—cellar, picture, coal, rail—in the same way that water, birds, flowers, colors, and so on recur in various forms in *Portrait*, symbolizing stages of Stephen's growth.

The dark cellar serves as a literal manifestation of the fear of sexuality brought to the surface in the first book's key episode, David's sexual "initiation" with a neighbor girl in a dark closet, and the confinement of the two spaces is associated with death when David sees a coffin in the street. In the familiar manner of children, David makes the cellar the repository of all his general anxieties, from which his mother affords protection. She cannot protect him from the fear of sex, however, which he cannot articulate, and when circumstances force him to seek refuge in the cellar, thus confronting his fear, the necessity of his psychic independence is brought home to him.

The picture, which Genya, the mother, brings home and hangs, represents cornstalks and blue flowers that are for her symbols of the old country, specifically of the field from which she last saw her gentile lover. For David, who has overheard parts of this story, the picture, like the cellar, is associated with the mystery and danger of sexuality—specifically his mother's—and it also represents the less threatening geographical and historical aspects of his origins. A counterpart of the picture is supplied by a set of bull's horns, hung up by Albert as a memento of his peasant past, symbolizing his aggressive virility. The picture and horns, as focuses of David's concern, represent a psychological progression from the cellar: unlike the formless dread that beset him earlier, these provide external, public symbols that are accessible to his reasoned inquiry, to a certain degree. The move from cellar to picture is one away from isolated terror toward recognition of the reality of the family and its history.

The coal is the burning ember in the story of Isaiah that will become the central symbol of David's spiritual quest. It represents a further step outward, away from the family circle. It is discovered in the cheder, under the guidance of the rabbi—a spiritual father—and also represents the development of religious awareness, identification with a cultural heritage, and not least, a profound experience of literary interpretation on David's part. The coal, which David takes to be of the dark sort one would find in a cellar, becomes the symbol of the light and power that can overcome darkness and fear.

The rail, finally, is the streetcar track where David tries to attain divine light and power in all-too-literal form by shorting out the third rail. It represents David's final outward step, into the city at large and into the modern world of manufactured light and power.

The symbols and images that attend each of the thematic centers are not limited to the individual books, but play freely throughout the work. One of the crucial scenes in "The Rail" takes place in a cellar; in "The Cellar," there is mention of Albert twisting a rail, and so forth. The rail and its light are prefigured everywhere. As befits the urban setting, Roth finds ample opportunity to include images of shining metals and people touching metal. In the first chapter, David reaches for a "bright brass faucet that gleamed so far away." Elsewhere he walks down the street grasping at "every rail and post within reach," sees a boy leaning against a brass bannister, and himself feels "the chill of a tarnished railing under his palm." At times David consciously thinks about the effect of light and metal:

He paused awhile and watched the Hungarian janitor polish one of the brass banisters in front of the house. It had a corrupt odor, brass, as of something rotting away, and yet where the sun struck the burnished metal, it splintered into brilliant metal light. Decay. Radiance. Funny. (242)

A group of boys try to fish a shining coin from a sewer through the bars of a grating and build a fire in a small metal box. Images of shining metal as well as of candles, flames, lights, and the sun are practically innumerable in the book, forming a continuum that is much more pervasive than the usual use of motif in a novel; to extend the musical metaphor, one might qualify their recurrence as an ostinato.

Perhaps Roth's greatest achievement in *Call It Sleep* is his mastery of sustained focalization from the young boy's point of view, a focus that is abandoned only in the last section, first to travel across town with the rabbi, then, after a passage of conventional omniscient narration, to broaden into the focus on the night voices of the neighborhood before finally rejoining David. Like *Portrait*, *Call It Sleep* makes use of consonant narration, the blending of narrative and figural voices in the idiom of the character, as well as quoted monologue without quotes, in the manner of *Ulysses*. In *Portrait* the mimetic use of the character's language in narration is most evident in the first pages' baby talk. Once away from the preschool years, though, the novel is marked more by the mature narrator's voice than by the voice of the character's immediate experience. In *Portrait* Joyce's credo of artistic transformation takes priority over the more psychically realistic representation of experience found in *Ulysses*. Roth seeds his narration with thoughts and exclamations that convey sensation or perception as if they were inner articulations. Joyce frequently uses this technique in *Ulysses*, for example when Bloom looks inside his hat and the quoted monologue "says" "White slip of paper," as if he said those words to himself, whereas it is the transcription of a perception.

To illustrate the difference I am describing between *Portrait* and *Call It Sleep*, it will be useful to compare scenes in which the protagonists endure corporal punishment. First, the well-known pandybat scene from *Portrait*:

Stephen closed his eyes and held out in the air his trembling hand with the palm upwards. He felt the prefect of studies touch it for a moment at the fingers to straighten it and then the swish of the soutane as the pandybat was lifted to strike. A hot burning stinging tingling blow like the loud crack of a broken stick made his trembling hand crumple together like a leaf in the fire: and at the sound and the pain scalding tears were driven into his eyes. His whole body was shaking with fright, his arm was shaking and his crumpled burning livid hand shook like a loose leaf in the air. A cry sprang to his lips, a prayer to be let off. But though the tears scalded his eyes and his limbs quivered with pain and fright he held back the hot tears and the cry that sprang to his throat.

—Other hand! shouted the prefect of studies.

Stephen drew back his maimed and quivering right arm and held out his left hand. The soutane sleeve swished again as the pandybat was lifted and a loud crashing sound and a fierce maddening tingling burning pain made his hand shrink to-gether with the palms and fingers in a livid quivering mass. The scalding water burst forth from his eyes and, burning with shame and agony and fear, he drew back his shaking arm in terror and burst out into a whine of pain. His body shook with a palsy of fright and in shame and rage he felt the scalding cry come to his throat and the scalding tears falling out of his eyes and down his flaming cheeks. (50–51)

The poetic structure of this passage is obvious, in the sym-metry of the two sections separated by the prefect's order, the triads of verbal adjectives, the incessant repetition of shaking and burn-ing, and the use of similes. The first simile—"a blow like the loud crack of a broken stick"—transforms sensation into sound, and the next two—"like a leaf in the fire" and "like a loose leaf in the air"—transform sensation into visual imagery. The use of passives and impersonal forms—"a cry sprang," "the pandybat was lifted"—disso-ciates the actions from their agents. This distancing might be justified as reflective of the shocked detachment of the mind observ-ing bodily trauma, or of the boy's heroic attempt at self-control, but the overall effect of the poetic tropes is to shift the focal balance of the passage from the immediacy of experience to its quality as a representation.

The following passage from *Call It Sleep* describes David's first beating at the hands of his father, after he has bloodied a playmate in some boyish roughhousing:

> Answer me, his words rang out. Answer me, but they meant, Despair! Who could answer his father? In that dread summons the judgment was already sealed. Like a cornered thing, he shrank within himself, deadened his mind because the body would not deaden and waited. Nothing existed any longer except his father's right hand—the hand that hung down into the electric circle of his vision. Terrific clarity was given him. Terrific leisure. Transfixed, timeless, he studied the curling fingers that twitched spasmodically, studied the printer's ink ingrained upon the finger tips, pondered, as if all there were in the world, the nail of the smallest finger, nipped by a press, that climbed in a jagged little stair to the hangnail. Terrific absorption. . . .
>
> Suddenly he cringed. His eyelids blotted out the light like a shutter. The open hand struck him full against the cheek and temple, splintering the brain into fragments of light. Spheres, mercuric, splattered, condensed, and roared. He fell to the floor. The next moment his father had snatched up the clothes hanger, and in that awful pause before it descended upon his shoulders, he saw with that accelerated vision of agony, how mute and open mouthed Yussie stood now, with what useless silence.
>
> "You won't answer!" The voice that snarled was the voice of the clothes hanger biting like flame into his flesh. "A curse on your vicious heart! Wild beast! Here, then! Here! Here! Now I'll tame you! I've a free hand now! I warned you! Would you heed!"
>
> The chopping strokes of the clothes hanger flayed his wrists, his hands, his back, his breast. There was always a free place for it to land no matter where he ducked or writhed or groveled. He screamed, screamed, and still the blows fell.

"Please papa! Please! No more! No more! Darling papa! Darling papa!" He knew that in another moment he would thrust his head beneath that rain of blows. Anguish! Anguish! He must escape! (83–84)

It is significant that David shrinks within himself and deadens his mind because his body won't deaden. Unlike Joyce's passage, where the body seems deadened by the observing intellect, the emphasis here is on the somatic core of experience, the most fundamental, preverbal, instinctual self-awareness. David is reduced to the circle of his immediate perception and sensation. Contrary to Joyce's passage, here sound (the father's voice) is transformed into sensation (the bite of the hanger). His father's voice needs no narrative identification because it is presented from within the boy's perception, particularly in the opening phrase, where it appears without quotation marks. "Despair!" and "Anguish! Anguish! He must escape!" are articulations of inner sensation and impulse. The distance between the represented experience and the medium of representation is in this case minimized as far as language can permit, with the exception of the unnecessary third-person pronoun of the last enunciation.

I do not mean to suggest that Roth's language is not metaphorical or that it is devoid of poetic usage, far from it. But his similes—"like a cornered thing . . . as if all there were in the world . . . biting like flame"—all serve to isolate and intensify the experience; they do not elicit images that are as external to the event as Joyce's leaves do. Robert Alter notes a distinctly Melvillian influence in the "cosmic sweep" of Roth's "explosive power of hyperbole that enlarges and violently transforms the experience it describes." We see such power in this passage's "splintering the brain into fragments of light," etc. For Alter this Melvillian cast is a unique trait of American literature, presenting "images of humanity facing the absolute ultimacy of existence" (1988, 33–37). This ultimacy emerges in each of David's physical traumas—beatings, falling down stairs, and electrical shock—where we are shown the most primal seat of selfhood, awareness suspended between being and the void. Against this cosmic—or microcosmic—background, we view the world from the perspective of the boy's unrelenting effort to integrate his emerging ego in a confusing and hostile environment. David's every perception and experience derive meaning from the sole end of self-understanding imposed upon him as a human being. This makes him seem in a sense heroic beyond his years, but then, he is simply performing the task of self-integration accomplished by all children. Roth's genius lies in representing childhood as a metaphysical drama believably focalized in an everyday boy.

The story of David Schearl's inner development, through a series of traumatic experiences, intuitions, and false deductions, is nothing less than a mystical quest. Finding himself alone and threatened not only in the great city, but also within the family triangle, David sets out to attain enlightenment in the classic literal sense. He seeks an illuminating experience, a merging with divine light that will transmute his fear, purify his perception and integrate his self, and Roth portrays this quest through a sequence of events and insights that mark David's development from psychological crisis to spiritual awareness and finally to accommodation with the material world.

As the story begins, David has an uncommonly strong and rich bond with his mother, and from the day of their arrival in New York he is faced with the father's overt resentment and jealousy. His fear of his father, who is represented throughout the work in Vulcan-like images of a hammer-wielding menace, is crystallized in a vision the boy has after learning that Albert has been fired for nearly "braining" a coworker:

> David could almost see him, the hammer raised over his head, his face contorted in terrific wrath, the rest cringing away. He shuddered at the image in his mind, stopped motionless on the stair, terrified at having to confront the reality.... David never said anything to anyone of what he had discovered, not even to his mother—it was all too terrifying, too unreal to share with someone else. He brooded about it until it entered his sleep, till he no longer could tell where his father was flesh and where dream. Who would believe him if he said, I saw my father lift a hammer; he was standing on a high roof of darkness, and below him were faces uplifted, so many, they stretched like white cobbles to the end of the world; who would believe him? He dared not. (28)

This mythologizing of his father marks the beginning of David's separation from the symbiotic openness that had characterized his rapport with his mother, the first step toward his independent selfhood; from this moment, he begins to keep his own counsel. From the outset, then, David is troubled by his confusion of the symbol he created and reality, and by the impossibility of articulating his vision. The "sleep" where visions are crafted is the locus of his deepest self, and it is toward the reconciliation of his being in "sleep" with his being in the world that his quest will be directed.

The next traumatic occurrence is David's discovery of sex while "playing bad" with an aggressive neighbor girl in a closet. In this case it is no longer a vision, but his own experience that he cannot share with his mother. Sex is, of course, the greatest factor contributing to the boy's isolation: it is his secret from his mother, and also her secret from him, as he attempts to piece together the overheard fragments of a conversation between Genya and her sister (the most salient parts of which are spoken in Polish to prohibit his understanding) concerning the former's great love in Austria. This tale is central to the family dynamic, since it is the basis of Albert's hostility; his suspicion that David is not his son only awaits a proper moment of rage to become an open accusation. Sex is also, ultimately, the undeniable sphere of parental union, definitively separating the men from the boys, as it were. Albert Schearl is generally too bitter and vituperative to be imagined as having much of an intimate bond with his wife, but in one notable scene, David notices a certain unusual lassitude and contentment in his mother's features as she tells him that Albert (now napping) has acquired a new whip (he drives a horse-cart) and offers to show him the instrument. David demurs, and is left contemplating intuited connections among the whip, the bull horns on the wall, the force with which his father had earlier brutalized a man who stole from him, and the sudden change in his mother's bodily aspect.

The next intensifying step in David's growth occurs after he has knocked out a playmate, fled to and from the cellar, and run away altogether after hearing the arrival of Mr. Luter, a would-be seducer of his mother. Eventually arriving at a police station, David awaits Genya, who will be seen in a completely new light—frightened, inarticulate—when she has to deal with the authorities of the strange new world that will be David's. While waiting, though, David arrives at a new understanding of his situation:

> He understood it now, understood it all, irrevocably, indelibly. Desolation had fused into a touchstone, a crystalline, bitter,

burred reagent that would never be blunted, never dissolved. Trust nothing. Trust nothing. Trust nothing. Wherever you look, never believe. Whatever anything was or did or said, it pretended. Never believe. If you played hide 'n'-go-seek, it wasn't hide 'n'-go-seek, it was something else, something sinister.... Don't play, never believe. The man who had directed him; the old woman who had left him here; the policeman; all had tricked him. They would never call his mother, never. He knew. They would keep him there. That rat cellar underneath. That rat cellar! That boy he had pushed was still. Coffin-box still. They knew it. And they knew about Annie. They made believe they didn't, but they knew. Never believe. Never play. Never believe. Not anything. Everything shifted. Everything changed. (102)

Thus David attains the skepticism that is a prerequisite of any search for enlightenment: the world is not as he sees it, he is not as he sees himself; unless he can somehow be changed, he will never find certainty.

David's turn from despair and cynicism occurs as he begins attending Hebrew school, under the direction of Reb Yiddel Pankower (whose invectives against dull-witted students are classics of linguistic creativity). After two months at cheder, David finds "a curious pause in himself as though he were waiting for some sign, some seal that would forever relieve him of watchfulness and forever insure his well-being." He attributes this calm to his increasing nearness to God. He no longer worries about his father, and his mother seems at peace. Even the secrets of his mother's past have "submerged within him."

Everything unpleasant and past was like that, David decided, lost within one. All one had to do was imagine that it wasn't there, just as the cellar in one's house could be conjured away if there were a bright yard between the hallway and the cellar stairs. One needed only a bright yard. At times David almost believed he had found that brightness. (221)

The search for brightness becomes paramount in David's mind when he hears the story of how Isaiah saw God—"Gee! And he saw

Him. Wonder where?"—and His terrible light, even though he was unclean, for the Jews of that time were sinful, as the rabbi says. "Clean? Light? Wonder if—? Wish I could ask him why the Jews were dirty. What did they do? Better not! Get mad. Where?" (227). David's nascent concept of the Almighty takes a sudden Bloomesque turn— "He was sitting on a chair. So he's got chairs, so he can sit. Gee! Sit Shit! Sh! Please God, I didn't mean it! Please God, somebody else said it!" (230)—but the logical implications of anthropomorphizing the deity are not as interesting to him as the detail about Isaiah's purification by means of a burning coal applied to his lips by an angel, using a *zwank*—pincers or tongs. Earlier in the work, when David quizzed Genya about death, she held up a sugar cube with tongs to demonstrate the narrow breadth of her understanding, and later he will observe a blacksmith handling hot metal with his pincers, and *zwank* will again appear as one of the apocalyptic words/sounds that attend David's great shock. The more immediate relevance of this passage, though, is in the boy's deduction that God is accessible, and accessible through burning light.

The pace of incidents leading to David's decisive action begins to quicken with two epiphanies—one sacred, one profane—that occur during the first day of Passover. By sacred and profane, I refer to Roth's constant juxtaposition of elements of the sacred text and their modern, secular counterparts, marking the distance between David's religious heritage and the world as he finds it. In another sense, this opposition is one of nature and industry, God's light versus electricity. In the first incident, David sits on a dock, feeling unusually good (in the moral sense) after having burned the family's last leavened bread crumbs according to tradition. Earlier in the day, Genya had answered a question of David's by saying that God was brightness (a moment profaned by Albert, who then entered the dark room saying, "We need some light in here"), and as he stares at reflecting sunlight on the river David becomes entranced with the "fire on the water . . . brighter than day . . . Brighter . . . Sin melted into light." When he emerges from his revery, he doesn't know just what he has seen, but he knows that it was a world "complete and dazzling."

Immediately thereafter, a group of gentile toughs (whom he tells he is Hungarian, not Jewish) bully David into dropping a scrap metal "sword" into the groove concealing the third rail of the car tracks, promising that he will see "de magic" and "all de movies in de woil! An' vawderville, too!" What he sees, in fact, is "Power!" and "light, unleashed, terrific light bellowed out of iron lips." The "sword" is "consumed with radiance," and David is "blinded, stunned by the brunt of brilliance" (252– 53). The scene is in every detail a foreshadowing of his later volitional summoning of the light. Aside from the evident sexual symbolism, the lips recall Isaiah's, touched by the coal.

David excitedly tells the rabbi of his discovery of the meaning of Isaiah and is admonished that God's light is not to be found between car-tracks. While reading scripture he is taken with paroxysms of laughter, a release of his own bound energy, leaving him with a "deep untroubled gentleness . . . a wordless faith, a fixity, mellow and benign." When he reaches home, he discovers that he now possesses the self-mastery—insurance of well-being—that he had sought, in the form of illuminated perception. As he enters the dread hallway of the cellar door, he notices that it is no longer so dark:

> Funny. Gee! Look! Look! Is a light! in the corner where baby-carriages—No. Looks like though. On the stairs, too. Ain't really there. Inside my head. Better is inside. Can carry it. Funny! Ain't so dark anyway. Ain't even scared. Remember how I was? Way long ago? Scared. . . . Funny I was. I'm big now. . . . Funny. Still can see it. There. And over there. And over in the corner where it's real dark. It sticks inside all the time, gee, can't never be scared. Never. Never. Never. (261)

The "nevers" in this passage are an echo of the litany of nevers—never play, never believe, etc.—that earlier marked David's disillusionment. His first "enlightenment," then, in its afterglow, brings David out of his crisis with a feeling of stability and certainty.

Soon enough, though, David notices that fear still distorts and clouds his perception whenever he is around his father, as if "his mind had slackened its grip on realities." His new-found clarity is lost completely when his father beats the thief and threatens to kill the boy if he tells Genya of the incident. The final indignity comes when he learns that his pals had watched his mother bathing from the roof. So David is once again threatened by his father, distanced from his mother by shame, blinded by rage and fear. He must begin his quest again, this time fleeing to the roof, as he had previously fled to the cellar. There he finds a respite from fear in the bright sunlight, and meets an older Catholic boy in whose apartment he discovers a picture of Jesus with a heart full of light and a box marked "God" that contains various religious icons. David learns from his friend that "Chrischin light is bigger than Jew light" (322), and feeling that he must find a solvent for his fears or be lost, he strikes a deal that will indeed have the desired effect, but not in any way he intended. Before his fears can be dissolved, they must first be brought out into the light of day; as Dante and all mystics know, the ascent to the light must begin with a descent into darkness.

In exchange for some rosary beads, then, David agrees to facilitate the older boy's "playing bad" with his cousin Esther, and the plan blows up in the worst possible way, leaving David again cowering in a dark cellar, implicated in the sin of sex. His fear of his father's likely reaction to the event causes him to tangle the threads of Genya's story and declare to the rabbi that his real mother is dead and his father was a church organist in Austria, a bit of fabulation that amounts to a classic resolution of the dilemma of the family romance. Paradoxically, it is the very sight of the rosary David hoped would protect him that triggers Albert's blind rage, sending the boy fleeing for his life into the night streets. Thus he discovers that there is no escaping his fear; he is once again the victim of his father, his mother can afford no protection, and he cannot return home. In a passage of frantic stream of consciousness he rehearses a possible explanation for his behavior that amounts to a recapitulation of the sequence of his epiphanies and realizations. What he sought through all of this, he says, was to regain the ball in his head, his inner illumination: "That's why Papa! That's why! Didn't—Ow! Ain't! Ain't! Ain't lit yet! What'll I do? Ain't lit yet!"

What he will do is return to the car-tracks, in the apocalyptic scene, drop in a milk dipper, and shock himself into near-death. In a "Circe"-like fantasy, the book's key images and motifs are replayed through the meaningful distortion of the unconscious as David lies with his foot (Oedipus's maimed foot?) in contact with the rail and is gradually revived. The intensely powerful free verse of Roth's rendering of electrified oblivion deserves a much more detailed examination than I can give here. Interspersed with the voices of the assembled crowd, Roth presents in David's awareness—now completely detached from the body—a dreamlike review of the elements of the boy's own mythography: a whirling hammer, a coal, the letters "*G-e-e-e*

o-o-o d-e-e-e," etc. Finally his awareness recedes to the last, most min-
uscule particle of being that can signal itself:

> (. . . *Down! Down into darkness,*
> *darkness that tunneled the heart of*
> *darkness, darkness fathomless. Each*
> *step he took, he shrank, grew smaller*
> *with the unseen panels, the graduate*
> *vise descending, passed from stage*
> *to dwindling stage, dwindling. At*
> *each step shed the husks of being,*
> *and himself tapering always downward*
> *in the funnel of the night. And now*
> *a chip—a step—a flake—a step—a shred.*
> *A mote. A pinpoint. And now the seed*
> *of nothing, and nebulous nothing, and*
> *nothing, And he was not* . . .) (429)

One last ember glows through oblivion, however, as David is being
revived, becoming the long-sought radiant coal of Isaiah.

The drama and artistry of the shock scene are such that it might
tend to overshadow the remaining chapter, but the latter is much
more than a simple winding down. My purpose in reviewing the plot
at such length is to show that David's story does not just depict growth
in the more conventional sense, but the growth of something quite
specific that would be the "it" of the title. This is revealed in the final
paragraph, in David's reflection after responding in the affirmative
to his mother's question of whether he were sleepy.

> He might as well call it sleep. It was only toward sleep that every
> wink of the eyelids could strike a spark into the cloudy tinder
> of the dark, kindle out of shadowy corners of the bedroom such
> myriad and such vivid jets of images—of the glint on tilted
> beards, of the uneven shine on roller skates, of the dry light on
> grey stone stoops, of the tapering glitter of rails, of the oily
> sheen on the night-smooth rivers, of the glow on thin blonde
> hair, red faces, of the glow on the outstretched, open palms of
> the legions upon legions of hands hurtling toward him. He
> might as well call it sleep. It was only toward sleep that ears had

power to cull again and reassemble the shrill cry, the hoarse voice, the scream of fear, the bells, the thick-breathing, the roar of crowds and all sounds that lay fermenting in the vats of silence and the past. It was only toward sleep one knew himself still lying on the cobbles, felt the cobbles under him like the black foam, the perpetual blur of shod and running feet, the broken shoes, new shoes, stubby, pointed, caked, polished, bun-iony, pavement-beveled, lumpish, under skirts, under trousers, shoes, over one and through one, and feel them all and feel, not pain, not terror, but the strangest triumph, strangest acquies-cence. One might as well call it sleep. He shut his eyes. (441)

It is significant that the state David describes is not sleep itself, but near-sleep, the dreamy semiconsciousness between sleeping and waking when the conscious mind is aware of the associative imagery of the unconscious. This is the state of Stephen Dedalus, whose soul is "waking slowly, fearing to wake wholly," when he is inspired to compose his villanelle, and it is the state of Marcel, whose somniative reflection at the beginning of the *Recherche* serves as both catalyst and paradigm of recapturing the past. Toward sleep, then, David finds the power to kindle images, cull and reassemble sounds, and know himself in memory. This ability corresponds to Stephen's ideal of "disentangling the subtle soul of the image from its defining circum-stances" and to Marcel's notion of deepening impressions in quietude and isolating the sensorial essence of experience.

It is instructive to recall that David's first image-making experi-ence, the vision of his father wielding a hammer, occurred when the vision "entered his sleep." With pain and terror overcome, however, David's image-cultivating is no longer governed by panic and dread, but by aesthetic pleasure. The images are no longer imposed upon his threatened ego as symbols of annihilation; they are rather sought out in calm self-recognition. The crowd is now turned toward him, not toward his father, as in the fearful vision. The people are no longer "stretched like white cobbles to the end of the world"; it is David who is stretched out on the cobbles, with the people running to his aid. The outstretched palms of the legions are reminiscent of the extended arms of roads and ships in one of Stephen's last diary entries, whose voices say to him: "We are your kinsmen." The sense of anticipation and self-possession is similar in the two cases, but

Stephen is running away from his people, whereas David's people are running to him.

Moving toward sleep is an act of self-possession for David. In reassembling his experience from the vats of the past in the form of the impressions his psyche presents to his watchful awareness, he finds the "strange triumph and acquiescence" of meaning, of giving shape to his identity as he knows himself within and as he fits into the world. In "sleep," at last, he comes to know himself, as Stephen would say, in relation to himself and in relation to others. It matters little that becoming an artist is not David's goal; what he attains is the requisite ability of a Stephen or a Marcel, but David's life in images does not need to be validated by means of external representation. For an immigrant boy in the melting pot, securing a stable sense of self and community is redemption enough.

While *Call It Sleep,* as I indicated in my introduction, does not meet the criteria of simularity—it is not a formally fictional representation of actual autobiography in the sense that *Ulysses,* the *Recherche,* and even *Under the Volcano* are, although its basic situation and characters are autobiographically derived—Roth does borrow techniques from Joyce's aim of representing as nearly as possible the actuality of Dublin on a specific day. Roth stops short of the exhaustive research that would be necessary to identify specific businesses and personages that would have been encountered in the neighborhood on the day in question, but he does bring the area within earshot of David's calamity to life in this scene to a degree unseen elsewhere in the novel. With minimal narration, he introduces a host of figures and alternates their voices as we join their conversations or interior monologues in medias res. There is Bill Whitney, an aging warehouseman; Jim Haig, a British sailor scheming to open a fish-n-chips on Coney Island; the prostitutes Mimi and Mary; a group of Jewish card players; an old peddlar who implores the "founder of the universe" as he schleps his baby carriage full of pretzels; Motorman Dan MacIntyre and the passengers of his Tenth Street car, including a kind-faced American woman telling everyone about the accessibility of the Statue of Liberty ("You can go all the way up inside her for twenty-five cents"); and Callahan, the barkeep, and his customers, including one O'Toole, a self-aggrandizing blowhard straight out of "Cyclops" who combines the Citizen's stature and belligerence with the Nameless One's style of racontage ("So I says..."). Like the

Nameless One, O'Toole knows the pain of urinating when afflicted with a "dose" ("I twisted all the pipes I wanna we'en I'm pissin'!"). Roth succeeds in conveying the impression that each of these fragmented characterizations represents but a moment, to which we are privy, in the continuous narrative of the character's life. Each voice reveals part of an ongoing personal drama—accidents, abortions, loves lost and found, prejudices and petty vexations—while a communist speaker and the Salvation Army compete for their attention and the city bustles. Like Joyce, Roth portrays the urban scene via the diversity of its voices and the least common denominator of the motives and concerns they reveal. O'Toole and his motley court in Callahan's, in particular, suggest a tip of the cap to the Dubliner.

The disparate cast of the chapter finally becomes an "umbiliform" crowd—a community—when they are interrupted and united by David's "accident." Whitney throws down a broom from his warehouse, and O'Toole uses it to push David from the rail. As a policeman administers artificial respiration, members of the encircled crowd begin speaking to one another in a babel of dialects and degrees of broken English, like a haphazard village born of curiosity and compassion for the boy. In the urban American environment of competing ethnic groups, especially in the age of immigration Roth depicts, shared values and cultural identity are not assumed—they are not the background condition they would be in Dublin, for instance—but emerge only in crisis, and the question of community marks a particularly American aspect of the novel. Roth was anything but a believer in the solitary, defiant heroism of the artist. In a 1969 interview (Bronsen 1969) he expressed his belief that the individual disintegrates unless associated with some larger entity. In his childhood, Roth suffered a loss of community when his family moved from the Jewish Lower East Side to a mixed area of Harlem, causing him to become socially maladjusted and to reject his faith and customs. *Call It Sleep* is a recreation of the lost community. After writing it, however, Roth did not regain any sense of communal identity in American culture, he says, and was subsequently unable to write until the 1967 Israeli-Arab War gave him a sense of identification with a people.

If there is anything dramatic about all this, I suppose it can be explained as the way a fictioneer does things. Significant for me is that after this vast detour, the once-Orthodox Jewish boy has returned to his own Jewishness. I have reattached myself to part of what I had rejected in 1914. (Bronsen 1969, 279)

This, then, is what enabled him to write again: the sense of communal identity that Joyce seemed to sustain on his own and Malcolm Lowry never found.

According to a number of pieces published in *Shifting Landscape* (1987), Roth came to harbor a great deal of resentment toward Joyce, who had been his artistic idol as a young writer. Roth feels that following Joyce's credo of "silence, exile, cunning" led him astray, into the realm of autonomous art and away from community and history, but it is difficult to see how this would be true of *Call It Sleep*. Roth seems inclined to see the work as essentially a product of the twenties, born of primarily aesthetic rather than social concerns, but it seems to me that his criticism must apply more to an attitude of his than to his realized novel. Whether or not the author felt himself to be a detached, cosmopolitan figure, *Call It Sleep* is not a story of exile, as I have tried to show. David finds community; he does not abandon it in pursuit of the great artificer.

Hurston

Zora Neale Hurston's *Their Eyes Were Watching God* belongs in the tradition of thirties novels I am describing on several counts: its regional focus and use of vernacular, its systematic use of a symbolic pattern (in this case taken from Haitian voodoo), and a protagonist whose attainment of self-possession is coincident with her capability of recounting the novel's story. Like David Schearl, Janie Woods comes to "cull and reassemble" the events of the plot in a state of rest, having acquired a stable identity. Hurston's equivalent of Roth's "strange triumph and acquiescence" is the peace that Janie finds at the novel's end, as she pulls in her horizon and "call[s] her soul to come and see." The story is framed in her return home, after having been "to the horizon and back," and is presented in the guise of a memoir in indirect discourse, as she is formally telling it to her friend Phoebe, though a third-person narrator quickly takes over. Thus Janie, too, represents a case of a self constituted in and through the art of telling her story. She, too, is a definer of herself in relation to herself and others.

Ellease Southerland (1979) has detailed the influence of voodoo in Hurston's work. In *Their Eyes Were Watching God,* voodoo symbolism and numerology function much like the Cabala in *Under the Volcano,* endowing the fictional world with a sense of Manichaean order, portents and signs of harmony and fearful symmetry. In Hurston's work, this all remains on the level of symbol and is not extended to devise an underlying structural design. That is, she draws upon her experiences as a voodoo initiate in developing a system of numbers, colors, celestial bodies, plants, and mutations that lend value and meaning to events and characters, but she does not use these to determine the form of the work in the way that Lowry, for instance, decides his number of chapters. Southerland shows, among many other things, that the number nine recurs as an emblem of safety and good fortune, while six is the sign of danger and death. In the same manner, the sun is of good omen, the moon of evil. Tea Cake, Janie's third husband and true love, is "the son of the evening sun" and dies waiting for a moon to plant by. His favorite color, blue, is the color that attends Janie's blissful visions.

Just as Joyce adapts Homeric lore to his realist premise by depicting metaphorical equivalents for some of its myths (e.g., suggesting Homer's literal transformation of men into pigs by describing the diners in Burton's restaurant as "animals . . . swilling, wolfing . . . suetfaced," etc., in "Lestrygonians" [169]), Hurston draws on the voodoo belief in metamorphosis, describing gossiping neighbors as mules, for example. In one comic scene, a dead mule is given a mock funeral and eulogized as a man, and there is recurrent reference to Janie's grandmother's perception that the black woman is "de mule uh de world."

Hurston's novel, as much as *Call It Sleep* and *Portrait,* can be termed a spiritual biography, insofar as she sets out to know herself, and to relieve her "cosmic loneliness." Her growth is symbolized in images of a road, the horizon, and a pear tree. At the beginning, she is "looking down the road, waiting for the world to be made" (25), and the man who awakens her sexuality as well as two of her three husbands come to her from the road. In the framing scene, it is she herself who has just come up the road, having been to the once unattainable horizon and back. Hurston says explicitly that Janie "saw her life like a great tree," and recurring images of a pear tree are used to illustrate both her sexuality and the state of her spirit. In a first scene, Janie lies beneath a real pear tree watching bees and blossoms in a figurative description of an orgasm. In the general sense of portraying a moment of adolescent sexual awakening, the scene calls to mind Stephen's "bird-girl" epiphany, but, significantly, it does not lead to the latter's sort of aestheticizing sublimation or poetic displacement. Janie's desire, though frustrated, remains desire for sexual fulfillment, and for much else besides. She is, like Davey, seeking a kind of stability and secure selfhood on both the social and existential levels. The former will be attained by assuming her position in the community as an independent woman, after having found herself in relation to Tea Cake, and the latter will be the product of self-recognition in assimilating the meaning of the whole of her trajectory.

At the end of her round trip to the horizon, Janie says she "now can live by comparisons," i.e., understand her existence in time, or, in terms of Eliot's description,[4] having arrived where she started, she now knows the place for the first time. Phoebe, the reader's stand-in, who has heard the story, suggests something of its value, and by implication, of the value of novels, with her comment "Lawd! Ah done growed ten feet higher from jus' listenin' tuh you, Janie. Ah ain't satisfied wid mahself no mo!" (284). Janie then contrasts "empty talkin'" with what I would call bearing witness. As she says, "It's uh known fact, Phoebe, you got tuh *go* there to *know* there.... Two things everybody's got tuh do fuh theyselves. They got tuh go tuh God, and they got tuh find out about livin' fuh theyselves" (284; Hurston's emphasis). Unstated but implicit are the necessity and the value of the telling itself, of bearing witness once one has found out for herself and found herself. When Janie finally sits down alone to pull in her horizon and "call her soul to come and see," she has attained the condition of Davey when he "calls it sleep."

Like *Call It Sleep,* then, *Their Eyes Were Watching God* gives a dimension of spiritual questing to the protagonist's story, and Hurston, too, implies a cosmic scope. Early in the book, Janie wonders whether her impending marriage will end her "cosmic loneliness," and the eventual answer to her question proves to be that the loneliness is relieved in a new relationship to herself, alone. As in Davey's case, this relationship is characterized by its implicit analogy to authorial power. It is notable that in these cases, the power is only implied, and never becomes a factor in first-degree characterization.

There is no question here of literary ambitions for the characters, let alone joining the high priesthood of art.

Of course, the socioeconomic context of the United States in the thirties was far removed from that in which Proust and Joyce worked. The coming to terms with Aestheticism that they had to work out was in part conditioned by their being caught between the belletristic tradition and the advent of mass circulation publications brought along by the new public, the rising middle class. Their particularly self-definitional fiction reflects the refusal of certain social roles and the assignment of another role to oneself, based on a concept of the artist available in Western Europe, and most especially in Paris, at the time. That is to say, there is a social and historical component behind the heroic fictionalized autoportrait of the artist that is played out by the succeeding generation. There is also a psychological aspect to such autoportraiture that might be understood in terms of gender and help explain why, while neither male nor female authors were focusing on the process of artistic arrival in the first degree by the thirties, it does not seem that women writers ever did, in fact, portray their accomplishments with anything like the special aura Proust and Joyce confer on their protagonists.

First of all, on the broadest level, one can say that glory of any sort, as a social construct, has never been as readily available to women as to men. So, one man's artistic triumph becomes a woman's eccentricity in the public judgment. The high priesthood of art would seem to be as exclusively a male dominion as the Catholic priesthood, in other words. While it has been possible for centuries for women to be writers and poets, the particular sort of recognition Proust and Joyce imply they deserve was not open to women in society, thus was not a conceptual option in fiction. One can appreciate this point in light of Marthe Robert's idea (1972) that Napoleon, as the consummate world shaper, is the paradigmatic model behind nineteenth-century realism. This is certainly not to say that Jane Austen, to name but one, is in any way lacking as a creator of fictional worlds, merely that she has no particular motivation to toot her own horn while doing so.

For Janie Woods, in any case, the value of the process she has undergone is strictly personal, a function of an internal striving that lends her life a continuity that both underlies and transcends her social being. The fruits of her struggles are shared in intimacy with an understanding friend (admittedly the formal pretext of our "hearing" the story). The ability to see a meaningful pattern and continuum in her life and the ability to express it contribute, as they did for Davey, to a sense of peace that comes from self-recognition. Public recognition—in the form of an eternal monument or admittance to a literary pantheon—are not at issue.

The notion of a private value drawn from artistic creation is also evident in Virginia Woolf's *To the Lighthouse,* where Lily Briscoe's painting functions as a microcosmic emblem of the novel's world, which is in a sense "framed" on her canvas. When Lily completes the picture (a figurative characterization of Mrs. Ramsay, among other things), she speculates that it is destined for some attic, but this does not trouble her in the least. "Yes, she thought, laying down her brush in extreme fatigue, I have had my vision" (310). Here, once again, is a novel ending with an image of the artist persona in restful self-awareness upon the completion of a representation that is a figure for, or recapitulation of, the novel itself. For Lily, Janie, and Davey, the vision itself—the meaning-conferring, ordering process, or "reading" of the events in the novel—is the thing. Lily's example makes the clearest statement about locating the value of art in the creative process itself. Quite obviously, however, the appearance of any novel in the world is testimony to the author's belief in the postcreational value of art, and the desire to reach an audience.

It may or may not be that Woolf, Roth, or Hurston privately envisioned their creative acts as sources of personal triumph or immortality. What is clear is that while many authors in the wake of Proust and Joyce created protagonists of varying degrees of autobiographical resonance as implied self-reflexive figures, none exhibit quite the same kind of "simularity," the incorporation of the connection of life to art as a formal principle in the work. That is, they do not use the coming into being of the novel (hence the novelist) as a plot-generative principle. The place of plot in Proust and Joyce, as I have said, is taken over by the special value accorded to arriving at the work's condition of possibility. Faulkner, Lowry, Roth, and Hurston tell stories of inherent dramatic interest, while in Woolf character study is of greater importance than drama. All of them, however, add a kind of simular depth to the novel by including in its form the protagonist's own reading/composition of the story—i.e., selecting, ordering, assigning value, finding meaning—which "builds in" the experience of both writer and reader, making the character an intermediary figure in a process, rather than a flat marionette.

Certainly in the depth of the Great Depression the last vestiges of decadence were gone; the mere fact of attaining the status of artist no longer conferred any special aura. The notion of living artistically quickly loses its luster when superseded by the difficulty of living, period, and the notion of the artist alone against the world would certainly be untenable for Roth, for instance, whose membership in the Communist party made him uneasy about the personal dimension of art to begin with. The larger point here is that the heroic type of author persona, in the Proust-Joycean vein, becomes somewhat outmoded, historically, but we can trace its evolution in two directions, which at times merge. On the one hand, there are manipulative pseudoauthors and other metafictional figures who point to the author's immediate presence behind the text in the act of writing (best exemplified by Nabokov), and on the other hand, there are writers who, in accord with Roth's ideal, portray themselves in authorial figures for whom the act of writing is a means of social integration. First, though, it will be necessary to follow the development of techniques of formal artifice in novels whose primary focus is not on the experiential, autobiographical matrix.

Chapter 4

Homunculì, Homunculà:
Meta- and Cosmicharacters,
Missing Persons

Raymond Queneau

Of the generation of novelists that matured in the immediate shadow of Joyce and Proust, it is Raymond Queneau, an assiduous student of English-language literature in addition to the French linguistic questions for which he is more widely known, who first articulated a fundamental aspect of the pair's legacy to his contemporaries. In a 1938 essay, "La symphonie inachevée" (1965a, 223–28), Queneau corrects what he considers to be a critical oversight on the part of writers such as Edmund Wilson and Henry Miller, and ranks Proust along with Joyce as "one of the first to have *constructed* a novel" (225; Queneau's emphasis). Queneau, like Lowry, believed that a novel should be a rigorously constructed poetic whole, but he was much more interested in the construction itself and in the novel as a product of imagination (as evidenced in the preface to *Mosquitoes* quoted in the previous chapter) than in a rendering of the author's experience. Aside from the collection of poems *Chêne et chien* and the roman à clef *Odile* (both 1937), Queneau abandons the use of an experiential matrix in favor of more strictly "poetic" principles in fashioning his works. Thus his Joycean influence, which he (unlike Lowry) is quick to acknowledge, is derived from the mythic, rather than the simular, dimension of *Ulysses*. Queneau is not, then, in the lineage of the "poet of experience"; his characterization is marked by epistemological inquiry rather than mimesis of subjectivity, putting him, in part, in the

143

lineage of Pirandello and Unamuno. Queneau's interest in a poetics of the novel leads directly to his work with the Oulipo group, making him a pivotal figure in a movement toward the priority of form over representation that has characterized a major current in the novel from the *nouveau roman* to the later works of Oulipian Italo Calvino.

The standard set for the novel at the beginning of the century, particularly by Joyce, is one of conscious structuring. It was no longer sufficient just to tell a story, to give oneself over to the seductive process of fabulation, leaving questions of form and style to the unconscious. In an essay from 1937, Raymond Queneau credits Joyce with having taught him that there was a technique of novel writing. The essay, "Technique du roman" (1965a, 27–33), makes the argument for deliberate ordering and then offers the author's own *Le chiendent* (1933) as a case in point. First, Queneau describes the status quo ante:

> Anyone can push before him like a flock of geese an indeterminate number of apparently real characters across a landscape measured in an indeterminate number of pages or chapters. The result, whatever it may be, will still be a novel. (27)

Likewise:

> It can no longer be a question of letting the characters of a novel run loose like homunculi escaped from their broken bottles, nor to consider them as pieces on a chessboard, the sequence of moves constituting the transition between chapters and the final check the author's victory. (32) (pace Nabokov!)

Queneau, never a doctrinaire sort, but a great ironist, goes on in his own fiction to unbottle a few such homunculi himself, including one who escapes from his assigned work, but the important point here is that the essayist is signaling the extreme limits of characterization: if one can no longer naively project oneself into a formless make-believe, neither is one likely to identify with flat widgets of some combinatorial machine. If it takes little art to indulge in freeform fabulation, it takes just as little to assign proper names to points on a graph; neither approach is likely to produce a satisfying novel.

Formal design comes to provide another answer, beyond autobiography, to Queneau's question about the source of novelistic material. That is, one might select a model first and then select and shape material to fit it. From Joyce one learns to shape a novel to a conceptual paradigm; with the example of everyday Dublin cum *Odyssey*, the way is open for writers to choose from among any number of seminal texts—from the Cabala to Dante to Descartes—and to fill in their general lines with figures and details. One of the basic issues to be decided by authors taking this route is the degree of adherence to and visibility of the subtext. At one end of the spectrum would be works of maximal dependence on the subtext, creating fictions that wouldn't be understood without recognition of it. These tend not to be novels, however, but rather shorter pastiches such as Zora Neale Hurston's "Cock Robin Beale Street," a jive version of the children's story with the animals characterized as Memphis ghetto figures speaking dialect, or "Book of Harlem," a pastiche of biblical narrative set in Harlem ("And in those days when King Volstead sat upon the throne in Hokum, there came a mighty drought upon the land" [1985, 101]). At the other extreme, Roth's *Call It Sleep* makes use of explicit allusive references to both biblical and mythological texts and motifs, but familiarity with the source texts is not an indispensable requisite to comprehension, nor do those texts determine the lines of the plot in the way that Joyce's overriding Homeric paradigm decides, for example, that Bloom should meet up with a young girl in his travels, or reclaim his home at their end. Between these extremes are *Under the Volcano* and *Le chiendent,* which each use, in addition to their respective Dantean/cabalistic and Cartesian paradigms, numerological schemata that are completely determinate of the works' structure but do not presume or require the reader's recognition. In fact Queneau, like Lowry, expected these schemata to function invisibly, something on the order of Joyce's more arcane signatures (organs, etc.), although he, too, would leave behind extratextual explanations. The brief sketch that Queneau provides in his essay is greatly amplified by Claude Simonnet (his Stuart Gilbert) in his *Queneau déchiffré* (deciphered) (1962).

Le chiendent exhibits none of the simular novel's highlighting of autobiographical reference; it is more a novel of ideas, some of them quite absurd. Queneau's original pretext was to render Descartes's *Discours de la méthode* in colloquial French, but rather than create a single voice that would simply paraphrase Descartes in *argot,* he de-

cided to embody the philosopher's principles in characters, to novel-
ize them, in effect. Along the way, Queneau settled for depicting a
general meditation on the nature of appearances, leading to a
metatextual denouement in which the characters' accumulated insights into being are applied to their peculiar circumstance of being
in a book. From there, the narrative has nowhere to go but back to its
starting point, not just conceptually, as in Proust, but literally, as in
Finnegans Wake (then still the incomplete *Work in Progress*), by returning to its first sentence.

   Le chiendent's Cartesian reflections take place in the mind of the
protagonist, Etienne Marcel (i.e., Stephen Marcel ... curious!), presumably named for the Parisian Provost of Merchants, assassinated
in 1358, for whom a street in the capital is named. The basic developmental principle behind Etienne's characterization is that as he
thinks, he therefore is. He gains consistency and depth as a character
to the degree that he becomes self-reflexive, in a series of steps reminiscent of E. M. Forster's taxonomy of characters in *Aspects of the
Novel:* he is first a mere shadow, then a "flat being," then a "being of
minimal reality," and eventually a "being of choice." His stages of
self-awareness are at first abetted by the presence of the mysterious
Pierre Le Grand, who stands in for the author, in part, and also for
the reader, as the arranger and observer of the action. At each level
of self-awareness, Etienne gains a correlative increase in awareness
of the outer world, represented in the form of such typically Quenel-
lian kitsch as plastic duckies, cheap potato peelers, and suburban
french-fry stands. In short, Etienne's illumination amounts to a divi-
sion of the world into rational subject and external objects.

   Once underway, Queneau puts much more into the work, including structural and allusive encoding of Gnostic notions and
figures, all nicely detailed by Simonnet. Like Proust, Queneau had a
great appreciation of Gothic design, and drew from it many ideas for
the architecture of his book. Having decided on a pretext and a
numerological scheme to regulate the number of chapters, subsec-
tions, styles, techniques (dialogues, monologues, letters, newspaper
stories, etc.), and the number and nature of the characters, as well as
the timing of their entrances and exits, Queneau then faced the problem of endowing the characters with human characteristics, given the
arbitrary mode of their genesis (as opposed to characters "drawn
from life"). In *Le chiendent,* he comes upon the two characteristics

that will become hallmarks of all his subsequent creatures: loquacity and preoccupation with the ordinary pleasures of daily life.

Queneau's characters are first and foremost speakers; they love to hold forth and they exhibit no small pride in their verbal style and *bons mots*. He is justly renowned for his ear for everyday spoken French, and gets a lot of mileage from mixing registers—from the pedantic to the baroque to the roughest *argot*—within a speech or even within a single sentence, and from occasional phonetic spelling that mimics the true sound and usage of the language. To a great extent, then, his characters are simply known by what they say, especially in his later novels, which are practically devoid of description. Discourse in these works is never indirect; the characters' inner voices are always externalized.

The second of Queneau's techniques is to give his characters banal habits that identify them as typical Parisians of the working- and lower-middle-class *milieux* he so loves depicting, and reveal affective qualities as well. The later works all feature characters who devote a great deal of time to imbibing their particular drinks (these vary from grenadine, to beer, to *pastis*, to *kir*, to absinthe), which serve as leitmotifs. The characters are, paradoxically, made eminently human by their very improbability as "realistic" characters. Etienne Marcel is one of very, very few of them to have anything like a regular job; when they do work, it is usually at such unlikely endeavors as fortune telling, transvestite dancing, leading the Etruscan Army, or making sure that female patrons of a fun house step over the forced air vent that will elevate their skirts for the delectation of a suspect group of connoisseurs known as the "philosophers." Mostly, they pass their time with talk and such esoteric pursuits as trying to catch the minute hand on a huge clock in motion. Despite the eccentricity of these activities, the characters are, in essence, involved in the most universal and thoroughly human pursuits: attainment of modest pleasure and speculation on the nature of existence. What they all inherit from Etienne Marcel—and they are not terribly far from Bloom in this respect—is an unassuming curiosity and sense of observation: they watch and speak. Queneau's characters are, however, drastically different in kind from Joyce's, and from those of any of the other authors thus far mentioned. They are cartoonlike, without past and without pain, although they do betray much "existential anxiety," a philosophical hobby horse of Queneau. Like Sterne, he

approaches the grimmest realities obliquely, through comically absurd scenes such as the suddenly dying waitress Ernestine's farewell
speech to her assembled wedding guests in *Le chiendent,* or the transvestite dancer Gabriel's Hamlet-like soliloquy, delivered atop the Eiffel Tower in *Zazie dans le métro* (1959).

Aside from the use of pretexts and formal design, there is another important lesson to be learned from *Ulysses,* one that would be
of particular interest to Queneau, who was for a time associated with
the Surrealists. This lesson concerns the possibilities for both character and narrative development opened up by the dreamscape of
"Circe." Here again, let it be said at the outset, what Joyce does
internally (characterizing the unconscious), Queneau does externally.
That is, while Queneau regularly employs Circean devices, they cannot be interpreted (at least not more than *very* hypothetically) as the
projections of the characters' unconscious because, for one, there is
no interposed realistic narrative that lets us, as in Joyce, follow or
reconstruct the "real time" events that trigger the fantasies, and, for
another, Queneau's surreal scenarios are depicted as occurring
around the characters, in history, and ultimately in the narrative itself.

The chief Circean devices used by Queneau are mutability of
characters and apocalyptic fantasy. In *Le chiendent,* while civilization,
history, and the plot dissolve around them, the three main characters
endure by changing roles and identities while maintaining their Cartesian skepticism. By the time the Franco-Etruscan War has wiped
out virtually everything, they accept as reliable only their own cognitive processes, which are then applied to the text itself as the characters review the story and their roles and agree to start it all over again.
Of the three characters, it is Cidronie Belhôtel Cloche, a.k.a. Miss
Aulini, the Abbey Rouvère, and the Queen of Clocks, who establishes
a pattern of mutation followed in most of Queneau's subsequent novels. In six of the novels, one finds thirteen characters who appear in
about forty separate guises. These changes accelerate near the ends
of the works, at times culminating in catastrophes of varying intensity—the forces of good and evil punching it out in an after-hours
cafe in *Zazie,* a flood in *Les fleurs bleues* (1965b), and the aforemen-
tioned war in *Le chiendent*—that cause, in Blake's expression (quoted
in "Circe"), "Time's livid final flame" to go out.

It is instructive to recall that *Le chiendent,* wherein Queneau
works out the techniques that see him through much of his career,

was written even as segments of *Finnegans Wake* were beginning to circulate as *Work in Progress*. Queneau's work shares the *Wake*'s Viconian notion of the circularity of history, and its manifestation in character, a single archetypal essence depicted in successive identities. The suggestion of metempsychosis is seen first of all in the names of Etienne Marcel and Pierre Le Grand, and of minor characters like Yves Le Toltec or Themistocle Troc. *Zazie* features, in addition to its transvestite dancer, a character represented first as the female Marceline and later as the male Marcel, calling to mind Bloom's gender change in "Circe." Another of *Zazie*'s characters undergoes four changes of identity before emerging in the final battle as Aroun Arachide (peanut), Destroyer of Worlds. Haroun al-Raschid was the historical caliph of Baghdad who found his way into the *Thousand and One Nights,* of course, but Queneau may well have found him in *Ulysses,* where he appears in "Proteus," leading Stephen through the street of whores, in a remembered dream, and twice in "Circe," where Bloom assumes his identity.

Such are the techniques of the novel that Queneau adopted from Joyce, put to use in his first novel, and drew upon throughout his career, while choosing not to follow Joyce in the use of realistic detail, autobiography, or acerbic social criticism. Queneau's artistic temperament is colored more by the Enlightenment—one thinks of Diderot's encyclopedic interests and fundamental good humor—than by the nineteenth century; he is much closer in spirit to his contemporary Jacques Prévert than to Baudelaire. That is to say that his work is governed more by reason, a scientific curiosity, and his love of common *milieux* than by a need to live artistically or transmute experience. Queneau was a philosopher by schooling, and a linguist by avocation; his motivation as a novelist was epistemological, not personally lyrical. When he portrays a character as an author, it is to play with the formal logic of the genre, not to depict his own arrival.

When Queneau does portray himself as a character, it is literally. In *Les enfants du limon* (1938), the character Chambernac turns over the manuscript of his biographical essays on literary madmen—which have constituted a large part of the novel's narrative—to a chance acquaintance who happens to be a novelist, and gives the latter permission to attribute the work to one of the characters in the novel he's working on, even going so far as to supply details of his own life so that the novelist will be able to create a believable character. As the pair part company, we learn that the novelist is, of course, a certain Monsieur Queneau. In reality, Queneau had written a book on literary madmen, for which he could find no publisher; his solution: put it in a novel, the genre that will gobble up and incorporate any alien text. Thus Queneau smuggles his original rejected work past the publisher and on to the public as a second-degree text, jokingly passing off the credit/blame to Chambernac, even making him responsible for Queneau's own characterization. Logically, the author has switched places with his character: the character supplied the text and characterization, and the author is a mere figure in the novel, a cowriter at best. *Les enfants du limon*'s implied coauthors are, then, both Queneau: the fictional Chambernac, the substitute author of Queneau's treatise on literary madmen, himself made into one of the species, and Monsieur Queneau, the nominally literal figure of the author of the rest of the novel.

I have said earlier that protagonists of the simular novel and its modernist heirs are identified with the authorial persona. Queneau, on the other hand, moves away from autocharacterization toward metacharacterization, i.e., portraying characters who are characters by their condition and aware of the fact. In general, Queneau employs fictional self-consciousness with much discretion, avoiding the vertiginous sorts of infinite regression that will later become the staple—and cliché—of postmodernism. In *Le chiendent,* the surviving trio become aware of their literary status only in the final, apocalyptic scene, affording Etienne the opportunity to review his performance. Most of Queneau's novels are punctuated with characters' nods and winks in the direction of the reader; they frequently mimic the narrative voice, and otherwise show signs of recognizing the true nature of their existence *in biblio,* but they only occasionally let slip explicit metacommentary of the sort displayed in Gabriel's Eiffel Tower soliloquy from *Zazie:* "This whole story [is nothing but] the illusion of an illusion, the dream of a dream, hardly more than a delirium typed out by an idiotic novelist (oh! pardon)" (90).

It is not until *Le Vol d'Icare* (Flight/Theft of Icarus, 1968) that Queneau creates a fully self-conscious character, although even in this case it is necessary to qualify the use of the term. Icare is a character who accidentally escapes from his novel and goes off into Paris to pursue his own destiny (although we learn at the end that he has fulfilled his written destiny after all). He is fully cognizant of being a character, but he's not shown to be a character in the book we're reading, as is Tristram Shandy, for example. In other words, Queneau does not foreground the reader's experience—"presence" in the narrative chain of transmission—as does Sterne.

Metacharacterization is a partial abandonment of the formal realist premises. It is partial because while it does expose and flaunt the conventions of formal realism, the characters—within the fore-grounded form—still carry on as mimetic figures for the most part. If they didn't, the startling effect of their self-consciousness would be lost. Icare underscores the essential verisimilitude of his kind: "For me, it's all the same. . . . Once we're free, don't we have the same desires? the same needs? the same faculties? Don't we have to obey the same necessities of living?" (218). The point is that metafictional representation doesn't replace the mimetic; it adds something to it. The character cognizant of his ontological status as a biblio-being is an analog of a human being at the limits of self-knowledge. Indeed, metacharacterization is a uniquely effective means of mimicking the existential quandary of a human attempting to grasp the formal limitations of being in the world. As Icare says, perhaps humans are the characters of some other kind of authors. As opposed to the simular novel's psychological mimesis—affect, perception, and thought seen from within—the self-conscious novel's mimesis could be qualified as ontological. Naturally the techniques employed toward these divergent ends are dissimilar beyond a certain point. In general, the narrative presentation of self-conscious characters is more straightforward than that of their simular counterparts, since the focus of metafictive works is on the formal and cognitive limits of the characters in the situation designed for them rather than on the nuances of their subjectivity. In *Icare,* Queneau reduces narration to a bare minimum, resorting to simple nominal indicators, as in a play, to identify the speakers of the constant dialogues.

It is apt that Queneau should borrow a technique from drama for this novel, in which several authors go off in search of a character. One of the authors goes so far as to point out the "Pirandellian" nature of the enigma facing them, even though the story takes place in 1895, long before Pirandello's characters went packing. In his preface to a 1948 edition of *Sei personaggi in cerca d'autore* and in *Colloqui coi personaggi* (1938), Pirandello offers theoretical observations on characterization that are useful in understanding self-conscious characters in the novel. Pirandello's metacharacterization hinges on his exploitation of the distinction between the elements of the form/content pairing contained in the two senses of the word *character* in English. The Romance languages maintain a distinction between *personaggio/personaje/personnage*—the role or figure—and *caratere/caracter/caractère*—personal attributes or qualities, and this is the opposition Pirandello focuses on, often with the terms *forma* and *vita*. For a human being, *forma* corresponds to the social role, identity as determined externally, while *vita* corresponds to essence, the self or spirit occupying the position, as experienced internally. To illustrate the mimetic utility of metacharacterization, Pirandello compares his five self-conscious characters with the sixth, the Mother, who is a conventional fictional figure:

> There is a character, the Mother, to whom having a life is of no importance whatsoever. . . . She hasn't the least doubt of already being alive, nor has it ever passed through her head to ask herself how and why, and in what way, she is alive. She hasn't, in sum, any consciousness of being a character: inasmuch as she is never, not even for a moment, detached from her "role." . . .
>
> In fact her role as Mother does not require in itself, in its neutrality, a spiritual element; and she has no life of the spirit. . . . She is unable to attain consciousness of her life, which is to say of her being a character. (20)

The distinction here is clear: conventional representation is only adequate for depicting unconscious entities. The Mother is completely identified with her role, as if there were no detached, observing self present; she is all form. Her opposite would be found in Pirandello's novel *Il fu Mattia Pascal* (1904), in which the hero, having escaped from the forms his life had assumed when a corpse is mistaken for him, tries to fashion a new identity from scratch, but fails; his self-designed alter-ego, Adriano Meis, is all content, i.e., being, undefined by social role and history.

Early critics of *Sei personaggi* missed Pirandello's point altogether, estimating that the Mother was the most sympathetic and human of the characters, whereas the author intended her to be pathetic and deficient as a person, if anything. In Pirandello's opinion, acute and paralyzing self-consciousness is the defining condition of modern humanity, and can best be depicted by analogy to characters cognizant of the formal artifice that marks the horizon of their possibilitics. At the same time, Pirandello believes in enhancing to the maximum the illusion of the characters' independence, as if they were invented without the author's conscious participation and behaved according to their own innate logic and destiny. Here, then, we reach the antithesis of simularity: Pirandellian characters and their kind bear no resemblance whatever to their creator.

Returning to *Icare,* we find that his consciousness of being a character is complete, down to recognition of his graphic genesis: "The ink flows on the white paper in thin and fertile streams from which friends, enemies, and relatives are born.... The pen leads a little world of objects and names toward a destiny that escapes me" (26). Soon, however, it's Icare who will escape his destiny, as he takes his stock of characteristics beyond the formal limitations of his assigned role. He explains to a new acquaintance:

> A draft of air carried me off. Instead of becoming reintegrated into that graphic domicile, I went my way until I found myself in the street. Then I wondered what to do, where to go, and by chance, attracted by that odor that I now know to be that of absinthe, I entered this tavern where I made your acquaintance. (33)

Unlike Pirandello's six, who are described as having a peculiar distinguishing aura that separates them from the play's conventional characters, and unlike Mattia Pascal, who in his fictional life as Adriano Mcis never feels quite at ease among "real" people who have a past and are rooted in a social role, Icare and the network of other literary escapees he meets up with are indistinguishable from and at ease among the "straight" characters (i.e., humans), whom they simply designate as "the others" or the "other people." The escapees all do rather well for themselves in the world, but most eventually return to their assigned roles in the works of Icare's creator, Hubert Lubert, and his colleagues. Icare himself becomes, predictably, a pioneer aviator, but offers to return to Lubert and accept his fate anyway. Lubert refuses, on the grounds that his original realist concept has been ruined. In a final ironic twist, when Icare perishes in a crash, Lubert announces that all has come to pass according to plan and his novel is now finished. Thus Lubert's novel, from which Icare first escaped and which has been a mere framed curiosity within Icare's story, becomes the frame in turn, swallowing up Icare's story with the stroke of a pen, vindicating authors everywhere.

There is another character of interest in *Icare*, the literary detective Morcol, who is hired by Lubert and his colleagues to track down their escaped characters. Morcol is the logical choice for the job, the authors feel, because he has himself appeared in a good many novels, under various names. He is, in effect, a generic type, representing the role aspect of character (corresponding to a narrative function). Like the characters in Pirandello's waiting room in the *Colloqui*, Morcol is a *caratere* for hire as a *personaggio*. In a notable scene, Morcol and Lubert argue over the nature of character, considering the specific question of whether the Manon of the opera is the same character as the Manon of the novel. Marcol, focusing on form, insists they are the same (i.e., the heroine named Manon), while Lubert, focusing on content—*caratere* or *vita*—insists they are different (e.g., one is a "ham who yelps *Adieu notre petite table*" [85], and the other doesn't even sing at all). Morcol, then, is something of a structuralist, for whom a character is nothing more than a narrative element designated by a proper name, whereas Lubert takes a character's mimetic qualities more seriously.

Pirandello and Queneau use metacharacterization as a means of philosophic and generic inquiry, respectively. Pirandello shows the self-conscious character to be ontologically analogous to a human viewing the "external" self—social, familial—with objective detachment. He focuses on the structural analogy in order to make a point about the nature of human existence. Queneau focuses more on content, on the experiential analogy between character and human (same desires, tastes, habits, qualities) in order to make observations about the literary genre. While simular fiction's focus is on the individual subject, metafiction's focus is on the species or the genre; the former represents the particularity of a given being, the latter the general shape and conditions of being. It would be far too simple to suggest that metafiction demonstrates an alleged futility, impossibility, or irrelevance of more referential literature; it happens to be the most expedient means of representing the unavoidable paradox confronting the mind's attempt to represent itself to itself. Although metafiction couldn't be farther from the subjective and lyrical purposes of the "poets of experience," at its best it, too, has the effect of counteracting the hegemony of scientific thought by playfully demonstrating the impossibility of reducing consciousness to a quantifiable, rational order. Simular novels such as *Ulysses* and *Under the Volcano* show that exacting attention to formal artifice does not in the least preclude a high degree of mimesis. On the other hand, when form takes complete priority over representation, as in combinatorial exercises (metafictional or otherwise) wherein representation becomes a fortuitous by-product, literature does indeed approach the sort of rational systematization that could be carried out by a "thinking" machine and becomes subordinate to the dominant, technological *épistème*. Thus it would abandon what, according to Langbaum, has been literature's unspoken purpose since the Enlightenment. These two tendencies, toward asserting literature's difference from or participation in the scientific *épistème*, are both embodied—often at cross-purposes—in the writing of Queneau's Oulipo colleague, Italo Calvino.

Italo Calvino

Calvino's writing—both critical and fictional—is very much concerned with the uses of formalism and the place of literature in the electronic age. In the early sixties, Calvino observed that existentialist literature had been undone by its failure to attain a certain type of literary rigor at a time when formal concerns were becoming dominant. By the same token, he also predicted the demise of structuralist experiments like the *nouveau roman* or the works of the *Tel Quel* group because of their lack of subjective interest. Calvino's own career is marked by a flirtation with sometimes quite arbitrary and mechanical generative devices and by an attempt to effect a marriage of scientific and literary discourses. A comparison of his theory and his practice will reveal how the latter—especially in the example of the character Qfwfq of *Le cosmicomiche*—ultimately undoes the former, demonstrating, willy-nilly, the degree to which science and literature are incommensurate. Within Calvino, then, one finds reflected the traditional conflict between rationalist and existential philosophy—exemplified in the persons of Descartes and Pascal—that underlies Langbaum's analysis of the Enlightenment/Romanticism opposition.

Calvino goes much farther than Queneau in eliminating personal experience from his works; indeed, the programmatic statements of his essays would seem to propose an absolute minimization of subjective authorial determinants in a work's genesis. It will be especially useful to consider at length his essay "Cibernetica e fantasmi" (1968; reprinted in Calvino 1980) since the attitude behind it is typical enough of a tendency in structuralist and poststructuralist theorizing to use cibernetic and combinatorial metaphors for mental processes, including artistic creation.

In the essay Calvino makes the fundamental error of unquestioningly accepting cybernetics as a model of human mental activity:

> Electronic brains, if still far from producing all of the functions of the human brain, are nonetheless already able to provide us with a convincing theoretical model for the most complex processes of our memory, of our mental associations, of our imagination, of our consciousness. (1980, 167)

Calvino's futurist euphoria leaves him far too easily convinced, too susceptible to the exaggerated claims of A.I. researchers hustling grants, it would appear. Many years after this essay, most of the things Calvino is taking for granted remain unrealized, but my immediate purpose is to follow the logic of his argument. From the mental sphere, Calvino passes to the biological, noting that biology has shown that

> the unending variety of vital forms can be reduced to the combination of certain finite quantities. Here again it is information theory which imposes its models. Processes which appeared to be the most refractory to a numeric formulation, to a quantitative description, have been translated into mathematical models. (169)

This may be the case, but the question Calvino needs to ask concerns the relationship of form to the whole. He is overlooking Pirandello's old opposition, contained here in the term "vital forms." Just as he earlier assumed brain functions to be the same thing as mental phenomena, he here implies an identity of the vital with the quantifiable forms it inhabits. Continuing on to transformational linguistics, neo-formalist criticism, and the work of Oulipo, Calvino compiles examples of what he calls procedures capable of being confided to a computer. These procedures are all based on the premise that by extrapolating from phenomena basic elements that can be formally systematized, one will be able to reproduce the original phenomena. It is faith in such processes that accounts for the confidence of early A.I. prognosticators and Calvino, who is given to tossing out uncritically such jargon as "the quantity of information of poetic texts" (169).

The reason for Calvino's adoption of the cybernetic model is to pose the question of whether confiding certain procedures to a computer will result in a machine-author:

> Thus, inasmuch as we already have machines that read, machines that carry out linguistic analyses of literary texts, machines that translate, machines that give summaries, will we then have machines capable of conceiving of composing poetry and novels? (170)

The degree to which the mechanical versions of these activities (where such indeed exist) approximate their human models is highly debatable, but in any case it will be more useful to follow Calvino's questions than his assertions, which frequently belong to the mythology of cybernetics. Calvino admits that the practical realization of a writing machine is irrelevant, that what interests him is rather the theoretical implications of its possibility (apparently he does not stop to consider that if the machine is an impossibility the theoretical implications are of little use).

> I am thinking of a writing machine that brings into play on the page all of those elements that are usually considered to be the most jealously guarded attributes of psychological intimacy, of lived experience, of the unpredictability of flashes of humor, of inner tremors, torments, and illuminations. What are these things if not so many linguistic fields of which we can well arrive at establishing the lexicon, grammar, syntax, and permutative properties? (170)

The first half of this statement proposes a mechanical poet of experience. The premises of the rhetorical question that follows are so blatantly erroneous that it is difficult to believe Calvino is posing the question seriously. He surely can't mean to say that lived experience is a linguistic field—although perhaps he does, given that he is merely repeating the reductive gesture of other "full blown" (absolutist) theorists, who might prefer to define lived experience as economic conflict, libidinal symbolism, or what have you. He is making the crucial mistake of taking language to be literal and opaque—nonsymbolic and nonreferential—as if meaning were somehow contained on its surface and not elicited in the referential context of a person's experience, linguistic and otherwise. Calvino's hypothetical machine would, he says, be capable of feeling in itself the need to produce disorder as a reaction to a previously established order, and capable of comprehending the referential totality of experience. It would be, in sum, a machine capable of producing "*la* letteratura" (Literature with a capital L). It is so obvious that this machine is the human being we already have that one wonders if Calvino is playing devil's advocate in order to point out ironically that his "literature corresponding perfectly to a theoretical hypothesis" (171) is a patent absurdity. He does admit to playing on the fears and prejudices of many literati in taking a position in favor of the machine, and he associates the gesture with an effort to demystify the Romantic notion of inspiration. But he persists in trying to reduce writing to a set of rational, programmable procedures, with the rationale that a writer is indeed a machine, and as such should at least know the rules of his own functioning. Again, we see here the classic error that Hubert Dreyfus has noted (see chap. 1): the assumption that human behavior takes place according to rules, and that these rules are somehow internalized and extractable.

Calvino's mechanical analogy is no more true or useful than a poet's analogy of a lightning bolt in providing a meaningful description of the creative process, but it does obtain a certain sanction insofar as it seconds the currently dominant paradigm, i.e., the technological as opposed to the Romantic.

A basic contradiction emerges in Calvino's argument at this point. Starting with assumptions rooted in classicism, he hypothesizes a machine that will, naturally, produce a kind of classicist writing, for which he praises it, but in the next breath he wants it to enact a break with the very order it would impose. In other words, the machine should break out of classicism into something very much like Romanticism. Why this rational Romanticism should be preferable to the Romanticism he objected to is a mystery, but it seems that what he seeks is a machine that will produce irrationality out of rationality, in a systematic way.

In a third section of the essay, Calvino explains the motive behind his adoption of the mechanistic model:

> In the vertiginous confrontation with the innumerable, the unclassifiable, the continuous, I feel reassured by the finite, the systematized, the discrete . . . [it is] almost an exorcism in order to defend myself from the vortex continually braved by literature. (174)

This "vertigo" is the same feeling that leads Mattia Pascal to formulate his personal oath, "cursed be Copernicus"; it is the feeling that gave rise to the Cartesian method in the first place, and Calvino, like Descartes, wants to reestablish himself at the center of an ordered system, insulated against the sort of anxiety in the face of the infinite spaces that Pascal (Blaise, not Mattia) speaks of. However, literature is at the same time always straining beyond its limitations:

> But the tension of literature, doesn't it always come to escaping from this finite number, doesn't it always try to say something that isn't known, that can't be said, that can't be known? A thing can't be known when the words and concepts for saying and thinking it have not yet been used in that position or disposed in that order, in that sense. Literature's battle is precisely an effort to get beyond the confines of language; it comes forth from the outer limits of the sayable; it is the call of what is beyond vocabulary which moves literature. (175)

Calvino is again equating experience—at least knowing—with language in a troubling manner, but otherwise his statement corresponds to Heidegger's conception of philosophy and poetry, which operate at the limits of the sayable and bring previously indistinguishable phenomena to our perception. He is not actually talking about knowing, but communication, a somewhat unpopular term for theorists who must treat language as an autonomous entity rather than a medium. For example, I know fully and in great detail the taste and texture of the mint presently in my mouth; it is my reader who cannot know it, at least not past my ability to come up with descriptive terms or analogies that will suggest similar sensations and approximations, not certain knowledge. The important point, though, is that I am drawing on my experience in formulating my description, not carrying out a combinatorial process; no machine can know the mint in the way I do. In other words, the unsayable is not located in language, the medium of its articulation, but in my experience of it.

It should be obvious enough that if I invent a new word, or put some words together in an unprecedented order, I have certainly not created a new thing, and most likely have not even created a new meaning, except through a fortuitous juxtaposition of referents. This is precisely Calvino's claim, though, as he tries unconvincingly to suggest a connection between myth and a combinatory process. Using Freud's theory of verbal slips and the meaning of jokes as a model, he suggests that a literary machine playing out possible combinations of elements will hit upon unintentional associations that will give rise to unsuspected meanings. The analogy is a poor one, however, since the machine would lack the key factor that makes Freud's model work, namely, the motivation (which Freud situates in the unconscious) to express a particular meaning; Freud's whole point is that the unconscious is anything but random in its associations. The notion that random associations of context-free elements would "produce new meanings," much less fill the role of myth in a culture, is akin to the old saw about chimpanzees and typewriters: in theory they might produce something intelligible (we don't even have to wait for *Hamlet*), but why would one bother? Calvino's metaphysical concept of language is at least as mystifying as anything the Romantics ever cooked up; it is only the technical gloss, combined perhaps with the prevailing intellectual winds in Paris when he wrote the essay, that could possibly make it seem any more sensible than the notion of inspiration or a visit from the Muse.

Happily, nothing refutes the basic premises of this inconsequential essay more demonstratively than some of Calvino's own fiction, particularly his character/second-degree narrator Qfwfq of *Cosmicomics*. The premise of *Cosmicomics* is as simple as it is clever: each story begins with an italicized epigraph that describes a scientific discovery or theorem, and then an unidentified narrator, whose only function is to present formally—with one italicized remark (e.g., *said Qfwfq*)—Qfwfq, the second-degree narrator who proceeds to tell a tale that illustrates the scientific principle in terms of everyday experience (e.g., how it was to be present at the Big Bang). Aside from his unusual name—inspired perhaps by an exercise from a typing manual—Qfwfq is an odd character inasmuch as he is not given a human form but has a human essence nonetheless. He has all of the attributes of a talkative, boastful old man, and he has apparently been around since before time began, in various forms. He seems to fulfill the cultural role of a singer of tales, offering explanations of the cosmos in human terms.

Calvino's great success is to have endowed this character with all of the traces of knowledge of finitude that characterize human beings (e.g., nostalgia, fear, instinct for self-preservation) while at the same time freeing him from corporal and temporal constraints. The important thing about Qfwfq is not that he has lived through eons in all manner of forms, like something from science fiction, but that he has done so in the manner of a human being; in other words, by taking Qfwfq out of a human context while preserving his ordinary human qualities, Calvino is able to depict what is most essentially human.

Actually, Qfwfq, in having a human way of being without human form, is very much like Heidegger's *Dasein*. In Heideggerese, Qfwfq's way of being is that of a self-interpreting being "always already" thrust into a world in which things are perceptible only in relation to that being's concerns. The humor of Calvino's stories stems from his representation of the referential totality of human concerns, in their most basic manifestations, even outside of human space and time. No matter how primordial or abstract the situation in which Qfwfq is placed, he has always taken the world—the human referential totality—with him. The point Calvino so playfully drives home is that without the whole package there can be no comprehension. In a statement from a 1968 interview, the author is explicit about the importance of context:

> What interests me is the mosaic in which man finds himself embedded, the play of relations, the figure to be discovered among the arabesques of the carpet [pace James!].... I know quite well that I certainly can't escape from the human.... The

stories that I write are constructed inside a human brain, by means of a combination of signs elaborated by the human cultures that have preceded me. (188)

Although I would myself make a distinction between brain and mind, and argue that stories are first constructed not from linguistic elements, but from conceptual, imagistic, even sensorial elements, this statement will nonetheless do as an explanation of precisely why whatever Calvino's writing machine produces will not be literature. In another essay, Calvino describes what he considers the most important attitude for a writer: "Only laughter—systematic derision, convulsive grimacing—guarantees that the discourse is up to the level of the 'terribility' of living and signals a revolutionary change" (1980, 214). Through all of the vertiginous play of *Cosmicomics*, a sense of the terribility of living—of change, separation, the inevitable solitude of a self-conscious intelligence in the universe—is never lost. Along the way, Qfwfq also points out the fallacies of the assumptions behind Calvino's cybernetics essay by demonstrating the priority of human being-in-a-world over any theoretical formulation about that world. Qfwfq shows at every turn the inevitable circularity of knowing and the inevitable frustration of desire, given the limits and conditions of human being.

The story "Quanto Scommettiamo?" ("How Much Shall We Bet?") provides a fine example of Qfwfq in action, as he reacts to the epigraph, which describes a cybernetic model of cosmogony:

> *The logic of cybernetics, applied to the history of the universe, is in the process of demonstrating how the galaxies, the solar system, the Earth, cellular life could not help but be born. According to cybernetics, the universe is formed by a series of feedbacks, positive and negative, at first through the force of gravity that concentrates masses of hydrogen in the primitive cloud, then through the nuclear force and centrifugal force which are balanced with the first. From the moment that the process is set in motion, it can only follow the logic of this chain.*

Yes, but at the beginning nobody knew it—*Qfwfq explained*—I mean, you could foretell it perhaps, but instinctively, by ear, guessing. I don't want to boast, but from the start I was willing to bet that there was going to be a universe, and I hit the nail

on the head; on the question of its nature, too, I won plenty of
bets, with old Dean (k)yK. (101)

The humor of Qfwfq's response obviously comes from the fact of his
having been "there" to speculate on the future coming-into-being of
the universe in which he must already have been, and it is com-
pounded by the copresence "there" of a Dean (along with all of the
institutions and other accessory entities that the title implies) and by
the fact that they are passing the "time" with such characteristically
playful activity as betting. In these few lines, Calvino signals a whole
world of human concerns including institutions, professions, inquiry,
speculation, and not least of all, false modesty, vanity, and competi-
tion, along with all that they suggest of selfhood and mortality. There
is something in the concessive tone of Qfwfq's "Yes, but..." that
seems to imply an affirmation of personal experience, indeed, of
self-esteem, over the possibly interesting yet lifeless details of the
preceding theory. Qfwfq's reply demonstrates that there is "always
already" a knower, immersed in a preexisting world, before there can
be an object of knowing. Qfwfq is in fact only playing on—thus humanizing, for play is a quintessentially human act—what one finds in
the theory itself upon closer examination.

The problem of the theory, insofar as it makes a claim to a
demonstration of the birth of the universe, is the problem that
plagues any gesture of originary explication. As the irreverent
Smerdyakov asks in the *Brothers Karamazov,* if God made the sun and
the moon on the fourth day, where did the light come from on the
first day? Calvino avoids this specific problem by letting there be not
light, but noodles in his version of the Big Bang ("All in a Point"), in
which a woman's loving impulse to serve noodles to her lovers causes
all that would be necessary for their realization to spring into being.
Returning to the example at hand, one might similarly ask where the
masses of hydrogen came from. In telling us that everything had to
happen as it did, the theory tells us nothing at all; its descriptions of
positive and negative feedbacks are simply descriptions of cybernetic
functioning. The most that the theory can do is advance us one step
in an infinite regression.

All of this is reminiscent of William James's celebrated quip
when he had explained the Hindu cosmology that situates the world
on the back of an elephant, standing on a turtle, standing on a rock,

and a wag asked what was under the rock. James's reply: "From there on, it's rock all the way down."[1] The student who posed the question might have been a simpleton or a genius; perhaps the distinction is meaningless in this case. What is clear is that Qfwfq is precisely this sort of wise guy himself. The anecdote helps to explain in what sense the Hindu and cybernetic models are compatible, thus showing the sense in which Calvino's desire to reconcile cybernetics and literature might be realized. It is first essential to see that the scientific theory is no more capable than the Hindu myth of "answering" the most fundamental of human inquiries. Each of them provides a model of interpretation grounded in the dominant conceptual frame of its particular world and time. As such, each might be said to belong to folklore, fulfilling the traditional tale-telling role Calvino so often speaks of; Qfwfq is the cosmic village elder. (His tone is, in fact, slightly paternal, studded with remarks like "You don't remember, but I do," and so on.) What Calvino does in the person of Qfwfq is link the more primordial and the most quotidian of our concerns, reaffirming the priority of human being along with all of its tragicomic paraphernalia.

The example from "Quanto scommettiamo?" is but one of many instances where we find the basic assumptions of information-type theories confounded. Teresa De Lauretis (1975, 416) has used the odd, unpronounceable names of the characters to propose a way in which the graphic reality of signs can give meaning to the otherwise senseless and phonetically inoperable combinations of letters, as if this were an example of a combinatorial process conjuring up new meanings along the lines suggested in Calvino's essay, but she overlooks a much more meaningful detail. The fact is that the combinations of letters are not presented as is, but are modified by kinship terms or other qualifiers; even Qfwfq is introduced as "old Qfwfq." It is not simply "Vhd Vhd" or "G'd(w)^n" we see, but rather "*Il Capitano* and *Signora* Vhd Vhd," "my sister G'd(w)^n," or "grandma Bb'b." Thus, the otherwise meaningless elements derive meaning from their insertion into a network of familial and social relations, and the star tlingly comical juxtaposition of the decontextualized letter combinations and their humanizing qualifiers enact my argument graphically.

One of Calvino's staple methods of fleshing out his scientific principles in the stories is to eroticize them. That is, Qfwfq's predominant concern—aside from playing games—is getting next to one female or other (I use the biological term, since they're not always human). At times his desires are more strictly physical—witness his compelling urge to seize Signora Vhd Vhd's breasts, or his obsession with the possibility of intersecting the trajectory of lovely Ursula H'x as they fall endlessly through space—and at other times his interest is more romantic or platonic. A number of the tales feature romance thwarted by cosmological, planetary, or biological mutation, as when his love-interest decides not to move onto dry land after all and remains aquatic, or when he must jump back to Earth, leaving Signora Vhd Vhd on her beloved moon, before that satellite reaches a prohibitive distance from its parent planet. In the latter story (the first in the original collection, entitled "La distanza della luna"), we see intimations of mortality in Qfwfq's nostalgia as he contemplates—from the moon—what he has lost in leaving the Earth to be with his love. What he describes, in effect, is the realization of meaninglessness (not unlike those moments of nauseatingly objective perception in existentialist novels) that results from isolating the human from its referential totality:

> It was all beyond my most luminous hopes, and instead, and instead it was exile. . . .
> I thought only of Earth. It was Earth that made it so that each person was precisely that someone and not another; up there, torn from the Earth, it was as if I were no longer that me, and she, for me, was no longer that she. . . . My being in love now knew only the estranging nostalgia for what we were missing; a where, a surrounding, a before, an after. (21)

Thus, Qfwfq, an apparently immortal being, paradoxically is threatened with a kind of nonbeing, and this sense of the tragic reemerges throughout the stories. One could say that each story repeats the general pattern of a human lifetime inasmuch as each typically begins with a sense of delight and play and ends on a note of pathos or anxiety. The most literal example of this is in "Giochi senza fine" ("Games Without End"), a cosmic variant on the "stayed-too-long-at-the-fair" theme, in which a boyish pastime—working all too well—takes an existential turn, as Qfwfq and his pal play compulsive tag around the edge of the universe, even though "we had lost all taste for chasing one another, and besides, we were no longer kids, but by now there was nothing else for us to do" (83). Many of the characters, and Qfwfq, too, in his many mutations (most convincingly when he's the last dinosaur), are portrayed as the last of a line, or the first, or otherwise removed and alienated from their communities. Qfwfq has the manner of a fun-loving raconteur, but like Tristram Shandy he shows a certain frantic apprehension under the surface, and this edge is the direct product of the self-awareness that no machine can have, and no amount of combinatorial shuffling can portray.

Cosmicomics, then, is predicated on an opposition of the rationalist and existentialist philosophical traditions that are the source of a great deal of tension in all of Calvino's later works, and that might otherwise be described as the formalist and representational aesthetics. The simular novel enacts a synthesis of these traditions in a way that is unfortunately lost on Calvino, whose notion of literary forms and history seems to extend only to folktales and formal realism as defined by Ian Watt. For example, in the essay "Il romanzo come spettacolo" we again see evidence of the structuralist enthusiasm that leads him to some faulty conclusions as he describes the state of the novel as he sees it:

> The first rule of the novel is to no longer refer to a story (to a world) outside of its own pages, and the reader is called upon to follow only the procedure of the writing, of the text in the act of writing itself; on the other hand there is a convergence of studies and analyses of what is (or was) the traditional story in all of its manifestations. (1980, 219)

Calvino's faith in structural analysis and his limited definition of the novel lead him to the conclusion that the genre is exhausted and irrelevant to the new "scientific" sophistication of the public:

> If we now know the rules of the "novelistic" game, we will be able to construct "artificial" novels, born in the laboratory; we will be able to play at the novel the way we play chess, with absolute good faith, reestablishing a communication between the writer, fully conscious of the mechanisms he is using, and the reader, who is in the game because he knows the rules and knows that he can no longer be taken for a patsy.

Calvino displays here the same sort of smug disdain we have seen in Culler and Valéry, when he discovers that characters are not real people. It is difficult to understand such bitterness and resentment toward the imagination; an easy answer would be the political one, e.g., that writers no longer wish to be complicit in an escapist, bourgeois genre that fosters the cult of individuality at the expense of the reader's "liberation." But the problem with this argument is that works of the sort Calvino describes have proven to be so reluctant and inept at coming to grips with sociohistoric reality that the contention is laughable. In any event, what Calvino proposes, based on his analysis of the state of the genre, is a sort of work that will respect the reader's formalist savvy and at the same time satisfy the basic desire for a plot.

There are two problems with this prescription, however. First of all, just how a novel might avoid refering to anything outside its pages certainly remains to be seen. "The text in the act of writing itself" has only one eminently predictable thing to say, and a rather high tedium quotient, as metafiction becomes a fad of epidemic proportions. Secondly, the public that has followed the novel is not the public concerned with folktales: people have been reading the novel to satisfy their desire for characterization, not just simple plots. It must be said, though, that Calvino does produce as admirable an exemplar of this aesthetic as one might desire in his *Se una notte d'inverno un viaggiatore* . . . .

The protagonists of *Se una notte* represent a milestone in characterization in one sense. After the simular novel's author-characters, and the metafictional novel's character-characters, Calvino introduces the reader-character, coming as close as the one-way communication of literature will allow to creating the illusion of the reader's actuality in his fiction. The protagonist, first referred to only by the second-person familiar pronoun *tu*, is reading *Se una notte*, and in alternating chapters is represented in the third-person as *Il Lettore* (the reader), who is in pursuit not only of the end of his continually interrupted novel, but also of his female counterpart, *La Lettrice*. In alternating chapters, then, we follow the plot of his pursuit of the woman and various abortive plots that comprise the novels, and we read what he is reading. Meanwhile, Calvino manages to carry metarepresentation to the *n*th degree, systematically deconstructing all of the logical borders between paired elements along a chain of literary transmission and reception. The effect is vertiginous in the extreme, as he compiles figure after figure to represent the notion of self-reflexivity. Indeed, one would say that the central figure of the work is that of the mind in an eternal present, watching itself watch itself as it watches itself, etc.

Calvino says of Boccaccio, his great predecessor in the frame-tale form, that his utopian framework, itself framed in the realistic context of a world lost to catastrophe, provided a pretext for the stories, which reproduced the variety and intensity of the lost world. The *Decameron* acted, in other words, to conserve the era's values in a time of great crisis, namely, the plague. One could say that *Se una notte* addresses a similar challenge, but in an opposite manner. That is, Calvino's frame does not hold up a fabulistic otherness to the world so much as a mirror, as if Boccaccio had his characters sitting around telling plague horror stories every day. The unpretentious Reader seeks narrative completion and love in a world of fraud, impossible bureaucracy, dehumanizing cybernetics, and mad, repressive police states. The "novels" that appear within this frame do not offer a vision of a less turbulent world, but rather repeat the conditions of the framing reality. In the end, though, the Reader attains both his goals, ending up reading peacefully in bed with the female Reader. Against a protean, menacing world, Calvino continually poses the spirit of the game and the immediacy of consciousness, valorizing reading as experience just as the simular authors highlight writing.

Calvino's writing is in many respects a logical extension of the concern for form that begins with Proust and Joyce's "construction" of novels. He is, at least theoretically, willing to turn over artifice to any arbitrary, mathematical procedure. He would, according to his essays, replace the values of the poetry of experience with random permutations of value-free elements, and he is left scrambling to find a source of value. In the end, his characters desert the "nightmare of history" for the ahistorical nightmare of signifiers. It is as if for Joyce and Proust the act of becoming a novelist ipso facto justified all representation, while for Calvino, there can be no possible justification for fictional representation. Happily, though, his prognostications for the novel have not been realized. Well before his 1968 essay, a certain Russian emigré professor and moth chaser was at

work writing novels that combine the best of experiential representation and formal experimentation, in his own Euro-American world,
where traditional poetics and advanced gamesmanship blend quite
well, as we shall see.

For Pirandello, Queneau, Calvino, and others of a more formalist orientation, formal experimentation is inseparable from episte-
mology, from the portrayal of consciousness aware of itself and its
limits. The shift in emphasis from subjectivity to consciousness (from
the self immersed in experience to the detachment of the self-observ-
ing mind) in novels can be interpreted as either progressive (a further
evolution in the representation of interiority) or regressive (a rejection of history, artistic solipsism), but such judgments must be based
on specific cases, not on the inherent qualities of the form itself. It
should be clear, however, that Calvino is right to recognize that the
ultimate logic of formalism by itself leads to cybernetic "art," and that
the extreme sort of suppression of authorial subjectivity he proposes
would entirely eliminate the historical voice of the artist (to the delight of totalitarians of all stripes, no doubt) and indeed amount to a
suppression of difference in general.

In an essay on French novelist Michel Tournier, Roger Shattuck
(1983, 8–9) implicates theorist Roland Barthes and practitioner Alain
Robbe-Grillet in what he terms a temporary deflection of the course
of fiction in an "anti-humanistic and neo-scientific" direction and
credits Tournier with returning to more literary values, and with
being unhampered by the imperative to be original at all costs that
seems to preoccupy certain of his contemporaries. Shattuck deems
the *nouveau roman* "a new art for art's sake looking toward an imper-
fectly defined social revolution" (9). This newly autonomous art differs from the old art for art's sake in its view of literature as a linguistic or semiotic, rather than an aesthetic, artifact, and the vague social
revolution it announces is precisely what Frederick Crews wryly dis-
misses as the belief in changing society by changing the rules of literary criticism (see chap. 1). Meanwhile, though, the old notion of art
for art's sake did not entirely disappear with the passing of decadence
or the prosperity of the twenties, but can be found—along with a
supreme degree of formal self-consciousness—in the long career of
Vladimir Nabokov.

Nabokov

Nabokov is a unique figure among twentieth-century novelists not only by virtue of his bilingual production, but also because of the way in which his works combine traditional aesthetic and anti-realistic elements. If anything, his novels would have to be qualified as anti-simular; it would be an understatement to say that he jealously guards his autobiography and constructs his novels as self-contained systems. Actually, Nabokov's various fictional explanations of the provenance of the text of the novels constitute something of a revival of the pseudofactual form. Nonetheless, the novels, aside from being replete with authorial signatures and other self-references, are to a large degree based on elements of refracted—as opposed to transmuted, in the Joycean sense—autobiographical representation. More than any other author, Nabokov gives proof of his schooling in both Proust and Joyce, whom he so admired.

Nabokov, the Russian aristocrat and American professor, enjoyed the unusual position of belonging to the nineteenth-century French tradition and to postmodernism; he embraced the highest standard of the canon (approaching literary snobbery at times) and radical innovation at the same time. Few other writers have been in a position to illustrate so convincingly both the aesthetic *frisson* and the vertigo of reflexive consciousness. If Nabokov belongs to the mid-century avant-garde—in his deconstruction of the border between frame and picture and his systematic frustration of conventional reception—he also belongs to a rear-guard, defending the tradition of belles lettres against common hackery. His strong opinions on literature sound not a little like Proust, in his idealization of art and castigation of Philistine vulgarity, and quite a bit like poststructuralist critics of realism:

> For me a work of fiction exists only insofar as it affords me what I shall bluntly call aesthetic bliss, that is a sense of being somehow, somewhere, connected to other states of being where art (curiosity, tenderness, kindness, ecstasy) is the norm. There are not many such books. All the rest is either topical trash or what some call the Literature of Ideas, which very often is topical trash coming in huge blocks of plaster that are carefully transmitted from age to age until somebody comes along with a ham-

mer and takes a good crack at Balzac, at Gorki, at Mann. (1970, 316–17)

For Nabokov, as for Stephen, art should be neither ideological nor kinetic in a mundane emotional sense. Like Joyce, he stands behind his creation, having left his calling cards and other indicators of the presence of the designing mind on the other side of the mirror. Nabokov does not use the novel to tell his own story, however; the job of artistically rendering his life is left to his autobiography, *Speak, Memory*. While the simular novel contains autobiographical fact in a fictional form, this work approximates the converse, an aesthetic artifice in the form of an autobiography.

As a conventional autobiography, *Speak, Memory* is an account of the author's journey from childhood to parenthood. It begins with his first awareness of himself as a temporal—i.e., mortal—being as he walks along with his parents, and ends with him and his wife and young son walking to the ship that will bring them to America. Thus, the first and last images are formally similar, but the narrating persona has come to occupy the paternal figure in the latter instance, in a nicely Pirandellian play of *forma* and *vita*. Although his courtship and marriage are not detailed in the book, at a point that would correspond to the time of those events in the narrative it becomes a direct address to the unnamed wife, who is designated only by the second person pronoun. This procedure is typical of the work's aesthetic, insofar as Nabokov's purpose is to portray not simply personal chronological history, but rather the development of a particular sensibility—an aesthetic self, one might say—which is the true subject of the autobiography. Early in the book, Nabokov provides a paradigmatic anecdote—concerning a general who once amused the boy with some match sticks, and who, years later, while fleeing the Revolution in disguise, happened to meet the boy and his father, whom he did not recognize, and asked for a match—that reveals his criterion of selection for events that will be included in his self-portrait. The true purpose of autobiography, he says, is to follow such thematic designs through one's life, to define one's life, then, in terms of an aesthetic order, as if it were itself an artistic creation. This amounts to a more elegant version of what Proust does across his three thousand pages, tracing the development of a self that can recognize a holistic meaning or design underlying the day-to-day disorder of historical existence, eliciting a sense of beauty or truth. In this sense, Nabokov's aesthetic is grounded in the classic Western notion of a temporally transcendent ideal. He describes the driving urge behind such an enterprise when he details for his wife the process set off in him by the feeling of love:

> When that slow-motion, silent explosion of love takes place in me, unfolding its melting fringes and overwhelming me with the sense of something much vaster, much more enduring and powerful than the accumulation of matter or energy in any imaginable cosmos, then my mind cannot but pinch itself to see if it is really awake. I have to make a rapid inventory of the universe, just as a man in a dream tries to condone the absurdity of his position by making sure he is dreaming. I have to have all space and all time participate in my emotion, in my mortal love, so that the edge of its mortality is taken off, thus helping me to fight the utter degradation, ridicule, and horror of having developed an infinity of sensation and thought within a finite existence. (1966, 297)

The particular stamp of Nabokov's genius is seen in his persistent and undaunted attempts to represent the mind's need to reconcile its awareness of its own finitude with its perception of an infinite universe, to create figures, in other words, for the paradox of consciousness in its temporal prison. The first paragraph of the autobiography describes the panic of a "young chronophobiac" looking at home movies made before his birth, revealing a world not one wit changed for his absence, and Nabokov's fictional protagonists are equally prey to such panic and indignation. Only Van Veen in *Ada* attains some measure of existential peace via requited love and artistic expression.

Nabokov does not represent becoming an artist as a defining and justifying condition of his existence. He had, of course, one equally demanding and absorbing preoccupation in his life, namely, Lepidoptera. *Speak, Memory* is more the story of an intelligence and sensibility than the chronicle of an artistic arrival; for Nabokov, the latter is significant as one—albeit major—of many life processes, valued as such and not as an end in itself. Thus, despite the obviously high premium he places on art, he does not portray himself as a heroic artist, and the mechanics and circumstances of his blossoming as a writer do not merit particular attention. Nabokov does, though, dedicate a chapter to the awakening of his poetic expression in adolescence, inspired—as was Stephen's—by the hope of passing through "certain very intense human emotions" (1966, 217), and he freely admits that the publication of this first volume was an unfortunate embarrassment. He goes on to describe himself at Cambridge University in terms Dedalus would appreciate: out of place, holding unpopular aesthetic and political opinions, and pursuing his solitary destiny. On the whole, though, personal history in the external sense is treated as rather incidental; it is not the ego—in the traditional "Viennese quack" sense—that is the subject of the autobiography, so much as the perceiving self that observes life in objective detachment. Nabokov's detachment from his represented self is such that at times it approaches fictionalization, as when he discusses his favorite among the Russian exile authors, V. Sirin, without giving the slightest indication that Sirin is, in fact, his own pseudonymous mask. Likewise, while Joyce and Proust use their characters to air their own aesthetic theories, Nabokov in his autobiography presents his theories only indirectly, in the guise of discussions of composing chess problems and gardening, for instance.

Nabokov is well known for his insistence on the autonomy of art from life, but the irony is that he must depend upon an implied connection between the two to make his point. That is, while his fictional works are intended to frustrate autobiographical interpretation, a central feature of their structure is the inclusion of the artist—more the fashioning mind than the historical person—within the frame, as in the many references to such shadowy personae as Vivian Darkbloom and Baron Klimadinov (his anagrammatic signatures) in *Pale Fire* and to the gentleman in the lawn chair in Ithaca. He must encourage the autobiographical connection in order to entrap the reader, and in so doing represents his formal aesthetic of showing the outside, the metadimension that makes perception of the contained fictional dimension possible. Thus his antirealism leads to a sort of hyper-realism on the next level, the realism of the work itself, as opposed to its framed representation. His stories are tales told by demented pseudoauthors foregrounded as creations of the toying artificer pretending not to be Vladimir Nabokov while signaling that he is. The result is that the only stable referential context of the tale is to be found in consciousness itself, "the only real thing in the world" (1964, 168). This explains Nabokov's impatience with the make-believe of traditional fiction, which does not include the observer in the picture. Where fiction has posed itself as a correlative of the real world, Nabokov insists that it is rather a correlative of the author's mind; as he says, the game is not between the author and the world, but between author and reader, between the representing and apprehending consciousnesses, a more dynamic process than that of an author who merely points through the window for a passive reader.

Like *Ulysses,* then, Nabokov's novels are marked by the presence of the artificer in the artifice; he, too, sets himself up as the lord of his creation, as the great unseen power behind the fictional world, but unlike Joyce, he is not concerned with entering the story as a character, with making the story his own in the personal sense. Nabokov is content to identify himself with the pervasive consciousness that envelops both picture and frame. His protagonists, so often authors or professors, are frequently in a position to grasp the higher reality that contains them. In *Bend Sinister,* for example, Adam Krug is relieved of his anxiety over his impending doom when he realizes, as the author explains in his introduction, that "he is in good hands ... death is but a question of style, a mere literary device, a musical resolution," and the character then "comfortably returns to the bosom of his maker" (1964, xviii). Through what he calls "impersonating an anthropomorphic deity," Nabokov consoles the character—his ontological, not biographical, analog—with the objective detachment of consciousness. In a notable passage Krug's observing "I" is suggestively conflated with the all-seeing eye:

> As usual he discriminated between the throbbing one and the one that looked on: looked on with concern, with sympathy, with a sigh, or with bland surprise. This was the last stronghold of the dualism he abhorred. The square root of I is I. Footnotes, forget-me-nots. The stranger quietly watching the torrents of local grief from an abstract blank. A familiar figure, albeit anonymous and aloof. He saw me crying when I was ten and led me to a looking glass in an unused room ... so that I might study my dissolving face. He listened to me with raised eyebrows when I said things I had no business to say. In every mask I tried on, there were slits for his eyes. Even at the very moment when I

was rocked by the convulsion men value most. My savior. My witness. (6)

Thus the detached observer—consciousness—is the character's particle of divinity. It should be noted that the whole of *Bend Sinister* is framed in a conflation of author and character. The book's first chapter and last page are first-person narratives enclosing a conventional third-person narrative. On the last page, "I" is the author at his desk, commenting on the demise of his character and describing the view from his window, which is identical to that described by the "I" of the first chapter, where only two brief phrases ("View from a hospital window" and "The operation has not been successful and my wife will die" [2]) locate the voice in the character who will be identified as Krug in the second chapter. As the author remarks on the last page of the book, the puddle he now looks at is "the one Krug had somehow perceived through the layer of his own life." Here, then, Nabokov is a benevolent deity, in a symbiotic relationship to his creation. Nabokov may play the deity in relationship to his characters, but he also makes it clear that their finitude is a reflection of his own, most explicitly when Kinbote announces at the end of *Pale Fire* that he could, in effect, escape to the next dimension and become Nabokov, but that he would only be done in by a meta-assassin in his turn. It is in this sense that the deity Nabokov impersonates is anthropomorphic; he does not recreate himself as a figure headed for Stephen's mansions in eternity.

There is a noteworthy difference between Nabokov's style of metafiction and that practiced by Calvino in *Se una notte,* for example. While the latter work, like *Lolita* and *Pale Fire,* presents its framed narratives as the products of somewhat demented and manipulative pseudoauthors, Nabokov differs both in his direct references to himself, the veritable author, and in the creation of distinctive worlds of refracted autobiographical details such as college towns, exiled literati, political assassinations, butterfly identifications, and so forth. The best example of this sort of refraction—or distortion of autobiographical detail to reflect not the actual, external world, but the inner world of the artificer whom it conditioned—is found in the curious world Antiterra in *Ada.* Antiterra amounts to Nabokov's inner reality projected onto the globe: a world with a Russian and French-speaking North America, it has the decor of a nineteenth-century French novel with twentieth-century technology added in. This combination of naturalistic description and suspension of historical verisimilitude creates a unique effect, that of seeing the private world of Nabokov's imagination given as a natural condition of the world we know. The process is quite the opposite of Joyce's exhaustive research of realistic details, but it is not a case of unconstrained imagination; it is rather an imaginative creation conditioned by, and logically corresponding to, the author's experience in the world. My larger point here is that unlike many postmodernists, Nabokov does not repudiate earlier forms and styles, but adds the postmodern dimension to them. While his metafictional pyrotechnics are perhaps quicker to attract attention, few writers since Proust have devoted such care to realistic visual detail, particularly in translating the semiotics of decor into revelations of character, from Charlotte Haze's Mexican kitsch in *Lolita* to the refined elegance of Ada's Ardis Manor.

In Nabokov's novels, literary tradition meets game theory, and games require two players. As the author says of composing chess problems, the object is not so much to fashion them according to the game's principles in the abstract as to anticipate the response of the solver at every turn. In other words, Nabokov designs his works for a "player" of his caliber, implying a certain respect for the reader as something more than a witness of one's attainments. He seems to find no particular sense of triumph in writing that would lead him to make his work the story of his arrival. The real is not a horror to be redeemed through artistic representation; if anything it is too imposing, too wondrous to be captured other than in particular details (a butterfly's wing as opposed to the conscience of a race). Details of the author's personal life are not in themselves any more worthy of interest than anyone else's, and should be no more relevant than they would be in a game of chess.

All is not intellectual gamesmanship in the novels, however. For example, in his introduction to *Bend Sinister,* Nabokov states that Krug's recognition of the "reality" of his world and the "dim-brained brutality" of the police state are secondary to the book's main theme, "the torture an intense tenderness is subjected to" (xiv), exemplified in the passages concerning Krug and his son. This might be a thoroughly maudlin theme in lesser hands, but, as always, Nabokov couches it in the observing consciousness, rather than in the emotional self of his character; the emotional dimension is framed in the mind that encompasses it.

> And what agony, thought Krug the thinker, to love so madly a little creature, formed in some mysterious fashion (even more mysterious to us than it had been to the very first thinkers in their pale olive groves) by the fusion of two mysteries, or rather two sets of a trillion of mysteries each; formed by a fusion which is, at the same time, a matter of choice and a matter of chance and a matter of pure enchantment; thus formed and then permitted to accumulate trillions of its own mysteries; the whole suffused with consciousness, which is the only real thing in the world and the greatest mystery of all. (168)

Krug then goes on lovingly to imagine his son growing up in a number of scenes—bicycling, playing ball, etc.—that are highly reminiscent of Nabokov's descriptions of watching his own son in *Speak, Memory;* but I do not wish to emphasize the implied connection so much as the intensity and mystery of it all. The parenthetical remark in the quoted passage makes a point that is especially significant in light of Calvino's essay cited previously, namely, that scientific knowledge does not reductively appropriate the phenomenon at hand, but actually deepens its mystery and our sense of wonder. Nabokov's articulation, compared to Calvino's contention that "the unending variety of vital forms can be reduced to the combination of certain finite quantities . . . translated into mathematical models" (1980, 69), reveals a very different perspective indeed. Calvino the author (not theorist), though, would surely agree that the passage is spoken from a profound sense of the "terribility of living"; a sense that finds expression through all of Nabokov's moments of refracted autobiography and manic gamesmanship. Nabokov's characterizations depict the aspect of a person that endures through historical trauma and cultural dislocation and can fight off the indignity of mortality by tracing its particular thematic design, whether embodied in a mad professor or a gentleman in his lawn chair in Ithaca. His lesson, as much as he would abhor the term, lies in his illustration of the place and power of creative intelligence of the literary sort in the postwar world; his long career forms a bridge—and the most direct route—

from Joyce and Proust to postmodernism. My point is that he demonstrates that being a resolutely contemporary writer addressing the concerns of the structuralist—and post—critical revolution need not imply a break with, or rejection of, the ongoing tradition of the novel.

Georges Perec

Georges Perec, a member of Oulipo along with Queneau and Calvino, had several things in common with Nabokov, not the least of which was a love of games and puzzles. Like Nabokov, Perec was an author of crossword puzzles and a master of verbal play such as anagrams and palindromes. Among his curious accomplishments are such tours de force as a novel written without using the letter *e* and a palindromic "story" some six pages long. The jigsaw puzzle is the controlling thematic and metaphoric paradigm of his monumental *La vie mode d'emploi* (1978), and in his "preamble" to the work he describes in thoroughly Nabokovian terms the "ultimate truth of the puzzle: despite appearances, it isn't a solitary game: every move made by the puzzle solver has been made by the puzzle-maker before him" (18). It is not, he says, the subject of the picture nor the technique of the artist that provides the challenge, but rather the subtlety of the cutting. Perec is indeed a subtle puzzle-maker: his novel is a labyrinth of intricate autoreferentiality (which I do not intend to detail), personal ciphers, and word games; and like Nabokov, he is extraordinarily attentive to detail, particularly elements of decor.

Unfortunately, though, Perec comes up short at making his puzzle resonate with the sort of ontological fervor characteristic of Nabokov. His novel, like the microcosmic artistic puzzles fashioned by his characters, seems in the end a somewhat hollow, if frightfully clever, exercise. The book is filled with literally hundreds of characters, all eminently forgettable, and his trio of obsessive artists—a painter, a puzzle-maker, and a writer—lack the engaging personality of a Humbert or a Shade. Worst of all, for a book that calls itself "novels" (although perhaps appropriate for a *mode d'emploi*—user's manual), there is virtually no dialogue in the entire seven hundred pages; the only "voices" appear mainly in the form of quoted letters and other texts. The problem is that Perec has taken the Joycean technique of structuring pretexts to such extraordinary lengths—creating such overwhelming constraints—that the novel is quite stiff and overconstructed. I will only refer the reader to his "Quatre figures pour *La vie mode d'emploi*" (Oulipo, 1981), where he details the structuring devices that result in a list of forty-two elements—allusions to specific authors, pieces of furniture, colors, paintings, thematic issues, etc.—that are to be included, in various permutations, in each chapter. Unlike Joyce, Perec is quite strict about following his schemata to the letter; suffice it to say that just meeting the terms of these all-encompassing formal constraints leaves little room for spontaneity or inspiration.

Thus, *La vie mode d'emploi* is the *ne plus ultra* of literary engineering, the logical end of a line from Joyce through Queneau, but it offers precious little to a discussion of represented experience. The same is not at all true, however, for Perec's *W ou Le souvenir d'enfance* (1975), which takes on the relationship of art and life in a most direct manner. The book is a unique meeting ground of autobiography and fiction in which we see the author coming to terms with his past through writing. Again like Nabokov, Perec's life was marked by historical trauma and dislocation, and he addresses the same question to which Nabokov's autobiographical "refractions" are a response, namely, how to deal artistically with unspeakable loss.

In Perec's case, the loss occurs at such an early age that it is less of a trauma than a vacuum, a hole in his past and identity. Perec was born in Paris in 1936, the only child of Jewish immigrants from Poland. In 1940 his father was killed at the front outside Paris, and in 1942, his mother put him on a train for the free zone in the south of France, where he would remain with various relatives until 1946. In the interim, his mother was taken prisoner in Paris, deported, and presumably killed in Auschwitz in 1943. After the war, Perec returned to Paris, having been adopted by a paternal aunt.

It was not until he had written three successful novels (*Les choses, Quel petit vélo à guidon chromé au fond de la cour?*, and *Un homme qui dort*) and a number of lesser, highly experimental works, that Perec approached the subject of his childhood. The materials at hand were his sketchy memories, a few photographs, stories told by his aunts, and a story called "W" (that letter being a symbol of his identification with his family and Jewish culture for reasons I shall not go into) that he had written as a teenager. Perec says that the idea of writing the story of his past arose in him at the same time as the idea of writing at all, but oddly enough, this first story was pure fiction, something of a fable for his past, whose true significance he would not assimilate until much later. The published *W ou Le Souvenir d'enfance*, then, contains the original story "W" and the author's memoir of his childhood, as the title implies. The memoir begins with a paradoxical, categorical statement: "I have no childhood memories," and by its end the author has enacted a defabulation, a transformation of his earlier fiction into the real world events from which it was derived.

The process of Perec's self-possession cannot be understood without considering the form of the work, which is as follows. The book alternates chapters of his original story with chapters of autobiography, and the whole is divided into two sections, separated by a page containing nothing but an ellipsis: "(. . .)." The book's real story lies in the unarticulated and subtle interplay of the two narratives. In the first section of the fable, Gaspard Winckler (later the puzzle-maker in *La vie mode d'emploi*) tells the story of his journey to W, an island in the Tierra del Fuego archipelago, in search of his namesake, a young boy lost at sea in very mysterious circumstances. Winckler had been a political refugee who was supplied with the boy's identity papers some time earlier by a humanitarian organization to which the boy's mother, Caecilia, belonged (Perec's mother's French name was Cécile, we later learn). All that is known is that a yacht was found with everyone dead (Caecilia had been trapped in her cabin, vainly trying to escape, as revealed by the deep fingernail scratches engraving the inside of her door, a detail that will become significant much later) and the boy missing. The ship's log had revealed an odd gap, suggesting that a detour had been made to one or other of the many nearby islands before the wreck. Winckler, upon learning of all this, agrees to undertake the journey by way of repaying his debt to Caecilia and her son.

The second section of the story, presumably narrated by Winckler like the first section although he is no longer named, describes the history and social conditions of the island, which he had described as a ruin in the retrospective first chapter. W is a society founded upon the Olympic ideal, organized entirely around daily athletic competitions and the glory of sport. At first the society seems merely unusual, but as details of its functioning are revealed in each succeeding chapter, one realizes that it is a complete Kafkaesque totalitarian nightmare, combining attributes of Hitler's grotesque pageantry and the barbarity of concentration camps.

The first section of Perec's memoir, meanwhile, covers the period leading up to his last view of his mother, as she put him on the train into exile. This section comprises mostly facts supplied by relatives and deductions based on photographs; it is the author's prehistory, of which he has no reliable memories. The second section details the childhood he does remember, encompassing his years in the South and his return to Paris, where he finally visits an exhibition about concentration camps and sees photos of the walls of gas chambers, engraved with the desperate scratch marks of the victims' fingernails.

In the book's last two chapters, the separate narratives reach their definitive conjunction. The last chapter of the fable describes, for the first time, the horror of life on W from the athlete/inmates' point of view, and we learn that they wear striped uniforms and are in fact "skeletal athletes, bent in the spine and ashen-faced, with bald, shiny skulls, panic-filled eyes, and festering sores" (1975, 218), and that, obviously, their athletic performances are utterly mediocre, thus making a complete mockery of the society's own abhorrent ideal and giving proof of its bankruptcy. Here, then, is the final reduction of any remaining distance between the imaginary and the historical. In the final chapter of the memoir (and the book), Perec tells how for years he made drawings of sportsmen with stiff bodies and inhuman facial features (219), "minutely detailing their incessant combats . . . obsessively listing their endless titles" (as in his fable), and how he later read David Rousset's *Univers concentrationnaire*, from which he supplies a page-long quotation describing how the structure of the camps was predicated not on the notion of work, but according to a perverse concept of "sport." The reader recognizes in the passage and in the boy Perec's uncanny intuition the source of W's guiding principles.

By the end of *W*, then, the reader will have fully grasped the story between the chapters, the artistic autobiography that is the story of Perec's coming into full possession of the significance of his boyhood drawings and fantasy, the story of how the search for a lost boy is superseded by the enormity of historical fact. Young Winckler, like young Perec, is irretrievable; the past cannot be recaptured, only approached through the testimony of its survivors.

While Perec is clearly not trying to "escape the nightmare of history"—quite the opposite—he is demonstrating, like the simular writers, the securing of a stable identity through artistic representation. Like Nabokov, he combines conventional autobiography and artifice to achieve self-characterization, and here again, the act itself is not endowed with any heroism other than that implicit in any human being who has endured.

> I do not know if I have anything to say, I know that I am saying nothing; I do not know if what I would have to say is unsaid because it is unsayable (the unsayable is not hidden inside writing, it is what triggered it to begin with) [Cyberneticists take note!].... I am not writing to say that I will say nothing, I am not writing to say that I have nothing to say. I am writing: I write because we lived together, because I was among them, a shadow amidst their shadows, a body near their bodies; I am writing because they left in me their indelible mark, and its trace is writing: their memory is dead to writing; writing is the memory of their death and the affirmation of my life.
>
> —Georges Perec (58–59)

> Whatever happens, whatever I do, I was the only depository, the lone living memory, the sole vestige of that world. That, more than any other consideration, is what made me decide to write.
>
> —Gaspard Winckler (10)

Perec's view of the relationship of literature and history is also expressed in *Un homme qui dort* (1967), which also presents an unusual exercise in characterization. The novel has a sole, second-person character, a young man with a severe case of existentialist anomie who spends most of his time in bed, in a state of passive self-reflection between waking and sleep. The second-person voice is used not so much to elicit identification on the reader's part, as in Calvino's *Se una notte,* as to heighten the sense of utter self-estrangement; it is actually an interior monologue by an observing self for whom the acting (barely) self has become horribly objectified, taking Adam Krug's dread dualism a good deal farther. The protagonist, conforming to the book's epigraph from Kafka, simply stays in his rather dismal room and waits for the world to come to him.

In the last chapter, the voice takes stock of the character's stratagem for living, revealing its hypocrisy and bad faith, just before he very matter-of-factly reenters the world. Perec's critique of the character consists largely of detailing unrealized expectations, all of a literary nature. It is as if the character had pridefully expected that he would, by mere virtue of his being, attain the sort of redemption accorded to the heroes of his favorite books (which happen to be Perec's favorites, too). Among others, the series of unidentified allusions refers to Lowry: "No merciful volcanoes have leaned to you"; Melville: "No errant Rachel has rescued you from the miraculously preserved wreck of the Pequod so that in your turn, another orphan, you might give witness"; and Joyce: "Your mother hasn't sewn up your clothes. You're not going forth to encounter for the millionth time the reality of experience, nor to forge in the smithy of your soul the uncreated conscience of your race," and "No old ancestor, no old artificer will help you now or ever" (155–58).

Proud solitude, the protagonist is told, like self-indulgent despair or alcoholism, leads nowhere; "You are such a small thing and the world is such a big word" (159). While he was trying to overcome time by removing himself from it, time had merely kept on flowing. The final paragraph summarizes the realization:

> No. You are no longer the anonymous master of the world, he over whom history had no hold, he who didn't hear the rain falling, who didn't see the night approaching. You are no longer inaccessible, limpid, transparent. You are afraid, you wait. You wait, in Place Clichy, for the rain to stop falling. (163)

The character joins, at last, the "thousands upon thousands" of other Earthlings. It is noteworthy that Perec connects his character's misguided visions of redemption to heroism of the Dedalian variety and forecloses it as an option, much in the way that another of the author's favorites, Flaubert, deflates Emma Bovary's equally novel-inspired romantic illusions. Perec does not refer to Proust, but he might well have added, "You did not stub your toe on any paving stone and learn at last the secret of recapturing lost time and 'making life real in a book'." It is not any inherent mediocrity of the character that makes it impossible for him to join the company of his literary heroes, so much as the fact that postwar culture no longer admits self-defining artistic heroism as a plausible paradigm.

Perec and Nabokov are exemplary mid-century authors insofar as their works span most of the forms and concerns of the era. The two are firmly in the tradition of architectonic fiction that goes back to Joyce and Proust. It is in their autobiographical works, though, that they participate in the simular novelists' other tradition, that of the poetry of experience. *Speak, Memory* and *W* highlight specific moments of artistic realization, what Nabokov calls the thematic design, that correspond to epiphanies. The difference, as I have been stressing, is that for Nabokov and Perec self-portraiture is no longer heroic.

John Edgar Wideman

In *W*, Perec makes explicit the connection of fiction and autobiography in defining his authorial voice in relation to family and community, a procedure also employed by John Wideman in his *Homewood Trilogy: Damballah, Hiding Place*, and *Sent for You Yesterday*. His non-fictional *Brothers and Keepers*, which recounts some of the events fictionalized in the trilogy, provides an instructive study of the artful transformation of fact into fiction and is a poetic work in its own right. Between the two works, and in the overt autobiographical references of the occasional first-person narrator (named, like Marcel, for the author) in the trilogy, one reads, as in the space between chapters in *W*, the story of the coincidence of acquiring the authorial voice with assuming one's place in the family, and by extension the community. For Wideman, as for Perec, self-possession is a question of moving from estrangement to social integration, and the telling of the story is the means.

It is beyond the scope of this chapter to attempt to do justice to the complexity of Wideman's oeuvre; I wish to concentrate only on the importance of tale-telling in the trilogy, and the place of gender roles and techniques of characterization therein. The first book of the trilogy, *Damballah*, opens with a story of the same name that serves as something of a parable for the fictionalized autobiographical stories that follow. It is the story of an American-born slave boy who undergoes an initiation into a primal African way of knowledge when, in a moment of psychic communion, an old African-born slave, Orion, thrusts the single word *Damballah* into his heart. The subsequent story of John, the narrator, up to the trilogy's final scene, when he gets up to do his signature dance, is very much the story of preservation of familial and cultural heritage in the face of pressure for assimilation and dissolution. In "Damballah," the magical, shamanistic power of Orion is countered by the authority of the unnamed boy's thoroughly Americanized and Christianized Aunt Lissy, who cautions him, with a slap to the head, to "talk Merican" when he repeats the African word. It is noteworthy here that what are commonly stereotyped as symbolically "masculine" and "feminine" ways of knowing are depicted across gender lines. The male character embodies the earthy, intuitive, "oceanic" power, while the female character is identified with the patriarchal authority of the white Master. Orion is finally put to death for his indomitability, for his failure to assimilate culturally, and, not incidentally, for frightening the Mistress with his naked body. He and Aunt Lissy in a sense prefigure the subsequent depiction of men and women in the stories. The men are frequently subjected to the dangerous lure of the street, the night world, the "magic" of drugs and alcohol, and white women who seal their fate, and the women try to preserve home and family by keeping them from that world. In another sense, though, it is the women who carry on Orion's role, since it is they, as the tellers of the stories John passes along to us in *Damballah,* who are the transmitters of the cultural heritage.

Indeed, most of the stories of which John, in turn, becomes the teller come through the matrilinear side of the family, although many of them do revolve around male figures, including the semilegendary maternal grandfather, John French. John the writer enters a line of succession descending from his great aunt, grandmother, and mother as he recounts the stories he heard from them. Through systematic analepsis and prolepsis, and with the aid of the occasional appearances of the first-person narrator John, nicknamed Doot, we are able, across and between the free-standing stories in the trilogy, to piece together his biography and family history as he learned it growing up, via the repetition of the family lore from many sources. The first-person passages also serve as chronicles of John's coming to terms with himself as a member of that community. Starting from an estranged position as an academic out of touch with his Homewood roots, John reaffirms his place in family and community through his representation of it. Implicit in the attention given to the family stories—repeated around kitchen tables and at funerals and other gatherings—is the notion of the family as a source of identity-conferring traditions and values that can only exist and endure by virtue of the stories passed from generation to generation. Wideman shows that the family is more than a formal relational network; it is in fact a literary construct, located in an evolving set of canonical stories.

> Past lives live in us, through us. Each of us harbors the spirits of people who walked the earth before we did, and those spirits depend on us for continuing existence, just as we depend on their presence to live our lives to the fullest. (Epigraph to *Sent for You Yesterday*)

In setting the oral tales down in print, Wideman is—aside from enacting an artful transformation of the material in terms of structure and voicings—memorializing the clan, fixing his place within it and its place in history. This is perhaps a more effective example of "life made real in a book" than Marcel's solipsistic dependence upon involuntary memory.

There is a decidedly Faulknerian aspect to Wideman's techniques of characterization, stemming from his pervasive use of character-centered focus rather than external omniscience. Like Faulkner, Wideman tells his stories from inside characters who are themselves characterized in the telling. They are above all stories of voice, highlighting not only varied vernaculars and idiolects, but oral composition itself. When the narrator uses indirect discourse—consonant narrated monologue[2]—the focalizing character (the one "telling" us the story) becomes, at least formally, responsible for the characterizations within the tale, thus creating both semiautonomous[3] and narrated monologues within the first-degree narrated monologue.

A fine case in point is the scene in *Sent for You Yesterday* when Lucy Tate is telling the first-person narrator Doot (whose viewpoint frames the entire book) the story of Junebug as she heard it from the boy's mother, Samantha, whom she visited in the hospital. The passage begins with an account of Lucy's walk up the hill to the hospital, from her point of view, then quickly moves to Samantha's perspective on the same walk, as seen from her window, and Junebug's story is told from within Samantha's character. Thus we have, formally, Doot's rendition of Lucy's telling of Junebug's story, as seen from within Samantha, in her voice. To add yet another layer, Samantha's interior monologue includes a dream that amounts to a version of the day of Junebug's death as he experienced it. It is, as it were, a narrated monologue of the mute toddler's perceptions and sensations (Wideman, like Faulkner, being a specialist in narrating from within idiosyncratic characters). In the passage, then, we have the inner voice and experience of each of the three characters, a further development of certain characteristics we have been seeing in them right along, and a triple perspective on one event and its meaning for the characters and the community at large. In relation to the work as a whole, the passage leads to the tragic core event that has shaped the characters and provides a major piece in Doot's coming to understand why Lucy's brother, Brother, is the way he is.

The mystery of Brother Tate's character functions as the plot-generative device of the novel, which opens with a prologue in the form of an after-death monologue by Brother. The novel proper begins with Doot (who got the name from Brother) recalling his first memories of Brother, and its frame is the story of his augmentation of those memories—of his coming to possess the rest of Brother's story—through the stories told by Lucy and her lover Carl, Doot's uncle. Not unlike Quentin Compson, Doot will be, as he unravels Brother's story, revealing the lives of its tellers and informing himself of the community from which he comes. It is a tribute to Wideman's masterful technique that he maintains the complex distinctions of voicing and focus throughout this book.

Like Faulkner, then, Wideman excels at recounting a dramatic anecdote from multiple points of view, in such a way that it becomes a vehicle for characterizing the ethos of a community, in this case Homewood during the author's lifetime, depicting the bonds among people and the entropic forces impinging on them all. Unlike Faulkner, though, Wideman explicitly emphasizes—in representing his arrival as teller of the tales—the affirmative value of the authorial power. The trilogy ends with Doot hearing Lucy's story of the first time he ever danced, at age three, to the song "Sent for You Yesterday." In the final image, that primal scene with Carl and Lucy is conflated with the present in a parallactic Proustian moment, as younger Doot and older Doot join in the dance:

> I'm on my feet and Lucy says, *Go boy* and Carl says, *Get it on, Doot.* Everybody joinin in now. All the voices. I'm reaching for them and letting them go. Lucy waves. I'm on my own feet. Learning to stand, to walk, learning to dance. (531)

"Learning to dance" in this scene is both acquiring independence and self-expression and, inseparably, taking a place in a community. Everybody is joining in with a contribution. Doot's reaching for the voices and letting them go recalls David Schearl's new-found ability to "cull and reassemble" sounds and images at the end of *Call It Sleep;* he is learning to negotiate that simular passage between character and author, where life is made real.

Character-focalized narration such as Wideman's, particularly with his emphasis on speech, can allow an author to avoid some of the thornier problems of gender representation. It should be said, first of all, that it does not necessarily "take one to know one" in literature any more than in the visual arts. Characterization, as an act of imagination, depends upon "negative capability," i.e., the capacity of the author to project him/herself into another persona. Granted, there will be cases where our sense of verisimilitude will be offended by an author who demonstrates too little ability in providing sufficient description, speech, and/or interior monologue to support our imaginative construction of a viable character, and it may well be the case that an inability to get beyond one's racial, social, or gender identification is at fault. For example, I earlier raised objections to Malcolm Lowry's rather weak characterizations of women. (Another sort of problematic gender characterization is found in the protagonist of André Pieyre de Mandiargues's *Le lis de mer,* who comes across as a bit too much of a male phantasm. This might be excusable if she were presented through the viewpoint of a male character, but she is instead presented as a free-standing character through the agency of an uncharacterized omniscient narrator.) On the other hand, there are abundant examples of perfectly successful characterizations across all of the above-named lines. It is evident enough, in any event, that disputes over charges of sexism in Joyce's portrayal of Molly

Bloom or the merits of Alice Walker's male characters are all implicit acknowledgements of literature's representational nature. My point is that a discussion of the representation of "otherness" will be more fruitful on the level of technique than of ideology.

The advantage of character-focalized narration is that it allows one to portray difference at the second degree, through a character closer to oneself. An outstanding example of this would be Virginia Woolf's characterization of Mr. Ramsay through Mrs. Ramsay's and Lily Briscoe's observations in *To the Lighthouse*.[4] As long as Mr. Ramsay is described externally, through the agency of a female character, we needn't be troubled with the "masculinity" of his inner life. Joyce, typically, jumps in where few dare to tread with his characterization of Molly, which constitutes a challenge both as one of the lengthier autonomous monologues on record and as a cross-gender characterization. I can add nothing to Brenda Maddox's discussion of feminist readings of Molly, and would only cite her contention that "the contradiction in Molly's character—life-affirming but male dependent—was present in Nora's" (1988, 210). It is known that many of Molly's thoughts were first spoken by Nora and duly recorded by Joyce, suggesting one method of capturing character, namely observation and transcription. In *Ulysses*'s other bit of relatively sustained focus on a female character, in "Nausicaa," Joyce avoids the problem of verisimilitude by casting Gerty McDowell's interior monologue in parody. Joyce's pervasive reliance upon natural models—for both details and characters—suggests an inversely proportional negative capability, whether by choice or necessity.

The problem of negative capability—of convincingly rendering the distinctive inner life of diverse characters—is one that comes to the fore with the increasing use of consonant narrated monologue, or what I have referred to in a more generic sense as character-focalized narration, to perform the informational role in characterization that was formerly the more exclusive province of the omniscient narrator. As narration tends toward formal objectivity—representing character as an observed experiential phenomenon, whether from within or without—the author's ability to render subjectivity becomes more crucial, since there is no longer a chatty narrator to interpret and comment upon a character's actions and state of being: it is up to us to see and to know.

For Proust, none of this is especially troublesome, since Marcel's perception and interpretation of other characters (or Swann's in his section) is the pervasive focus in any case, and the very unknowability of others is a central point to be made. Marguerite Duras's *Le ravissement de Lol V. Stein* offers a curious case, both in terms of the protagonist's unknowability and the fact that she is presented through a male first-person narrator. In the narrative present in which Jacques Hold encounters Lol, he finds her character unreadable: "My first discovery with respect to her was that to know nothing about Lol was already to know her. One could, it seemed to me, know even less, less and less, about Lol V. Stein" (81).

The void in Lol is the result of a trauma in her past, which is reconstructed by Hold as an imaginative act. That is, he accords himself authorial license in reconstructing her past, building it on a framework of observations reported to him by mutual friend Tatiana Karl and Lol herself, which he then fills in with speculation. Like Marcel, Hold sprinkles qualifiers and disclaimers throughout his narration: "perhaps," "might have," "I think I see what she must have seen," "I see it this way," "I believe," etc. For the reader, Hold's uncertainty makes him scarcely more knowable than Lol.

Along with her refusal of omniscience, Duras declines to ground the narration in the certainty of any stable subjective center. In Proust, Marcel may be uncertain about what he observes, but we are indeed certain about his own thoughts, motivations, and reactions, however mutable. In *Lol V. Stein*, though, we are no more sure of Hold than he is of Lol. At times, Hold is in effect characterized through Lol, as he reports to us her experience with him as he imagined it looked from her point of view. Formally, then, we have Hold, the source of our information about Lol (or her "author"), constituting himself as a character through the focus of the character he is "creating." The only certainty here is in actual, externally observed phenomena, which afford scant indications of character; all else is speculation.

The story's setting, a vague colony with only partially knowable place names (S. Tahla, T. Beach, U. Bridge), aside from corresponding in the most general sense to the colonial world of Duras's youth, has the advantage of being removed from the dominant cultural context of the characters, for whom estrangement in an unknowable world is a given background condition. No detail whatsoever of the indigenous culture is provided. The sequence of initials in the odd place names, which is completed by Lol's *V.*, suggests something on the order of an Oulipo combinatorial exercise, as practiced by Perec, perhaps, or a meaningfully minimal gesture toward a naturalistic pretense. As Hold says of Lol, we can only know less and less about this world.

Lol V. Stein, built around a void of character, shares Proust's notion of the unknowability of others, but not his belief in finding a ground of certainty in the observing self. Lol's memory is inaccessible and Hold's is irrelevant, since he has only just met her. When he returns with her to the scene of her trauma, the casino at T. Beach where she was abandoned by her fiancé, he tries to exercise negative capability: "Lol looked. Behind her I tried to accord my vision so tightly to hers that I began to recall, more each second, her recollection" (180). His recollection of her recollection is a recapitulation of details earlier provided by eyewitness Tatiana Karl. Hold is able to envision the scene, but in the end this ability can provide no ground for establishing character. He cannot know Lol, for there is nothing to her but the void that is the sign of the trauma.

> A monumental calm covered over, swallowed everything. A trace remains, one. Alone, indelible; one doesn't know where at first. But what? Doesn't one know? Not a trace, not one, everything has been enshrouded, and Lol with it. (181)

At the end of the sequence, Hold gives up "fighting against the mortal vapidity of Lol's memory," and goes to sleep. One might be tempted to say that the novel thus makes a statement about the futility of negative capability, and the (non)viability of literary representation, or the impossibility of knowing "otherness" at all. Conversely, one could make the case that Duras has mimetically portrayed a character suffering from a kind of emotional autism or dissociation. Of course if we choose the latter path, we will be committing the sin of naturalistic recuperation as castigated by Jonathan Culler (see chap. 1). Again, I would contend that it strains credibility to suppose that novelists devote themselves to their art for the purpose of demonstrating its futility, and that there is no way not to read a novel as a character-centered representation, any more than one could read a dictionary as a novel.

All of the protagonists I have discussed thus far have been endowed by their creators with a certain alienated condition, that is, an awareness of a troublesome specificity, whether social, sexual, political, or existential. The striving writers, the cuckolded Jew in a Catholic land, the ghost of the South lost in Cambridge, the abandoned alcoholic expatriate, the immigrant boy caught between cultures, the black woman trying not to be the world's mule, the orphan of the Holocaust, the political exile, and the human sensibility turned loose in an indifferent cosmos all appear in works in which the particularity of the protagonistic perspective—the *quidditas* of character—is itself a focal point, apart from the plot, or general laws or judgments one might apply to them. The history of the twentieth-century novel as compiled here can be read in terms of the stand taken by the various authors with respect to the singularity or marginality of the protagonists. Proust and Joyce affirm the exceptionality of their artists, offering their novels as proof and vindication of it. Quentin Compson and Geoffrey Firmin are made to die for their irreconcilable difference. David Schearl and Janie Woods attain a quiet, if violently facilitated, integration of self and world, via the ability to perceive order and meaning in the events of their lives, with an implied analogy to the authorial function. For Perec in *W* and John in the *Homewood Trilogy*, authoring the story becomes a means of identification with family and community, a reinsertion into the "nightmare of history" against which Joyce and Proust proclaimed their heroic individuality, even while laboring to record its details.

The most illustrative example of an actual author-protagonist attaining a personal and social identity through self-representation, though, is found in the simular biography of Joseph Meehan, alterego of Christopher Nolan in *Under the Eye of the Clock* (1987). For Nolan, a quadriplegic incapable of speech, the ability to tell his story (written with the aid of a special typing device; a happier conjunction of literature and technology than anything suggested by Oulipo) is the only means of having a voice in the world, of leaving the most extreme sort of isolated individuality and joining the rest of the chattering earthlings. The acceptance of his first book by a publisher is "his moment of birth . . . [he] bestowed birth to himself. He birthed an author" (92). Now, says Nolan, Joseph would share the same world as everyone else; "his voice would be his written word," his book "made sense of his life" (93). While the traditional notion of artistic transcendence has the author's written voice ensuring him a place in the future, Nolan uses his to enter the present. At last, he says, he will be able to let people know what it is like to be him:

> He saw life recoil before him, and using the third person he rescued poor sad boyhood and casting himself inside the frame of crippled Joseph Meehan he pranked himself a storyteller, thereby casting renown on himself by dangling disability before the reader. Look, he begged, look deep down; feel, he begged, sense life's limitations; cry, he begged, cry the tears of cruel frustration; but above all he begged laughter, laugh, he pleaded, for lovely laughter vanquishes raw wounded pride. (28)

Nolan presents the ultimate case of artistic self-definition, inasmuch as it is only through his written self-characterization that he can make himself known at all. More than any other author, he makes clear the difference between the observing, expressing self and the form in which it is captive.

When Joseph becomes a student at Trinity College, he salutes his countryman and predecessor in autoportraiture: "Crying hurrah for lilysweet knowledge he frowned at the greatness of Joyce; wanting to emulate him for boyhood's fame" (161). While Joyce, like Proust, used the novel to affirm his difference, Nolan stands at the opposite end of the simular tradition, using it to affirm his similarity. The authors at the beginning of the tradition took for granted the place of the literary artist in society. For them, the act of artistic transformation deserves greater emphasis than its particular objects; it is what gives them value. Applied to the author, insofar as the authorial self is the object of representation of the simular novel, this would mean that the author, an otherwise undistinguished person, acquires value in becoming the artist, in representing himself as such. Ireland may be important because of Stephen, as he says, but he is only important because he will become (or is the past of) the artist. Life, in a sense, acquires meaning as raw material, to become real only when in print. For Nolan, by contrast, writing is not such a self-validating end; his autoportraiture memorializes his ability to enter not mansions in eternity, but the chorus of voices around him.

All of these cases, though, share the legacy of the simular novel in fashioning characters and voices that artfully convey a sense of actuality, of the experience of the author behind the work, speaking through fictive surrogates. Authors have continued to develop the novel as a medium of authorial expression even as theorists, pursuing their own interests, have disavowed the possibility.

Notes

Chapter 1

1. I shall use the term in the sense described by Jonathan Culler (1982, 8).

2. See Rader 1974, 81.

3. The expression is Y. Bar-Hillel's, quoted in Dreyfus 1986, 7, 11, 141, 204.

4. See Bordwell 1988 on the misapplication of pseudo-Proppian analyses to films.

5. See Alter 1989, 52ff, for a critique of Cixous's rather vehement attack on character.

6. Cf. Fish 1985:

Paradoxically, the triumph of Chomskian theory from an institutional point of view is an illustration of its failure from the point of view of its fondest hope, the hope to transcend point of view by producing a picture of the language that holds for any and all institutions and is beholden to none. Chomsky is in the position of every other theorist: the consequences he seeks are impossible, and the consequences to which he has clear right and title make him indistinguishable from any other political agent and render theory a category about which there is nothing particular—because there is nothing general—to say. (455)

7. Alter 1989, 70.

8. See Battaglia 1968 and Cohn 1978 for the philosophic/thematic and technical backgrounds, respectively, of this claim.

9. An excellent example of this is Barthes's second cited case (1984, 167), Michelet's inclusion of much "irrelevant" detail in his historical account of the last moments of Charlotte Corday before she was executed. Michelet's "additions" illustrate precisely the nature of literature, as opposed to history in this specific case, but that is not my point. The details, as Barthes says, do not contribute to the "plot" of the piece as a historical narrative, but they do create a sense of the event—stemming from impressions of duration and of foreboding. Corday sits "for an hour and a half" for the portraitist, there is "a gentle knock" on the "little" door "behind her," etc. All of these details

serve to establish character by introducing psychological, affective, and spatial indicators that facilitate an empathetic involvement in the scene—nothing so obvious as the arousal of sympathy for Corday, but simply the rendering of the scene to our inner awareness, based on our experience of the world, and not just to the intellect.

10. Barthes 1984, 171. His choice of jewels: "masts like a forest of needles," "islands like big, immutable black fish," "clouds like aerial waves breaking silently against a cliff."

11. Or, as Baruch Hochman points out (1985, 46), character is reducible to type in exactly the same way in which human beings we encounter may be.

12. See Watt 1957.

Chapter 2

1. For example, see Johnson 1979.

2. For conflations of Stephen and Bloom as emblems of Joyce, see Rader 1989, Rader 1984, and Rader 1978.

3. All citations of Proust are from the 1987 *Pléiade* edition, and in my translation, unless otherwise indicated.

4. For Dantean allusions in *Ulysses*, see Reynolds 1981.

5. See Painter 1978, vol. 2, chap. 3 for Proust's reaction to the death.

6. Reprinted in Proust 1921, 211–25.

7. See also Henry 1981.

8. Reprinted in Joyce 1959. Hereafter referred to in text as *CW*.

9. Dorrit Cohn (1978) calls these passages quoted monologue, although they bear no markers of quotation. I feel they more properly belong to the first-person form to which she assigns "Penelope," i.e., autonomous monologue. They are not completely autonomous, as is Molly's monologue, since they are interspersed with external narrative indications. I do not think that Cohn is precise enough in distinguishing quoted inner discourse from what would seem to be the content of a character's perception, seen from within his focalization, reported in his words, but which upon closer examination should be understood as stylized, discursive equivalents of nonverbal awareness that cannot, of course, be represented as such. For example, in the sequence "He peeped quickly inside the leather headband. White slip of paper. Quite safe," the first sentence is obviously external narration, but the second, and perhaps the third, are not actual quotes. There is no need to suppose that Bloom, looking inside his hat and being relieved to find his note secure, hears or says these words in his head. Indeed, it would be odd for someone to say "white slip of paper" upon seeing the note; it is not, in fact, a white slip of paper to him as it would be to someone ignorant of its content or affective significance. The words, then, are the necessary verbal correlative of his perception, and even of his sense (not verbal expression) of relief. Rather than quoted, I would say that the content of Bloom's mind is reported. The passage is a reported bit of autonomous monologue (intermit-

tent autonomous?) interspersed along with a continuous series of others into the narration.

10. For metalepsis in Proust, see Genette 1972, 243-45.

11. There is, according to the Grandgent and Singleton edition of the *Commedia* (Dante 1972, 47–48), no evidence that Dante knew Francesca, although her nephew had aided the poet's children and would host him in the last years of his life.

12. Cf. Painter 1978, vol. 2, chap. 10, and de Chantal 1967 on the fictionalization of Agostinelli's demise.

13. Robert de Montesquiou, Charles Haas, Antoinette Faure/Marie Benardaky, Alfredo Agostinelli, Count Cholet, Gogarty, Vincent Cosgrave, J. F. Byrne, and Matthew Kane, respectively. For Proust's characters see Proust 1965.

14. Joyce is hardly the first since Dante to use the device; Diderot's *Neveu de Rameau* and *Le rêve de d'Alembert* come to mind as prominent examples.

15. "Gazelles are leaping, feeding on the mountains. Near are lakes. Round their shores file shadows black of cedar groves. Aroma rises, a strong hairgrowth of resin. It burns, the orient, a sky of sapphire, cleft by the bronze flight of eagles. Under it lies the womancity, nude, white, still, cool, in luxury. A fountain murmurs away among damask roses. Mammoth roses murmur of scarlet winegrapes" (477).

Chapter 3

1. Written for the *Minuit* edition, reprinted in Queneau 1965a, 125–33.

2. Queneau may be forgiven for assuming that Faulkner's fictional war exploits were autobiographical, when it appears that Faulkner himself went limping around Oxford in uniform for some time, posing as a returned hero, whereas he had actually been in flight training near Toronto for the most part. See Oates 1987.

3. "*¿Le gusta esta jardin que es suyo? Evite que sus hijos lo destruyan!*" "Do you like this garden which is yours? Do not let your children destroy it!" Firmin's version: "Do you like this garden? Why is it yours? We evict those who destroy."

4. Eliot 1986, 2:299.

Chapter 4

1. My source for this anecdote is Hubert Dreyfus.

2. Again, the term is Dorrit Cohn's.

3. Once Wideman's narrated monologues get rolling, the pervasiveness of the character's viewpoint and idiom approach autonomy, although, as in Faulkner, we can recognize a certain unifying lyricism that is that of the veritable author, and the narrator is always at hand to facilitate external description and scene-setting.

4. While on the subject of Woolf's technique, it is worth noting a certain weakness in her interior monologues, compared to Joyce's studied attention to the mimesis of mental phenomena, for example. In a typical case, Mrs. Ramsay's thoughts while reading aloud to her son (1955, 93) are not only unconnected with her outward activity, but they seem altogether incommensurate with it. That is, the thoughts are not presented in a way that is convincingly mimetic of the character's awareness (unless she happens to be extraordinarily adept at splitting her attention). As elements of characterization, the thoughts function perfectly well in informing us of her feelings, attitudes, and observations, but as presented they arrive not as if from within her, as form suggests, but rather as if from outside via the agency of the narrator. In other words, to use Cohn's terminology, the representation has the form of a consonant narrated monologue, but the lack of coordination between the inner and outer activities (particularly given that both involve the use of voice) creates a note of dissonance.

Bibliography

Ackerley, Chris, and Clipper, Lawrence J. *A Companion to "Under the Volcano."* Vancouver: University of British Columbia Press, 1984.

Adams, R. M. *Surface and Symbol: The Consistency of James Joyce's "Ulysses."* London: Oxford University Press, 1962.

———. *After Joyce.* London: Oxford University Press, 1977.

Alter, Robert. *Partial Magic.* Berkeley: University of California Press, 1975.

———. *Motives for Fiction.* Cambridge, Mass.: Harvard University Press, 1984.

———. "Awakenings." *New Republic*, January 25, 1988, 33–37.

———. *The Pleasures of Reading in an Ideological Age.* New York: Simon and Schuster, 1989.

Barthes, Roland. *"L'effet de réel."* In *Bruissement de la langue.* Paris: Seuil, 1984.

Battaglia, Salvatore. *Mitografia del personaggio.* Milan: Rizzoli, 1968.

Beebe, Maurice. "Ulysses and the Age of Modernism." *James Joyce Quarterly* 10, no. 1 (Fall 1972): 172–89.

Biasin, Gian-Paolo. *Italian Literary Icons.* Princeton: Princeton University Press, 1984.

Binns, Ronald. *Malcolm Lowry.* London: Methuen, 1984.

Blamires, Harry. *The Bloomsday Book.* London: Methuen, 1966.

Bordwell, David. "ApProppriations and ImProprieties: Problems in the Morphology of Film Narrative." *Cinema Journal* 27, no. 3 (September 1988).

Bredin, Hugh. "The Displacement of Character in Narrative Theory." *British Journal of Aesthetics* 22, no. 4 (Fall 1982): 291.

Bronsen, David. "A Conversation with Henry Roth." *Partisan Review* 36 (1969): 265–80.

Calvino, Italo. *Le Cosmicomiche.* Turin: Einaudi, 1965.

———. *Se una notte d'inverno un viaggiatore...* Turin: Einaudi, 1979.

———. *Una pietra sopra.* Turin: Einaudi, 1980.

Canadian Literature 8 (1961). Special Issue on Malcolm Lowry.

Cancogni, Annapaola. *The Mirage in the Mirror.* New York: Garland, 1985.

Clarac, Pierre, and Ferre, André. *Album Proust.* Paris: Gallimard, 1965.

Cohn, Dorrit. *Transparent Minds.* Princeton: Princeton University Press, 1978.

Crews, Frederick. *Skeptical Engagements.* New York: Oxford University Press, 1986.

Cross, Richard K. *Malcolm Lowry: A Preface to His Fiction.* Chicago: University of Chicago Press, 1980.

Culler, Jonathan. *Structuralist Poetics.* Ithaca, N.Y.: Cornell University Press, 1975.

———. *On Deconstruction.* Ithaca, N.Y.: Cornell University Press, 1982.

Dante, Alighieri. *La divina commedia.* Ed. C. H. Grandgent and Charles Singleton. Cambridge, Mass.: Harvard University Press, 1972.

Day, Douglas. *Malcolm Lowry.* London: Oxford University Press, 1973.

de Chantal, René. *Marcel Proust: Critique littéraire.* Montréal: Les Presses de l'Université de Montréal, 1967.

de Lattre, Alain. *Le personnage proustien.* Paris: Corti, 1984.

de Lauretis, Teresa. "Narrative Discourse in Calvino: Praxis or Poiesis?" *PMLA* 90, no. 3 (May 1975): 414–25.

de Veroli, Elena Mortara. "Da Babele al silenzio: il romanzo sinfonico di Henry Roth." *Letture d'America* 5, nos. 24–25 (Fall 1984).

Dreyfus, Hubert. *What Computers Can't Do.* New York: Harper/Colophon, 1979.

———. *Mind Over Machine.* With Stuart Dreyfus. New York: Free Press, 1986.

Dujardin, Edouard. *Le monologue intérieur.* Paris: Messein, 1931.

Duras, Marguerite. *Le ravissement de Lol V. Stein.* Paris: Gallimard/Folio, 1964.

Dusoir, Ilse Lind. "Design and Meaning in *Absalom, Absalom!*" In Hoffman 1960.

Eliot, T. S. "Little Gidding." In *Norton Anthology of English Literature,* 5th ed., vol. 2. New York: Norton, 1986.

Ellmann, Richard. *James Joyce.* London: Oxford University Press, 1983.

Epstein, Perle S. *The Private Labyrinth of Malcolm Lowry: "Under the Volcano" and the Cabbala.* New York: Holt, Rinehart, and Winston, 1969.

Faulkner, William. *The Sound and the Fury.* New York: Random House, 1956.

———. *Absalom, Absalom!* New York: Random House, 1974.

Fish, Stanley. "Pragmatism and Literary Theory, I: Consequences." *Critical Inquiry* 11, no. 3 (March 1985): 433–58.

Flaubert, Gustave. *Madame Bovary.* Vol. I of *Oeuvres.* Paris: Pléiade, 1951.

Forster, E. M. *Aspects of the Novel.* New York: Harcourt Brace and World, 1927.

Genette, Gérard. *Figures II.* Paris: Seuil, 1969.

———. *Figures III.* Paris: Seuil, 1972.

Gifford, Don, and Seidman, Robert. *Notes for Joyce.* New York: Dutton, 1974.

Gilbert, Stuart. *James Joyce's "Ulysses."* New York: Random House, 1955.

Goldberg, M. A. *The Poetics of Romanticism.* Yellow Springs, Ohio: Antioch College Press, 1969.

Grace, Sherrill E. *The Voyage That Never Ends.* Vancouver: University of British Columbia Press, 1982.

Hamon, Philippe. "Pour un statut sémiologique du personnage." In *Poétique du récit,* ed. Gerard Genette and Tzvetan Todorov. Paris: Seuil, 1977.

Harkness, Marguerite. *The Aesthetics of Dedalus and Bloom.* Cranbury, N.J.: Associated University Presses, 1984.

Harvey, W. J. *Character and the Novel.* Ithaca, N.Y.: Cornell University Press, 1965.

Henry, Anne. *Marcel Proust: Théories pour une esthétique.* Paris: Klincksieck, 1981.

Hill, Art. "The Alcoholic on Alcoholism." In Wood 1980.

Hochman, Baruch. *The Test of Character.* Rutherford, N.J.: Farleigh Dickinson University Press, 1983.

————. *Character in Literature.* Ithaca, N.Y.: Cornell University Press, 1985.

Hoffman, Frederick J., ed. *William Faulkner: Three Decades of Criticism.* East Lansing: Michigan State University Press, 1960.

Hurston, Zora Neale. *Their Eyes Were Watching God.* Urbana: University of Illinois Press, 1978.

————. *Spunk.* Berkeley: Turtle Island Foundation, 1985.

Jameson, Fredric. *The Political Unconscious: Narrative as a Socially Symbolic Act.* Ithaca, N.Y.: Cornell University Press, 1981.

Johnson, J. Theodore, Jr. "Against 'Saint' Proust." In *The Art of the Proustian Novel Reconsidered,* ed. Lawrence D. Joiner. Rock Hill, S.C.: Winthrop College, 1979.

Joyce, James. *The Critical Writings of James Joyce.* Ed. Ellsworth Mason and Richard Ellmann. New York: Viking Press 1959.

————. *Ulysses.* New York: Random House, 1961.

————. *Stephen Hero.* New York: New Directions, 1963.

————. *Letters.* Ed. Stuart Gilbert and Richard Ellmann. 3 vols. New York: Viking, 1966.

————. *A Portrait of the Artist as a Young Man.* New York: Viking, 1968.

Kain, Richard M. "The Significance of Stephen's Meeting Bloom: A Survey of Interpretations." *James Joyce Quarterly* 10, no. 1 (Fall 1972): 147–61.

Kilgallin, Tony. *Lowry.* Erin, Ont.: Press Porcepic, 1973.

Kimball, Jean. "The Hypostasis in *Ulysses.*" *James Joyce Quarterly* 10, no. 4 (Summer 1973): 422–39.

Knowles, A. Sidney, Jr. "The Fiction of Henry Roth." *Modern Fiction Studies* 11 (Winter 1965): 393–401.

Langbaum, Robert. *The Poetry of Experience.* New York: Norton, 1957.

Levin, Harry. *Gates of Horn.* New York: Oxford University Press, 1963.

Lowry, Malcolm. *Hear Us O Lord from Heaven Thy Dwelling Place.* Philadelphia: Lippincott, 1961.

————. *Selected Letters.* Ed. Harvey Breit and Margerie Bonner Lowry. Philadelphia: Lippincott, 1965a.

————. *Under the Volcano.* Philadelphia: Lippincott, 1965b.

————. *Dark as the Grave Wherein My Friend Is Laid.* New York: New American Library, 1968a.

————. *Lunar Caustic.* London: Jonathan Cape, 1968b.

————. *October Ferry to Gabriola.* New York: New American Library, 1971.

Lowry, Margerie Bonner, ed. *Malcolm Lowry: Psalms and Songs.* New York: New American Library, 1975.

Lyons, Bonnie. *Henry Roth: The Man and His Work.* New York: Cooper Square, 1976.

Maddox, Brenda. *Nora: A Biography of Nora Joyce.* New York: Fawcett Columbine, 1988.

Maddox, James H., Jr. *Joyce's "Ulysses" and the Assault upon Character.* New Brunswick, N.J.: Rutgers University Press, 1978.

Magazine Littéraire 193 (March 1983). Special Issue on Georges Perec.

Mandiargues, André Pieyre de. *Le lis de mer.* Paris: Gallimard/Folio, 1956.

Markson, David. *Malcolm Lowry's "Volcano": Myth, Symbol, Meaning.* New York: Times Books, 1978.

Mayoux, J. J. "The Creation of the Real in Faulkner." In Hoffman 1960.

Mein, Margaret. *A Foretaste of Proust.* London: Saxon House, 1974.

Nabokov, Vladimir. *Pale Fire.* New York: Putnam, 1962.

———. *Bend Sinister.* New York: Time/Life, 1964.

———. *Speak, Memory.* New York: Putnam, 1966.

———. *Ada.* New York: McGraw-Hill, 1969.

———. *Lolita.* Ed. Alfred Appel, Jr. New York: McGraw-Hill, 1970.

———. *Strong Opinions.* New York: Random House, 1973.

Nolan, Christopher. *Under the Eye of the Clock.* New York: St. Martin's Press, 1987.

Nuttall, A. D. *A New Mimesis.* London: Methuen, 1983.

Oates, Stephen. *William Faulkner: The Man and the Artist.* New York: Harper and Row, 1987.

Oulipo. *La littérature potentielle.* Paris: Gallimard, 1973.

———. *Atlas de la littérature potentielle.* Paris: Gallimard, 1981.

Painter, George D. *Marcel Proust: A Biography.* 2 vols. New York: Random House, 1978.

Peake, C. H. *James Joyce, the Citizen and the Artist.* Stanford, Calif.: Stanford University Press, 1977.

Perec, Georges. *Un homme qui dort.* Paris: Denoel, 1967.

———. *W ou Le souvenir d'enfance.* Paris: Denoel, 1975.

———. *La vie mode d'emploi.* Paris: Hachette, 1978.

———. "Quatre figures pour *La vie mode d'emploi.*" In Oulipo 1981.

Picon, Gaeton. *Lecture de Proust.* Paris: Mercure de France, 1966.

Pirandello, Luigi. *Maschere nude.* Milan: Mondadori, 1939.

———. *Sei personaggi in cerca d'autore.* Milan: Mondadori, 1977.

———. *Il fu Mattia Pascal.* Milan: Mondadori, 1984.

Proust, Marcel. *Pastiches et mélanges.* Paris: Gallimard, 1921.

———. *Contre Sainte-Beuve.* Paris: Gallimard, 1954.

———. *Album Proust.* Paris: Gallimard, 1965.

———. *A la recherche du temps perdu.* 4 vols. Paris: Gallimard/Pléiade, 1987–89.

Queneau, Raymond. *Le chiendent.* Paris: Gallimard, 1933.

———. *Les enfants du limon.* Paris: Gallimard, 1938.

———. *Le vol d'Icare.* Paris: Gallimard, 1959.

———. *Bâtons, chiffres, et lettres.* Paris: Gallimard, 1965a.

———. *Les fleurs bleues.* Paris: Gallimard, 1965b.

Quennell, Peter, ed. *Vladimir Nabokov: A Tribute.* New York: William Morrow, 1980.

Rader, Ralph. "Defoe, Richardson, Joyce, and the Concept of Form in the Novel." In *Autobiography, Biography, and the Novel,* with William Matthews. Los Angeles: University of California Press, 1973.

————. "The Concept of Genre in Eighteenth Century Literature." In *New Approaches to Eighteenth Century Literature*, ed. Philip Harth. New York: Columbia University Press, 1974.

————. "Exodus and Return: Joyce's *Ulysses* and the Fiction of the Actual." *Toronto Quarterly* 48, no. 2 (Winter 1978): 149–71.

————. "The Logic of *Ulysses;* or, Why Molly Had to Live in Gibraltar." *Critical Inquiry* 10 (June 1984): 567–77.

————. "Why Stephen's Hand Hurts: Joyce as Narcissus." *James Joyce Quarterly* 26, no. 3 (Spring 1989): 440–45.

Reynolds, Mary T. *Joyce and Dante*. Princeton: Princeton University Press, 1981.

Rivers, J. E. *Proust and the Art of Love: The Aesthetics of Sexuality in the Life, Times, and Art of Marcel Proust.* New York: Columbia University Press, 1980.

Robert, Marthe. *Roman des origines et origines du roman*. Paris: Grasset, 1972.

Roth, Henry. *Call It Sleep*. New York: Avon, 1964.

————. *Shifting Landscape*. Philadelphia: Jewish Publication Society, 1987.

Sartre, Jean-Paul. *Situations I*. Paris: Gallimard, 1947.

Searle, John. "The World Turned Upside Down." *New York Review of Books*, October 27, 1983, 77–79.

Segre, Cesare. "Se una notte d'inverno un critico...." *Strumenti Critici* 13, nos. 39–40 (October 1979): 177–215.

Shattuck, Roger. *Marcel Proust*. New York: Viking, 1974.

————. "Why Not the Best?" *New York Review of Books*, April 28, 1983, 8–16.

Simonnet, Claude. *Queneau déchiffré*. Paris: Julliard, 1962.

Smith, Anne, ed. *The Art of Malcolm Lowry*. London: Vision, 1978.

Southerland, Ellease. "The Influence of Voodoo on the Fiction of Zora Neale Hurston." In *Sturdy Black Bridges*, ed. Roseann P. Bell, Bettye J. Parker, and Beverly Guy Sheftall. Garden City, N.Y.: Anchor Doubleday Press, 1979.

Spitzer, Leo. *Etudes de style*. Paris: Gallimard, 1970.

Sultan, Stanley. *"Ulysses," "The Waste Land," and Modernism.* London: Kennikat, 1977.

Theoharis, Theoharis C. *Joyce's "Ulysses" and the Anatomy of the Soul.* Chapel Hill: University of North Carolina Press, 1988.

Thiher, Allen. *Raymond Queneau*. Boston: Twayne, 1985.

Valéry, Paul. *Tel Quel*. In *Oeuvres II*. Paris: Pléiade, 1960.

Varese, Claudio. "Italo Calvino: Una complessa continuità." *La Rassegna della letteratura italiana* series 7, nos. 1–2 (January–August 1980): 252–57.

Watt, Ian. *The Rise of the Novel*. Berkeley: University of California Press, 1957.

Wideman, John Edgar. *Brothers and Keepers*. New York: Holt, Rinehart and Winston, 1984.

————. *The Homewood Trilogy: Damballah, Hiding Place, Sent for You Yesterday.* New York: Avon, 1985.

Wilson, Rawdon. "The Bright Chimera." *Critical Inquiry* 5 (Summer 1979): 725–49.

Wood, Barry, ed. *Malcolm Lowry: The Writer and His Critics*. Ottowa: Tecumseh Press, 1980.

Woolf, Virginia. *To the Lighthouse*. New York: Harcourt Brace Javonovich, 1955.

Wright, David G. *Characters of Joyce*. Dublin: Gill and MacMillan, 1983.

Index